Crossroads between Culture and Mind

Continuities and Change in Theories of Human Nature

Crossroads between Culture and Mind

Continuities and Change in Theories of Human Nature

Gustav Jahoda

Harvard University Press
Cambridge, Massachusetts
1993

Printed in Great Britain

10 9 8 7 6 5 4 3 2 1

ISBN 0-674-17775-4

Library of Congress Catalog Number 92-15901

To the memory of

JEAN

who made it all possible.

Contents

Preface

Authors commonly feel the urge to explain why their own work is not just 'yet another book' on the topic – and I am no exception. The past two decades have seen the appearance of a considerable number of texts on the history of psychology, and the reader might understandably suspect that this could be another such text masquerading under an esoteric title. Now I must admit that the main theme of the present work is the history of psychology, but it focuses generally on aspects most other histories choose to exclude.

In a well-known article intriguingly entitled 'Does the history of psychology have a subject?', Roger Smith (1988) pointed out that textbook history of psychology 'projects back' the subject as it is at present rather than portraying it as the meaningful activity it was in the past. In other words, such history mainly traces the development of the currently dominant paradigm of 'scientific psychology'. The history of psychology as a cultural discipline tends to be largely neglected. One hears little, if anything, of the great nineteenth-century debate about the place of psychology in the world of knowledge; and the echoes of this debate increasingly reverberate today, though participants often remain unaware that they are echoing.

Until the latter part of the nineteenth century, what Alexander Pope called 'the proper study of mankind' was not divided up into separate academic disciplines. Thinkers of the most varied backgrounds, including philosophers, historians, philologists, anthropologists, biologists, and many others, were concerned with what may broadly be termed 'psychological' problems. Not only did they claim a legitimate interest in such issues, but they often made notable contributions. While these do not usually figure prominently, if at all, in texts on the history of psychology, they have been recorded by social historians, historians of anthropology, and others. I cannot, therefore, claim that the material is new, except perhaps in some minor particulars; numerous specialist scholars have covered most of the ground to be surveyed, and I shall have occasion to refer to them. On the other hand, I have not relied entirely on secondary sources, but have gone back as far as possible to original writings, sometimes venturing to offer my own interpretations. What is relatively new – or at least somewhat unusual – is the particular perspective from which the material is being viewed.

Many of the original sources are in French or German, and when translated versions existed and were accessible I made use of them, unless they appeared inadequate. In other cases, where the references are to French or German originals, the translations are my own and the titles appear in the Bibliography in the original language. In general – and particularly with German texts that have elaborately nested clauses which would be practically unreadable in English – these translations are not literal. My objective has been to convey an adequate rendering of the sense, though of course I may not always have succeeded.

The germ of the idea for the present book dates back about a decade to my stay at the Netherlands Institute of Advanced Studies. There I came into close contact with a group of professional historians from whom, as an amateur, I learnt a great deal. Later, in Geneva, I had useful advice from Fernando Vidal, a historian of psychology with a broad vision. As far as anthropology is concerned, I owe much to discussions over the years with Bill Epstein and Ioan Lewis, and was helped by Jean Jamin's extensive knowledge of the history of French anthropology. Maurice Mauviel, whose special interest is the history of French psychology and related problems of culture, drew my attention to some early work.

My conversion from merely 'cross-cultural' to a wider 'cultural' psychology is largely due to the influence of Michael Cole, who also has a sophisticated appreciation of historical issues. When he discovered that I was working in this field, he generously placed at my disposal some of the material he himself had collected. I also owe a great debt to Bernd Krewer, widely read in the history of German psychology and anthropology. Not only did he help me to clarify my ideas, but he was tireless in obtaining copies of all kinds of now obscure publications.

I would like to thank Gün Semin, editor of the series, for suggesting the present title, and to make special mention of the invaluable assistance received from Farrell Burnett, senior editor at Harvester Wheatsheaf; she patiently provided advice and guidance at every stage of the preparation.

A grant from the British Academy, for which I am grateful, enabled me to obtain copies of rare material from various libraries.

Lastly, I wish to acknowledge the support from my family and friends, which enabled me to carry on at a difficult time.

1

Introduction
Mind, Culture and History

What is matter ? Never mind.
What is mind ? No matter.
(Punch, 1855)

T he relationship between 'mind' and 'culture' has emerged as a prominent issue during the last quarter of the twentieth century. It could be said to have become fashionable, and followers of fashion commonly feel themselves to be modern and up to date, in complete contrast to their predecessors. Those who are better informed are well aware that fashions tend to be cyclical, so that similar themes recur in different guises in successive periods. The aim of the present work is to provide a broad perspective of the elements of continuity and change in ideas about culture and mind, mainly over the past three centuries. I shall seek to show that while some questions have been answered and others recognized as false or meaningless, there are some important ones we continue to ask; and, moreover, that there are at least two basically different styles of approach to these questions that divide opinions to this day. Any historical survey of this kind encounters certain difficulties and pitfalls that must be explained at the outset, beginning with history itself.

On the History of Ideas

Contrary to an illusion widespread among the lay public, 'history' does not consist mainly of a collection of 'facts' ready to be consulted. Rather, it involves the selection and interpretation of relevant material in the course of which some degree of subjective bias is unavoidable. Much has been written about the principles that should govern this process, and one version of so-called 'historicism' – there are many different ones (D'Amico, 1989) – holds that specific ideas are embedded in a broader context and can be understood and adequately interpreted only *within* that context. In fact some would maintain that any idea is constrained by what Foucault called an *episteme*, an intellectual framework which determines the conditions and the very possibility of kinds of knowledge in a particular place at a particular time.

Fortunately it is neither necessary – nor would I be competent – to enter into the technical details of these issues. The existence of a flourishing tradition dealing with the history of ideas indicates that one need not worry unduly about the more extreme claims that one needs, as it were, to get into the skin of past writers. There is no way in which one could exchange one's twentieth-century mind with an earlier one; and therefore, as George Herbert Mead (1956) rightly noted, each generation discovers a somewhat different past. Moreover, even within the same generation it is possible to find totally divergent interpretations of the past. Thus Philippe Ariès (1973), in his well-known history of childhood, pictured the Middle Ages and early modern period as the good old times when children were not isolated but integrated into adult life. By contrast, Lloyd de Mause (1976), in his 'psycho-history', claims to unravel a horrific tale of child murder and physical as well as sexual abuse. Fortunately, the risk of such radical divergences is much smaller in a sphere of the history of ideas. For unlike the history of childhood, where inferences based on fragmentary materials are entailed, the history of ideas can draw directly on the writings of the various thinkers whose positions are to be examined. Yet quite apart from the ever-present possibility of the distorting effect of personal bias, complex ideas expressed by past writers are frequently open to alternative interpretations.

The Meaning of Words: 'Mind' and 'Culture'

One particular aspect of this general problem demands some detailed discussion – namely, terminology. The problem is a pervasive one in the history of science:

> Meticulousness in the translation of sources is particularly important when dealing with older specialist terms whose meaning has changed in the course of time. Linguistically speaking, several of the central expressions used are the same today as they were in the past, but their meaning might have changed radically so that a direct translation in such cases would be misleading indeed. (Kragh, 1987, p. 136)

The issue is further complicated by the fact that in addition to changes over time, the ideas to be discussed in this book are those of writers in languages other than English. Dictionaries are not much help even for current usage. For instance, if one looks up 'mind' in an Anglo–German dictionary, one finds '*Seele*', '*Verstand*' and '*Geist*' which, retranslated, are 'soul', 'reason' and 'spirit'; the corresponding terms listed in an Anglo–French dictionary are '*âme*', '*intelligence*' and '*esprit*'. There is thus no exact equivalent of 'mind' in German or French, just as there is no precise equivalent of '*esprit*' in English, as the expression '*esprit de corps*' indicates.[1] In practice this is not an obstacle to current international psychological communication, but it does become important in discussing ideas of even the relatively recent past, such as those of Wundt. The meaning of a term is commonly embedded in theoretical assumptions, such as that of a distinction between 'soul' and 'spirit' or 'mind', which were taken for granted at the time but no longer make sense to us. I might illustrate this in relation to Kant, a philosopher who influenced psychological theorizing from Herbart to Piaget. Kant referred to the study of the soul as '*Pneumatologie*', while his '*Anthropologie*' broadly corresponds to what is now called psychology.

The way I have tried to handle this problem, particularly acute in German, was either to explain the meaning but to add the original term, so that the informed reader can make her or his own translation, or – in the case of well-known terms such as *Völkerpsychologie* – simply to use the original one.

When it comes to 'culture', additional problems of a somewhat different kind are encountered. While a shared understanding of the meaning of 'mind' can be taken for granted, so that there is no need to try and define it, the same cannot be said of 'culture'. Paradoxically, this term was comparatively straightforward initially, but becomes increasingly difficult to grasp as one approaches the present. Originally it stems from 'cultivation', as in 'agriculture', although Cicero already used *cultura mentis* figuratively to refer to philosophy. But for centuries it meant producing or developing something, such as 'the culture of barley' or 'the culture of the arts', and it is still applied in this sense, as in the phrase 'culture of bacteria'. It was only in eighteenth-century France that the single term *culture* began to be used and to acquire the sense of training or refinement of the mind or taste, rapidly extended to refer to the qualities of an educated person. All this, of course, is far removed from the current usage in the social sciences.

An allied expression that recurs in the literature is 'civilization'. The *concept* can perhaps be traced back to the Greek orator Isocrates, who proclaimed in the fourth century BC that it was Attic education and the attainment of a humanitarian ideal, rather than mere descent, that made a person a Hellene as distinct from a barbarian (Jüthener, 1923). The word 'civilize' in the sense of 'bringing out of a state of barbarism' had already been current in the seventeenth century, but the noun 'civilization' was also coined in the eighteenth century and, unlike 'culture', has not undergone any radical change of meaning. The noun, it should be noted, existed only in the singular and was more or less equivalent to 'enlightenment', an ideal of intellectual and moral progress; its opposite was 'barbarity', a term not confined to 'savages'; thus Russia and even Sweden were said to have emerged from 'barbarity' (Braudel, 1980, p. 180).

For most of the nineteenth century and beyond, 'culture' and 'civilization' were often treated as more or less synonymous,[2] 'culture' sometimes being used in the sense of 'rudiments of civilization'. Around the middle of the century the plural forms began to emerge, a significant change that marked a transformation in world-views: the normative ideal had given way to a recognition that 'cultures' or 'civilizations' can vary in time and space.

Primitive Culture (1871) by Edward Burnett Tylor (1832–1917) is usually regarded as a turning point. Its famous first paragraph begins with the words 'Culture or Civilization' and then defines culture as 'that complex whole which includes knowledge, belief, art, morals, law, custom, and any other capabilities and habits acquired by man as a member of society' (Tylor, [1871] 1958, p. 1). It was no accident that Tylor used the singular, since he was concerned with the characteristics of human culture in general rather than with cultural variations. At any rate, modern usage of the term is generally taken as having started to crystallize from Tylor's formulation, subsequently becoming transformed largely owing to the influence of Franz Boas (Stocking, 1982). However, the phrase 'modern usage' is in need of qualification. The term 'culture' is now one of the most frequently used terms in the social sciences, its meaning normally being taken for granted. This tends to create an impression of universal consensus – to some extent justified in so far as there is probably a core of common meaning, but somewhat misleading because different writers, even within the social sciences, vary quite considerably in their handling of the concept. There is no single agreed definition of 'culture'; the well-known monograph by Kroeber and Kluckhohn (1952), which also contains a comprehensive history of the term, lists no fewer than 161 different ones.

Since 'culture' is central to the present theme, this nettle will have to be grasped. I shall not try to select one out of the plethora of definitions, nor be so foolhardy as to attempt yet another. Instead, a rather rough-and-ready effort will be made to discuss what, at the present time, seem to be taken as the *necessary* attributes of the concept, and to point to variations in some of the more peripheral aspects.

There is, first of all, complete consensus that nearly all innate, biologically determined aspects of humans are excluded from 'culture'. There are two slight provisos to this, one being that clearly all normal humans have a built-in potential to acquire culture (Trevarthen, 1983). The other concerns language, generally considered as part of culture:

although the basic capacity for language is innate, becoming a speaker of any particular one is a cultural matter. There is also agreement that 'culture' is, in Tylor's classic phrase, something 'acquired by man as a member of society'; and, furthermore, that something is transmitted, with modifications, through the generations. Views tend to vary as to what exactly that 'something' is, and there has been a substantial change over the past generation. During the 1950s the emphasis tended to be on patterns of *behaviour*, but later 'culture' came to be conceptualized mainly in terms of knowledge, meaning and symbols. For instance, Rohner (1984, p. 119) called it a 'symbolic meaning system', while Sperber (1985, p. 74) referred to 'culture' as essentially 'widely distributed, long-lasting representations'. Others regard affective systems as equally important aspects of 'culture'; some would also include cultural *products* in the form of artefacts. Since these include buildings, roads, and so on, such usage tends to blur the boundary between 'culture' and the physical environment.

The frequent use of such terms as 'system' or 'structure' in connection with 'culture' also implies that it is generally seen as not just a random assembly of specific features, but as having some coherence and organization (for a more extended discussion, see Shweder and LeVine, 1984). These, then, in broad outline, are the main features of 'culture' in modern social science discourse.

Words and Concepts

At this point readers might well begin to doubt whether the implicit promise of the title is really capable of being fulfilled, since it entails a retrospective application of the concepts of 'mind' and 'culture'. Now except for the terminological intricacies discussed above, there seems to be no fundamental difficulty with regard to 'mind' as long as one thinks of it broadly as the key feature of 'human nature'. Ideas and beliefs about 'human nature' not only go back to the beginning of recorded history, but exist in some form in all known human groups; and they are being increasingly studied under the heading of 'indigenous psychologies'. For earlier periods, long before the advent of specialization, one can draw freely on the writings of a wide range of thinkers including philosophers, physicians, naturalists, travellers and, later, anthropologists and sociologists. Such usage is sanctioned by the practice of most conventional histories of psychology. For in spite of the fact that the term itself dates back only to the late sixteenth century (Lepointe, 1970), authors usually have no compunction in tracing origins back to Antiquity.

By contrast, there appear at first sight to be strong objections to the retrospective use of the elusive term 'culture', which has undergone radical changes. Let me try to show that, quite apart from the cumbersomeness of a constantly changing vocabulary, there is a case for using the term 'culture', at least as a kind of rough-and-ready shorthand for past ideas.

The argument rests on the fact that the absence of a term does not preclude the presence of concepts, otherwise articulated, that – at least broadly – correspond to or overlap with what we understand today by 'culture'; and I would submit that even before the eighteenth century, and certainly by then, such concepts were available to all prominent thinkers. Since this will be documented more fully later, it will suffice here to cite the example of Montaigne's famous essay 'On Cannibals', written in the sixteenth century:

> ... il n'y a rien de barbare et de sauvage en cette nation ... sinon que chacun appelle barbarie ce qui n'est pas de son usage; comme de vray il semble que nous n'avons autre mire de la vérité et de la raison que l'exemple et idée des opinions et usances du pais ou nous sommes. (Montaigne, [1580] 1954, p. 33)

In the above, reproduced in its original archaic French, Montaigne is saying that everyone calls 'barbarism' whatever does not correspond to their own customs; and he states that we have no other criterion of truth and reason than the example of the opinions and customs of the country in which we find ourselves. Now these 'opinions and customs' are important aspects of what we still mean by 'culture'. As late as 1872 Walter Bagehot employed the expression 'the cake of custom' to refer to cultural traditions. The view that Montaigne can be regarded as having been concerned with culture is widely shared, and a number of commentators have described him as one of the first 'cultural relativists' – that is, taking the view that each culture should be judged only in terms of its own standards. Corresponding notions, such as Voltaire's '*mœurs et esprit*' or Hume's 'moral causes' of differences between peoples, were widespread in the eighteenth century. This, of course, should not occasion any surprise. A term like 'culture' is a kind of construct that groups together a set of phenomena, and what makes up the set will largely be a function of implicit or explicit theoretical assumptions. Past thinkers held different theories and applied different labels, but they were concerned with similar phenomena.

Thus I would submit that it seems defensible to employ the term 'culture' diachronically to designate a certain commonality of meaning. This usage is not intended to imply direct lines of intellectual descent, but it will be instructive to show what are at least suggestive parallels in the ways different thinkers have handled certain concepts, and how they have struggled with fundamental problems that are by no means fully resolved even today. In doing so, they often employed arguments that have a familiar ring; but whether or not the meaning is exactly the same and they really anticipated modern debates is not always easy to decide. My own view is that in many cases the arguments were effectively identical. This, perhaps, is not altogether unexpected, since in the social and psychological spheres knowledge is not cumulative in the way it is in the natural sciences; hence similar issues tend to recur in different historical periods.

Plan of the Book

At the outset it will be useful to say something about two of the major themes that will be encountered, involving issues that have preoccupied people in different ages. Perhaps the most fundamental of all is the question of what it means to be 'human', and where the boundaries lie between the human and the non-human. Far from being a merely theoretical issue, this has vital practical consequences. Thus the Spanish Conquistadors regarded the American Indians as mere beasts and, as such, open to unrestrained exploitation and extermination until the Pope (only after long and careful consideration) decreed otherwise. There is hardly any need for a reminder that the notion of 'others' as subhuman survived into the twentieth century.

Then there is the theme of the nature and significance of differences between 'us' and 'others', and here it is important to note that this is an issue that arises only when there is contact with 'others'. For a culture is to its members rather like what water is to fish: felt as the natural element, not merely unquestioned but unquestionable. Hence the expansion of travel and colonial conquests played a key part in stimulating reflections about one's own culture in relation to others. The differences between human groups – not merely physical but in their customs, beliefs and world-views – prompted speculation about their origins. It should be noted that such contacts can, of course, be indirect: by oral transmission in non-literate cultures or through writing in literate ones. The images created thereby were not infrequently grossly distorted, and this applied not only to the distant past and not merely to the ignorant. For instance, Hegel wrote about the frightful things one can find in Africa, which he saw as a kind of counter-world to Europe where everything is turned upside down.

These two general themes, I venture to suggest, are probably pan-human. Many traditional, non-literate cultures applied to themselves a name that can be translated as 'the people', implying that they saw themselves as the only truly human beings. Many myths of origin also deal with differences between 'us' and 'them', often purporting to account for the way they came about. The reason for mentioning this is to indicate that some of the basic issues, to be considered here from a 'Eurocentric' standpoint, are almost certainly not confined to the European part of humanity. Scholars familiar with historical writings of other civilizations, such as the Indian or Chinese, would probably be able to trace essentially similar modes of thought. It was mainly from the Renaissance onwards that European thought developed along its own particular lines, though some of these were already foreshadowed in Antiquity.

Accordingly, the first, preliminary chapter follows the usual pattern of beginning with the cradle of European culture. The Greeks and Romans had a great deal of intercourse with other peoples and a lively – if somewhat condescending – interest in their cultures. During the Dark Ages the European mind became closed, peopling the unknown outer world with fabulous creatures with only partially human attributes. Its horizon initially extended very gradually until the Renaissance, which saw a burgeoning of voyages of discovery that continued apace. Encounters with strange peoples and their exotic customs stimulated lively debates on the causes of such diversity. Another leap forward came with the scientific revolution of the seventeenth century which, by the threshold of the eighteenth century, had brought about a transformation of ideas about nature and human life.

The main body of the work consists of three parts, each preceded by a general overview. Part I surveys the eighteenth-century antecedents of the two traditions: 'positivism' and what might be called the 'sociohistorical' approach. It shows how the orginators of these approaches conceptualized the relation between culture and mind.

Parts II and III both cover nineteenth-century developments. Part II starts with a sketch of biological race theories. Although these are positivist in character, this is not the reason for including them. Since the culture–mind relationship is unproblematic for such theories, they could be considered as falling outside the scope of the present discussion. However, some background had to be provided, since those positivists who rejected racial explanations needed to deal with their opponents' arguments. In doing so they raised the banner of 'psychic unity'. The development of what is commonly known as 'theories of social evolution' (as distinct from biological evolutionism) is described, followed by an account of the gradual adoption of empirical methods. This early research was the precursor of modern positivistic cross-cultural psychology.

Part III deals with the growth of the alternative sociohistorical tradition, whose nineteenth-century origins were mostly in German Idealist and Romantic philosophy, and in philology. The first, mid-nineteenth-century version of *Völkerpsychologie* arose from these sources. It sought to provide, if not an actual solution to the problem of the relation between culture and mind, at least a path towards it. The emergence at that period of a positivist experimental psychology gave rise to an intensive debate about the status of the discipline – whether it belonged to the sciences or the humanities.

Wundt's changing positions on this issue are discussed, as well as the manner in which the culture–mind relationship was conceptualized in his own formulation of *Völkerpsychologie*. This whole movement was the forerunner of modern cultural psychology, which opposes the dominant positivism of mainstream psychology.

A brief epilogue then reviews the range of issues discussed over the centuries, which display considerable continuity. Moreover, while a few of the problems have been fully resolved, most are still on the agenda at the close of the twentieth century.

Notes

1. In Volume 1 of the *Trilingual Psychological Dictionary* (International Union of Psychological Science, 1975) the translations are, respectively, '*Geist*' and '*psyché*', neither of which is adequate.
2. This is not strictly true, since there were some national differences in the connotations of these terms. Elias (1977) presented an interesting analysis of the differences in shades of meaning between German *Kultur* and French and British 'civilis/zation', and examined their probable origins. I have to admit that my discussion of the concept has an Anglo-Saxon bias; as will appear in due course, German usage was and remains somewhat different (see also Greverus, 1987).

2

Frontiers of Humanity
The Changing Outlook from Antiquity to the Seventeenth Century

Greece and Rome

Since this story traces the development of European ideas about other peoples and their cultures, the starting point will be Ancient Greece. The Greeks called other peoples 'barbarians', because their languages consisted of unintelligible noises sounding like 'bar-bar-bar' or, as Herodotus more kindly put it, like the twittering of birds. Only Greeks possessed an articulate language, the mark of civilization; the notion of language as an index of the level of culture was one that survived until the twentieth century. Another such mark was the existence of the *polis*, the city, which uncouth tribes lacked.

The image of non-Greeks was not a flattering one. In Euripides's *Andromache*, they were portrayed as given to incest and indiscriminate murder without restraint by laws. Aristotle held that the *nature* of slaves and barbarians was inferior to that of free citizens; for instance, he claimed that they had no powers of planning or foresight (Adkins, 1970), just as was said later of 'savages'.

Towards the end of the fifth century BC Thucydides transcended the then conventional view of the contrast betwen Greeks and barbarians by conceding that in earlier ages the former were probably no different from the latter; at least implicitly, he referred to the uniform nature of humans, variations being relatively superficial. Even more radical was Hippocrates in his treatise *On Airs, Waters, Places*, which earned him the pejorative label *philo-barabaros*. Baldry (1965) summarizes his ideas as follows:

Differences in the character of the various peoples are the result of either the climate or the institutions under which they live, and this principle is equally valid everywhere. (p. 50)

The Stoic philosophy that began during the third century BC espoused a similarly 'modern' view of the basic unity of mankind, rejecting the absolute division between Hellenes and barbarians. Yet Stoics maintained – much as Victorian liberals were to do later – that the unity of mankind should come about by the universal adoption of Greek standards of learning and customs.

It is perhaps no accident that the early Stoics were mostly Syrian, and the later ones Romans, which made it easier for them to avoid the more extreme Greek chauvinism. A more esoteric version of the kind of environmentalism espoused by Hippocrates emerged later when, in the second century AD, Ptolemaeus of Alexandria put forward a kind of astrological ethnography, whereby the mental disposition and cultural states of peoples were attributed to cosmic factors (Hertz, 1925). This view had a long-lasting influence, and as late as the seventeenth century a professor at Tübingen used it to account for the various European national characters: the restless and frivolous character of the French is due to the influence of Mercury; the Germans and the English are governed by the moon and are therefore more sluggish, addicted to drink and less sharp-witted; Swabia is in the sign of Venus, so Swabian women have more permissive customs.

Generally, however, forms of climatic determinism were more common, as was noted by Voget (1973, p. 5), who muses on what might have been:

> The Greco-Roman equation frequently derives the institution from a national character, which in turn must be traced to geographic conditions. Had the equation been reversed, deriving national character from traditional institutions, the basis for a science of culture would have existed . . .

In addition to philosophical speculations, there were those who sought to give an account of peoples beyond the Greek cultural sphere. Outstanding among them was the fifth-century-BC historian Herodotus. Himself a 'colonial' Greek from Asia Minor, he is sometimes known as 'the father of ethnography'. While a good deal of his *History* consists of hearsay, he did travel extensively and was a keen and lively observer. He related the well-known story of the Egyptian king Psammeticus, who attempted to find out which was the oldest human race. Psammeticus is said to have ordered two ordinary children to be kept in isolation until they uttered their first word, which turned out to be in Phrygian. This was probably the first record of an – albeit apocryphal – experiment concerned with language and culture.

No doubt Herodotus was somewhat credulous by our own lights, but he did try to check the story by questioning Egyptian priests in several places to see if their accounts tallied. Moreover, his belief in the story of Psammeticus cannot be dismissed as merely naive, since some two thousand years later a brilliant group of French scientists and philosophers, who will be discussed in due course, proposed a very similar experiment to study child development.

Mention should also be made of the Hellenized Syrian Poseidonios who, during the first century BC, described the modes of life and psychological features of various peoples. He contrasted the Nordics (such as Germanic or Celtic tribes) with Mediterranean peoples. The Nordics he described as being characterized by an excess of *thymos*, which may be glossed as emotionality, including courage, passion; the southerners were said to be governed by *logos*, referring to reflection, moderation and instinct control. Similar claims about north–south differences – albeit with the direction reversed – may be found in twentieth-century 'race' literature. Poseidonios himself did not offer any racial interpretation but attributed the differences to climatic and other environmental factors. Indeed, he suggested that if northerners migrated southwards, they could learn to control their instinctive impulses.

Generally, much of Greek and Roman thought had a critical and rational tenor that was later to be lost.

The Transition to the Middle Ages

Herodotus did not accept everything his informants told him – for example, about men whose heads grow beneath their shoulders. Later writers were less critical, and travel writing that mixed fact with often sensational fiction became an established literary genre. During the first century AD such material was assembled in Latin by Pliny the Elder in his *Natural History*. There is a sense in which he may be regarded as the Ur-father of the Human Relations Area Files:

> by perusing 2000 volumes, very few of which . . . are ever handled by students, we have collected in 36 volumes 20,000 noteworthy facts obtained from one hundred authors. (quoted in Friedman, 1981, p. 7)

In one of his books he took over from Greek writers and further expanded accounts of fabulous races in distant parts of the world. Friedman (1981) has prepared an alphabetical list of some forty types, from which just a few specimen examples will be culled. Some are altogether fantastic: *Astomi* or 'apple-smellers', who neither eat nor drink but merely smell fruit or vegetables, and whom a bad smell kills; *Blemmyae*, who have their faces on their chests; *Cynocephali* or 'dog-heads', who communicate by barking; *Sciopods* who have only one huge leg, which they use as a sunshade while lying on their backs. While these are obviously mythical, others clearly have some foundation in fact. For instance the *Bragmanni*, naked wise men who live in caves, are probably derived from Brahmins. Or again, there are the *Pygmies* referred to by Herodotus, who tells a story of some men on an expedition to Africa who were captured by some 'dwarfish men'.

These 'monstrous races', as Friedman calls them, dominated the imagination of the Middle Ages, when they were depicted on illuminated manuscripts. The adventurous questing spirit of the Greeks was by then extinguished, intellectual life being confined to scholastic theology, which largely governed the outlook on the wider world. The picture was one of a stark juxtaposition of us, the Christians, and the others, the heathens. The humanity of the latter, commonly perceived as grotesque in mind and body, was often regarded as questionable. Pygmies in particular gave rise to much scholastic debate as to their status (which, incidentally, continued long after the Middle Ages): the question was whether they should be considered humans. In the thirteenth century Albertus Magnus placed the Pygmies between apes and men in the Chain of Being (a notion to be examined more fully later), just below the human level:

> the Pygmy is the most perfect of animals. Among all the others, he makes most use of memory and most understands the audible signs. On this account he imitates reason even though he truly lacks it. Reason is the power of the soul to learn from experience out of past memories and through syllogistic reasoning, to elicit universals and apply them to similar cases in matters of art and learning. This, however, the Pygmy cannot do . . . (cited in Friedman, 1981, p. 192)

It is astonishing how reminiscent these views are, on the one hand, of Spearman's (1923) definition of intelligence as the 'neogenesis' of abstract entities, and, on the other, of Jensen's (1973) distinction between memory tests, on which there are no significant black–white differences, and reasoning tests, where they are supposed to be present! Koch (1931), in his study of the teachings of Albertus Magnus, summarizes Magnus's argument: Pygmies, while living in groups, do not form ordered communities and lack science, art, morals and shame – in other words, they are devoid of culture.

While medieval scholars sought to find a place for strange and exotic beings in their theological picture of the world, on the more popular level a pervasive image was that of the 'wild man of the woods'. Distinct from both the Plinyan races and from devils and fairies, this is:

> a hairy man curiously compounded of human and animal traits, without, however, sinking to the level of an ape. It exhibits upon its naked human anatomy a growth of fur, leaving bare only its face, feet and hands. . . . Frequently the creature is shown wielding a heavy club or mace, or the trunk of a tree . . . (Bernheimer, 1952, p. 1)

The powerful presence, throughout the Middle Ages and beyond, of this figure of a wild man suggests, perhaps, a psychological need for symbolic expression of unbridled physical assertiveness. We may not have left this behind altogether – witness the continuing appeal of such images as Tarzan or the 'abominable snowman'.

It was not until the later Middle Ages that an expansion of commerce and the rise of missionary activity resulted in greater contact with non-Christian peoples. Yet this did not usually produce more realistic representations; the influence of the fabulous imagery prevailed. Moreover, these savage and evil creatures were not necessarily from distant shores, but could equally well be in the remoter European regions. One report about Latvians, for instance, describes them as tall and strong but lacking in skills; they are godless and addicted to sorcery; they change themselves into wolves and cats, fly through the air on the back of goats, take part in devilish dances and generally behave in an incredibly horrible fashion (Mühlmann, 1986).

The Renaissance

This fantastic picture of the outside world, portrayed as late as the fourteenth century in John Mandeville's *Travels*, was slow to change even after the dawn of the voyages of exploration. These began with Marco Polo, who visited India, China and Tibet at the end of the thirteenth century. During the fifteenth century the Portuguese explored the West Coast of Africa, later reaching the Cape of Good Hope shortly before the discovery of America. The following century saw the conquest of Mexico and Peru by the Spaniards, who also reached New Guinea.

It was a new breed of men, created by the Renaissance cult of the individual, who embarked upon these hazardous voyages of exploration. The all-embracing theological shell had cracked, opening the way for a renewed interest in the culture of Greece and Rome, which in turn liberated minds. Renaissance travellers eagerly sought personal fame as well as proclaiming the goal of converting the pagans. One can clearly discern the ethnocentric anchoring of the concern with exotic peoples. At the same time there was a search for a perspective whereby one might locate 'the others' in time and space for the purpose of systematic comparison, with a view to gaining a better understanding of one's own individuality and society (Rowe, 1965). A major obstacle to this quest was the fact that nothing like the distinction between nature and culture had as yet emerged.

The period was also characterized by an immense – albeit somewhat diffuse – curiosity, manifesting itself in a passion for collecting a wide range of natural objects and artefacts, as well as a receptivity to new ideas. The travel literature resulting from these voyages, therefore, found an avid public. Although much of it dealt with the adventures of the journeys, perils and deprivations overcome, there were also descriptions of strange lands and peoples: South American Indians, the Hottentots of the southern tip of Africa, Melanesians, and many others.

Although the first-hand accounts by travellers were often sober and factual, it did not follow that belief in the fabulous disappeared. Popular travel books embroidered the tales – describing, for instance, the inhabitants of the New World as 'blue in colour and with square heads'. One of the most successful of these collections, the *Cosmographia* by Sebastian Muenster (1544), presented an indiscriminate mixture of the old 'monstrous races' and the newly discovered 'savages'.

Yet despite the persistence of fables, the Renaissance saw an unprecedented expansion of the European intellectual horizon in terms of both the physical and the human world. As regards the latter, the 'monstrous races' gradually sank down to survive as mere popular superstitions, while the 'savages' became an important concern of philosophers and theologians.[1] Two quite different orientations prevailed: one was 'anti-savage', rooted in the Christian conception of savages as sinful and quasi-demonic beings; the other was based on an emerging humanistic tradition, harking back to Graeco-Roman thought, which viewed 'savages' as natural and unspoiled. This duality remained a persistent theme, re-emerging strongly in the course of the eighteenth century.

The impact of the discovery of a wide variety of human types and cultures on contemporary thought has been analyzed admirably by Margaret Hodgen (1964), who shows how the realization of human diversity presented a challenge to the biblical account of descent from Adam and Eve. The orthodox explanation was based on the eleventh chapter of Genesis, which recounts the multiplication of languages and the dispersion of peoples, some of whom degenerated.

Others were led to question – or at least to reinterpret – the biblical story. Sir Walter Raleigh's (1614) *History of the World* is of particular interest in the present context, since it was based upon 'the assumption of the uniformity of the human mind and the likeness therefore of past to present historical processes' (Hodgen, 1964, p. 243). Raleigh departed somewhat cautiously from the literal biblical account, revising the scales of time and place. A more radical stance, sailing close to heresy, was adopted by Jean Bodin (1577) in his *Of the Lawes and Customes of a Commonweale*. Essentially an environmentalist, he believed in an interaction between a people's disposition (their 'humours') and climatic and geographical factors. Bodin's view, unlike that of Hippocrates, was that institutions need to be fashioned in accordance with the prevailing 'humours'. He also placed great emphasis on migrations, with the consequent mingling of peoples giving rise to new institutions. Thus, with the minimum necessary bow in the direction of orthodoxy, Bodin explained human diversity in largely naturalistic terms.

There were those, however, who felt that the newly discovered remote peoples were so strange that they could not be the offspring of Adam and Eve; thus they were not truly human. In 1520 Paracelsus wrote:

> It cannot be proved that those men who inhabit the hidden countries are descended from Adam . . . in speech they are like parrots, and have no souls . . . (cited in J. G. Burke, 1972, p. 264)

Paracelsus was only the first among a long line of so-called 'polygenists' (as opposed to the 'monogenists', who followed the biblical version of a single creation). Far from being – as mentioned above – mere theoretical speculation, such views served to justify innumerable barbarities committed against what were classified as 'subhumans'.

There were numerous debates on these issues, and the attempts to make sense of the existence of exotic peoples took varied forms. An important one was a search for similarities with the known, strange customs and rituals being assimilated to the familiar. Thus a fourteenth-century Franciscan visiting a Mongolian temple described the image of a woman and child as that of the Virgin and Christ. Generally, similarities between certain features of 'savage' and 'true' religion were either attributed to the devil parodying Christian worship, or taken as evidence of common origins coupled with degeneration. This problem of similarities and parallels constitutes a major thread through the centuries, which later also inspired empirical research.

In addition to religion, a salient focus of discussion was language, including the ancient question of *the* original language. The issue was complicated by a recognition of borrowing and diffusion resulting from migrations. Some monogenists argued that Noah himself had travelled round the world, dispersing his progeny. Others compiled vocabularies of different languages, comparing them at different periods with a view to establishing their Hebrew origins; among them was Bodin, who sought to trace a connection between French and Hebrew, via Greek. After Columbus had brought some captured Indians to the Spanish court, an Italian scholar studied their language and questioned them about their way of life. He came to the conclusion that it was like the Golden Age, when people were simple and innocent. This foreshadowed the eighteenth-century picture of the 'noble savage', and swings in polarity between the 'good' and the 'bad' savage.

Towards the New Age of Science

With a vast expansion of travel, exploration and colonization during the sixteenth and seventeenth centuries, the material available for comparative studies grew proportionately. From the beginning of that period, advice to travellers began to be published. This advice included general admonitions of a vague kind – for example, to mark down things observed – and moral warnings about dallying with women. Other works listed various types of customs and institutions that should be recorded, and also mentioned the need to note the psychological dispositions of the people, their moral character, qualities and abilities. Bernard Varen's (1650) *Geographica generalis* achieved wide circulation among travellers. The topics it covered, reproduced below (from Malefijt, 1974, p. 45), are by no means outdated:

1. Stature, shape, skin colour, food habits;
2. Occupations and arts;
3. Virtues, vices, learning, wit [in the sense of intelligence];
4. Marriage, birth, burial, name giving;
5. Speech and language;
6. State and government;
7. Religion;
8. Cities and renowned places;
9. History;
10. Famous men, inventions and innovations.

It would, of course, be anachronistic to suppose that the authors of such guides were thinking in terms of anything like culture and psychology, since such categories were then nonexistent. All they do show is an interest in a range of topics we now include under these rubrics.

Such an interest was also displayed by the prominent philosophers of the period, notably René Descartes (1596–1650) and John Locke (1632–1704). Descartes's rationalist nativism left an indelible imprint on psychological conceptions of humanity. He was a dualist, who regarded the body as essentially a mechanical device, and animals lacking a soul as mere machines. Humans are unique in possessing a mind and a language capable of expressing reflective thought. Information about the physical world is transmitted to the mind through the senses, he believed, but basic ideas – such as those concerned with God, or logical concepts – are innate. Although these ideas are absent in small children, he viewed their later emergence as predetermined.

Curiously enough, he also voiced sentiments echoing those of Montaigne:

all those whose opinions are decidedly repugnant to ours are not on that account barbarians and savages, but on the contrary ... many of these nations make an equally good, if not better, use of their reason than we do. I took into account also the very different character which a person brought up from infancy in France or Germany exhibits, from that which, with the same mind originally, this individual would have possessed had he lived always among the Chinese or with savages . . . (Descartes, [1637] 1937, p. 14)

This clear statement of cultural influences on the psychological make-up of individuals is probably the outcome of Descartes's personal experiences as a soldier in the army of the German Emperor. It is hard to see how it could be reconciled with his nativism; but then, as Bertrand Russell remarked, the most fruitful philosophers have often been inconsistent.

John Locke, a friend of Isaac Newton, used that very same cultural argument to oppose the doctrine of innate ideas. He regarded humans as part of nature, and it is unlikely to be a coincidence that in his philosophy the 'primary qualities' of objects, such as number, shape or size – as distinct from the 'secondary' ones like colour or taste, which are in the mind – correspond closely to Newton's account of the basic properties of the physical world. Locke was an empiricist who stressed the need for observation rather than mere armchair speculation. Knowledge, for him, is based on experience and is gradually built up from birth. Sensation gives us information about the material world and a second process, reflection, transforms such information from mere reproduction into 'human understanding'. Reflection itself he conceived as a rather mechanical process of association.

Locke points to children and illiterates as exemplifying environmental determination, and the cultural framework of cognition is spelled out with great clarity in the following passage:

> Had you or I been born in *Oldania*, possibly our Thoughts, and Notions, had not exceeded those brutish ones of the Hotentots that inhabit there: And had the *Virginia* King *Apochancana*, been educated in *England*, he had, pe-haps, been as knowing a Divine, and as good a Mathematician, as any in it. The difference between him, and a more improved *English*-man, lying barely in this, That the exercise of his faculties was bounded within the Ways, Modes, and Notions of his own Country, and never directed to any other, or farther Enquiries . . . (Locke, [1690] 1975, I, IV, 12)

It should be noted that Locke postulated not only cultural determinism but also what later came to be known as 'the psychic unity of mankind'. Similarly he undermined, again on the basis of ethnographic evidence, the notion of an absolute morality that had long been the bedrock of Christian theology.

Other developments at that time contributed to the formation of a radically fresh perspective. One was the elaboration by Veit Ludwig Seckendorf (1626–92) and William Petty (1623–87) of a system of social statistics dealing with births and deaths, showing that human life is subject to order and regularity, and could be studied quantitatively. Another concerned the relationship between animals and humans, which had long been obscured by beliefs in more or less mythical beings. A landmark was the publication in 1699 of Edward Tyson's *Orang-Outang, sive Homo Sylvestris: or, the Anatomy of a Pygmie compared with that of a Monkey, an Ape and a Man*. Tyson's dissection of a 'Pygmie' (later shown to have been a chimpanzee) was the first attempt to deal with the anatomy of any of the anthropoid apes. He compared the structure of a man with that of monkeys, concluding that the 'Pygmie' is an intermediate animal between the two. Tyson further suggested that all the legends of Pygmy races, apemen and suchlike from Antiquity onwards originated from imperfect observations of what were in fact apes. While the myths lingered on for a while – and in his own time stuffed monkeys were displayed as supposed members of the Pygmy race (Montagu, 1943) – his work ensured their eventual demise, at the same time opening up a new field of comparative anatomy.

Lastly, a disciple of Descartes, Bernard de Fontenelle (1657–1757), propagated the notion of the immutability of the laws of nature and spelled out the consequences of the new astronomy. He was probably the first effective popularizer of science, and his *Entretiens sur la pluralité des mondes* (1686) was an important event that had a well-deserved success. Taking the form of a conversation between a savant and a lady in a country house park, it shows the *Weltanschauung* of the poor lady being completely shattered. It must be understood that at the time the ideas of Copernicus, Kepler and Galileo had not yet been widely disseminated; most people still believed that the sun revolved round the earth. The Marquise responds to the new revelation with utter disorientation:

> Voilà l'univers si grand que je m'y perds, je ne sais plus où je suis; je ne suis plus rien. La terre est si effroyablement petite!

Thus at the threshold of the eighteenth century humanity began to be regarded as part of nature within a vastly expanded universe that dwarfed its former pretensions. The stage was set for radically fresh thought about the place of humans in nature and society.

Notes

1. Park and Daston (1981) have discussed the significance of 'monsters' in medieval discourse, and the changes in the connotations of the term between the Renaissance and the seventeenth century (from marvels to medical pathology).

PART I:
Eighteenth-century Preludes

L'opposition entre Nature et Culture est
l'une des questions disputées de l'âge des
Lumières. (Gusdorf, 1972, p. 377)

Introductory Overview

The theme of nature versus culture in shaping human destiny constituted one of the major themes of eighteenth-century thought. The terminology is, of course, a modern one, and the theme was implicit rather than explicit. With some inevitable simplification of complex and varied sets of ideas, one can distinguish two major lines of thought about the approaches to what used to be known as 'the study of man', which gave rise to two distinct traditions.

The dominant ethos of the philosophers of the Enlightenment was, in our terms, a positivistic one: humans were regarded as essentially part of nature. Hence they were seen as open to the same kind of scientific study that had proved so strikingly successful in the case of physical nature. The ambitious aim of such an approach was to throw light on the past, present and future of humankind, and for this purpose an understanding of human psychology was seen to be necessary. Among the psychologies elaborated, the most significant one in the present context was sensationism, based on Locke and developed by Condillac. Though in retrospect it seems purely speculative, it was believed at the time to be strictly 'scientific'.

Most Enlightenment philosophers, not unlike a majority of their twentieth-century successors, regarded their psychology as universally applicable. One might say that they believed in what became known in the nineteenth century as the idea of the 'psychic unity of mankind'. But this ran counter to the inescapable fact – then becoming increasingly well documented – that there are vast differences between humans, in both time and space. These were accounted for, first, in terms of the doctrine of *progress*. Various parts of humanity had passed through a series of stages upward from savagery to 'civility' at differing rates – a process widely regarded as lawful, inevitable and continuous.[1]

Beyond that it was necessary to try to explain both the widely variable rates of progress of different populations, and also the less salient differences remaining between civilized European nations. The most popular and very ancient cause put forward was 'climate', often used as an umbrella term including a range of what we would call ecological factors associated with climatic conditions such as types of subsistence, diseases, foods, and so on. Food as such was important in view of the widespread notion that 'you are what you eat'. At the same time, various writers pointed out the weaknesses of purely climatic interpretations. Often combined with 'climate' were such factors as types of government and social institutions. With the exception of Hume, who contrasted 'physical' and 'moral' influences, no explicit distinction was usually drawn between what we would call 'ecology' and 'culture'. Yet the transmission of ideas, skills and values from generation to generation, a key element of our concept of culture, was commonly recognized. A further question addressed by Enlightenment philosophers was how change and progress actually came about. The answer was generally in terms of motivational factors, with people acquiring – for various not very clearly specified reasons – new 'wants', which stimulated their energy and released their intellectual powers.

Language was widely discussed, being regarded (with a few exceptions) as a uniquely human characteristic. The question of its origins gave rise to great deal of debate, as did the relationship between language and thought. As far as the character of peoples was concerned, language was usually taken to reflect rather than cause it. As will be mentioned later, language as such played a far more critical role within the rival humanistic tradition than among Enlightenment thinkers.

While most of the earlier writing was confined to 'armchair' theories, during the latter part of the century a growing awareness of the need for more systematic information developed. For instance William Robertson, whose *History of America* dealt mainly with American Indians, had no personal experience of these 'savages'; but in planning his work he prepared a questionnaire which he sent to many people who did have such experience. One of his French contemporaries, Constantin François Volney (1757–1820), stressed the need for first-hand contacts in order to research the causes of differences between peoples. He travelled extensively in the Middle East, coming to the conclusion that religion and government are the key determinants of a people's psychological disposition.

Volney later became a member of a group of outstandingly gifted French thinkers who made up the Société des Observateurs de l'Homme. Their aim was to found a genuinely empirical science of man, based on observation rather than speculation. While they did not jettison sensationist psychology, they modified it towards a more physiological orientation. One of their number, Degérando, wrote a field manual dealing with research on 'savages' that was so far ahead of its time that many of its principles were not put into practice until more than a century later. It was intended for use by an expedition, which saw the first application of cross-cultural hypothesis-testing, including measurements. The lead given by the Société towards an empirical social science based on a positivist philosophy was not followed up during the nineteenth century. With the rise of functional biology and evolutionary speculations in sociology, it faded away, to re-emerge with renewed strength in the twentieth century.

The dissenters shared a scepticism with regard to the idea of progress, and were out of tune with what appeared to them as the cold and inhuman rationalism of the Enlightenment. All of them were concerned with the relationship between mind and culture; but in the case of Rousseau this was confined to culture in general, while Vico and Herder sought to demonstrate the sociohistorical particularity of human minds.[2]

Chronologically, the alternative ethos was first introduced by Vico, though the full impact of his ideas was long delayed. Hence it seems preferable to start with Rousseau, who wrote in the midst of the Enlightenment, yet in an important sense was not part of it. Not for him the unbounded optimism which saw humans as ascending an infinite ladder of progress, thereby fulfilling a destiny laid down by nature itself. For Rousseau, humans had been, in a distant and mystical past, entirely natural creatures. Some little way along the path of their emergence from quasi-animal savagery they attained the peak of happiness, which progressively declined as they became civilized. Thus, in our terms, Rousseau drew a sharp distinction between 'nature' and 'culture', seeking to trace the transformation from one to the other. Although his equation of this alleged process with a decline from virtue to vice is simplistic, he did make shrewd comments on some of its psychological implications. Rousseau, with greater insight than most of his contemporaries, understood the intimate links between culture and mind. At the same time his Romantic vision was a brilliantly imaginative flight that paid scant attention to the facts about primitive life available even then. He was a man of ideas, unconcerned with methods of inquiry.

Vico's aim, by contrast, was to usher in a new era in the study of human affairs by divorcing them from the methods of the natural sciences. The thesis he put forward most forcefully was that totally different approaches are needed for studies of the human and physical worlds. He argued that we are in a specially good position to understand the human world, since we largely created it ourselves; therefore, the focus of the inquiry ought to be on the human mind and its historical development. Like the Enlightenment philosophers and Rousseau, Vico also envisaged stages of development from savagery to civilization, paralleled by a mental development that moves from the dominance of feeling via 'imaginative knowledge' – a kind of poetic apprehension – to full conceptual knowledge. Where he differed from them fundamentally was in his ideas relating to culture.

As we have seen, Enlightenment thinkers had already arrived at notions at least overlapping with modern conceptions of culture; but theirs – and also that of Rousseau – were mainly concerned with *culture in general* changing in the course of the development of humanity. Vico, on the other hand, envisaged *particular cultures* with their own specific characteristics, though he failed to develop this notion as far as Herder was later to do. Vico saw the historical changes cultures underwent as a function of changing psychological characteristics. And since he held that language constitutes the master key to mentality, he proposed the study of historical changes in language use as the method of choice for understanding particular cultures – recapturing, as it were imaginatively, modes of thought and feelings in different places and periods. Though his influence made itself felt only some time after his death, Vico inspired a long line of thinkers out of sympathy with the 'scientism' of those who believe that the study of humans should be no different from that of the rest of nature.

Herder's ideas are in many ways so similar to those of Vico that it has been suggested – but also disputed – that he simply took them over. Herder was one of the leaders of the Romantic rebellion against the rationalism of the Enlightenment and its unbounded faith in the scientific method. For Herder, even more than for Vico, human nature is not fixed and unchanging but capable of taking on a rich variety of different forms. The stress is not on individuals as such, but on their participation in a *Volksgeist* (literally 'spirit of a people') that comes close to what we mean by 'culture'. Herder explored the implications of being a member of such a unit – of 'belonging', as Berlin (1976) felicitously put it. Like Vico, he emphasized language as the cement that binds the group together and serves the transmission of common ideas and values through the generations. Singularly free of the prevailing Eurocentrism, Herder was widely read in the travel literature of his time. He went well beyond Vico in discussing the effects of environmental factors and culture contacts that contributed to the shaping of the specific psychological and social characteristics of different cultural groups.

Herder's ideas were later elaborated by Humboldt into the systematic historical and linguistic study of peoples and cultures. This in turn became the forerunner of the first (Lazarus and Steinthal) version of *Völkerpsychologie*, a theme that will be taken up again in Part III.

Notes

1. From an epistemological point of view this meant the substitution of temporal for spatial distance from 'the others', which seems to have constituted an obstacle to real communication with them. It has been suggested that this lay at the root of later positivistic anthropology, with its cleft between 'observers' and 'observed' (Fabian, 1983).
2. My decision to include Rousseau among the dissenters is admittedly a somewhat contentious one – he really straddled the two traditions. There can be no doubt, however, that he remained separate from the mainstream of the Enlightenment.

3

Philosophers of the Enlightenment
Nature, Human Nature and Progress

In the course of the eighteenth century, age-old dogmas and beliefs about the world and the place of humans within it began to be questioned, and radically new ideas emerged.[1] Among the major influences that contributed to the changes in outlook was the scientific revolution of the seventeenth century. Newton's prestige was high abroad as well as at home, and even in France Alexander Pope's lines were well known:

> Nature and nature's law lay hid in night;
> God said, 'Let Newton be', and all was light.

The existence of statistical regularity had already been demonstrated for demographic aspects of social life, and from there it was a relatively small step to envisage causal laws governing mind and society. One of those who first took this step was Charles de Secondat, Baron de Montesquieu (1689–1755). He had visited England and been introduced to the Royal Society – though Newton himself was then no longer alive – and he also met the translator of Locke. Montesquieu's attempt to establish a general theory accounting for the differences between human societies is spelled out in the introductory passage to his *De l'esprit des lois*:

> I have first of all considered mankind, and concluded that its infinite variety of laws and customs did not uniquely arise from arbitrary fancy. I have postulated the principles, and have seen how particular cases fit them neatly; the histories of all the nations merely follow them; and that every particular law is linked with another law, or depends on another more general one. (Montesquieu, [1748] 1964, p. 529)

The reference to 'the infinite variety of laws and customs' indicates an awareness of rich cultural diversity in time and place. The eighteenth century was a period in which the world seemed to shrink as never before. Already in the seventeenth century knowledge about peoples outside Europe had increased considerably, and thereafter the growth of interest in remote peoples was manifested in a spectacular expansion of travel literature. Towards the end of the century this prompted a comment from Herder that travel reports were becoming ever better and more numerous. Anybody who has nothing to keep him in Europe, he said, rushes across the globe in 'philosophical fury' and collects material from all parts of the world.

The popularity of travel literature encouraged almost immediate translations, which were widely diffused among educated people across Europe. The magnitude of the changes may be illustrated from the detailed analysis by Duchet (1971) of publications in French: the total numbers of books in that language alone in the sixteenth, seventeenth and eighteenth centuries were 21, 78 and 250 respectively. She supplemented this with a content analysis of the libraries of some prominent *philosophes*; thus she showed that Voltaire, for instance, possessed no fewer than 133 travel books. In most cases a large proportion of such books dealt with non-European cultures, either oriental or concerned with the 'savages' of America or Africa. The image of the savage, albeit an unrealistic one – played an important role in Enlightenment ideas of human nature.

It is also necessary to understand that such ideas took shape within a context – especially in France – of increasing discontent with existing religious and political institutions. The authority of the Church, one of the main pillars of the *ancien régime*, was no longer accepted by many of the outstanding thinkers, who adopted instead a vague kind of deism. The philosophical doctrines being forged, including conceptions of human nature, were to a considerable extent critiques of the status quo and attempts to provide blueprints for the path ahead. This accounts for the fact that a capacity for almost unlimited progress was attributed to human nature – though, paradoxically, that nature itself was generally regarded as remaining constant.

The psychologies of the time reflect a movement away from a spiritual view of humans towards a more material one. The most extreme manifestation of this trend is to be found in the writings of Julien Offray de La Mettrie (1709–51), a physician who boldly chopped off the spiritual half of Descartes's dualism, declaring in his *L'Homme machine* (1748) that humans as well as animals are mere machines. He tried to show that what were then called the 'faculties of the soul' are essentially dependent upon the organization of the brain and the rest of the body. In support of this claim he quite reasonably referred to the effects on the mind of bodily changes such as drugs, illness or fatigue; but a great deal of the supposed evidence consisted of irrelevant anecdotes such as the fact that beheaded chickens still continue to run about. La Mettrie concludes that the soul is nothing but an 'enlightened machine'. The faculties themselves are developed by education, which alone lifts us above the animals. Those who are unable to benefit from education – among whom he includes the blind and the deaf, imbeciles, madmen and savages – are mere animals in human form. This emphasis on the powerful effects of education was also a recurring theme of other writers who held quite different theories.

Few of La Mettrie's contemporaries took such an extreme view, though a vaguely mechanistic orientation was not uncommon. Montesquieu was by no means the first to stress climate as a major factor in shaping mentality, but he tried to identify the processes through which its effects were exerted: he speculated that heat and cold differentially affect nerve and muscle 'fibres', people in cold countries having 'stronger' fibres and also eating rougher kinds of food. From such differences in 'the constitution of the *machine* [emphasis added]', Montesquieu suggested, differences in the strengths of the passions result ([actual date unknown] 1964, p. 486)

Sensationist Psychology

Most of the philosophers writing after the mid eighteenth century dropped the crude mechanical analogies while adhering to the belief that a scientific approach to mind and society is not only possible but necessary. Their views were largely influenced by the writings of Locke, introduced in France by Voltaire, who had travelled in England as a young man. Locke's ideas were further elaborated by Condillac, whose psychological teaching known as 'sensationism' provided the psychological foundation, explicit or implicit, for most of the prominent philosophers of the Enlightenment.

Etienne Bonnot de Condillac (1715–80) was an admirer of John Locke's attempt to trace the development of the mind from its simplest beginnings to its fullest complexity. The twin pillars of Locke's theory were sensation and reflection, the latter accounting for the higher mental processes such as comparing, distinguishing, judging and willing. However, Locke had abandoned his genetic approach at that point, treating these as basic 'faculties' without seeking to trace them to their source.

Condillac, in *An Essay on the Origin of Human Knowledge* ([1746] 1971) and even more directly in his *Traité des sensations* (1754), set about to remedy this by concentrating on pure experience and, by means of a descriptive analysis, reducing everything to 'sensation' as the root of all cognition, feeling and action. While he recognized the physiological aspects of mental phenomena, Condillac resolutely set them aside; he began not with the senses but with sensation, the inner life. The resulting system had the virtues of logical simplicity and great elegance, and was therefore acclaimed by his contemporaries.

In expounding his system, Condillac made use of a thought-experiment, imagining a statue endowed only with a sense of smell, engendering the simplest possible sensations.[2] The statue is, of course, a kind of model of a person prior to any experience, and as such is not to be viewed as passive. If we present the statue with a rose to smell, its capacity for feeling is entirely taken up with the scent of the rose, and this Condillac called *attention*. The statue may enjoy or suffer but cannot as yet, of course, envisage any other state of being; nor has it any sense of its own identity.

Let us now offer a different flower, and the statue's whole 'attention' is given over to the second scent. If we now go on to repeated alternating presentations, something new emerges: the statue gains awareness of more than one state of being because of the *memory* of the other state, leading to a *comparison* of the two existences. At this mode of consciousness the stage of *ideas* is reached, and other operations can be performed: thus if one considers different things, qualities or parts of a whole, then it is *reflection*; if attention is focused on a memory, or brings together two or more ideas in a way not given by sensation, then we have *imagination*; when we note similarities and common properties, then we have *abstraction*. Condillac also discusses the conditions under which the statue acquires a sense or notion of self, this being the sum of the sensations experienced and recalled.

A similar analysis is devoted to the progression from the simple dichotomy of pleasure and pain to the whole gamut of emotions. Here again, memories and comparisons increase the richness and diversity of feelings. Thus, according to Condillac, the whole development of the psychic functions can be analyzed in terms of the single sensation of smell which, like taste and hearing, is a simple sensation. Touch is more complex, because it involves the idea of an external object; as is sight, because judgement enters into it.

The radical conclusion reached by Condillac was that such mental processes as remembering, comparing, judging, having abstract notions like those of duration or number, are all just different 'modes of attention'. Moreover, since attention and 'desire' can ultimately be reduced to 'sensation', it follows that 'sensation' is the fundamental element underlying all human faculties.

Condillac's attempt to show, within the context of the simple sensation of smell, how the association of ideas leads to the emergence of such functions as imagination and memory was, of course, a *tour de force*. As such it is apt to be misleading unless it is viewed within the broader context of his writings, where the association of ideas is not something free-floating but a process lawfully governed by human needs:

The connexion of ideas can arise from no other cause, than from the attention given to them, when they presented themselves conjunctly to our minds. Hence as things attract our attention only by the relation they bear to our constitution, to our passions, to our state, or, to sum up all in one word, to our wants; it follows that the same attention embraces at once the idea of wants, and of such things as are relative to those wants, and connects them together. (Condillac, [1746] 1971, p. 46)

The fundamental driving force of 'wants' constitutes a constant thread in Condillac's arguments. This may be illustrated in relation to one of the current themes: differences between peoples. According to Condillac, climate determines temperament, which in turn influences the type of government, and both jointly create the character of a people in terms of their passions and wants. The language of a people reflects their character by expressing their dominant interests and values (a notion often mistakenly believed to be a 'modern' one). On the other hand, the state of refinement of a given language also limits the scope of mental operations among 'rude and ignorant people', and a Newton among them would lack the conceptual tools for displaying his genius. Condillac's thesis may be summarized in modern terminology by saying that ecology determines culture, which in turn shapes mentality.

Even my brief sketch will, it is hoped, have conveyed something of the power and subtlety of Condillac's thought, which fails to emerge from the few lines usually devoted to him in histories of psychology; were it otherwise, it would be hard to account for the great impact he made on his sophisticated contemporaries.[3]

One important figure who accepted Condillac's empiricist theory of mind, and pushed it further by adopting La Mettrie's views on the overwhelming influence of education, was Claude-Adrien Helvétius (1715–71). His importance was due not so much to his doctrine – which was in several ways rather simplistic and rightly criticized by Diderot and others – as to his role in creating an intellectual climate favourable to the Revolution. In his *De l'esprit* (1758) he scandalized his contemporaries by his materialism, holding that humans have no divine soul but only senses and a passive, though receptive, mind that can be completely shaped through 'education'. It must be said, however, that he used the term 'education' in a very broad sense, meaning:

everything that serves for our instruction, and thus I say that no one receives the same education, because everyone has, if I dare say, as teachers, the form of government under which he lives, his friends, his mistresses, the people surrounding him, his reading, and lastly chance, i.e. an infinity of events whose causal change our ignorance prevents us from perceiving. ([1758] 1973, p. 208)

This long list indicates that Helvétius was really referring to what we would call 'sociocultural environment'. He denied the existence not merely of group or race but also of innate *individual* differences, claiming that given the right circumstances, anybody could achieve anything. In this he was a forerunner of J. B. Watson, the founder of twentieth-century behaviourism, who guaranteed that he could make a doctor, lawyer, artist or other specialist out of any healthy infant. But Helvétius also followed Condillac in believing that 'passion' is what drives us. Some passions tend to distort reason and thus lead to error, yet without passion, reason becomes ineffective. One of the chapters in *De l'esprit* is headed 'One becomes stupid as soon as one ceases to be impassioned'.

While Helvétius held that reason gradually develops in the individual owing to the influences of the social environment, others took the view that man is endowed with reason by Providence, 'reason' being a kind of disposition that is always there but overlaid or masked by unfavourable conditions. If people could only follow the dictates of reason, there would be no error. Now this harks back to Descartes, who held that any of our ideas which are clear and distinct are also bound to be true, since they come from a God who would not deceive us; errors come only from our imperfections (Descartes, [1637] 1937).

Perhaps the clearest and most interesting expression of this widely held view was by François Marie Arouet de Voltaire (1694–1778). In his *Essai sur les mœurs* ([1756] 1963) he writes:

> God has given us a principle of universal reason, just as he has given feathers to birds and fur to bears; and this principle is so constant that it persists in spite of all the passions that oppose it, in spite of the tyrants wanting to drown it in blood, in spite of the impostors who want to destroy it with superstition. (p. 27)

Voltaire did not confine himself to mere assertion, but tried to provide some supporting evidence. Thus he claimed that humans have an innate mechanical sense: 'The most ignorant peasant knows everywhere how to move the heaviest load with the help of a lever' (p. 26) without any conception of the physical laws governing its effectiveness. Another striking example is the following:

> Ask a child without any education, who has begun to reason and to speak, if the grain a man has sown in his field belongs to him, and if the thief who has killed the owner has a legitimate right to that grain; you will see if the child does not respond as would all legislators on earth. (p. 27)

(This story is reminiscent of those of Kohlberg.[4]) At any rate, Voltaire believed that certain basic aspects of 'reason' are inborn, even though they might have existed only as potentialities before the emergence of language.

The Constancy of Human Nature and the Causes of Progress

Voltaire also said that all peoples are similarly endowed, and all have passed through the stage of savagery. This was a generally held view in the eighteenth century, as stated by David Hume (1711–76) in *An Enquiry Concerning Human Understanding* ([1748], in Hume, 1894), where he wrote:

> It is universally acknowledged, that there is a great uniformity among the actions of men, in all nations and ages, and that human nature still remains the same, in its principles and operations. The same motives always produce the same actions. The same events follow from the same causes. . . . Study well the temper and actions of the French and English; you cannot be much mistaken in transferring to the former *most* of the observations which you have made with regard to the latter. Mankind are so much the same, in all times and places, that history informs us of nothing new or strange in that particular. Its chief use is only to discover the constant and universal principles of human nature . . . (1894, p. 358)

The idea that human psychology is the same at all times and in all places has some implications for the question regarding the ways in which humanity progressed from savagery to civilization. If people possessed the same 'reason' from the outset, why do they appear to have been so 'stupid' in some ways during the earlier stages? Hume attempted to deal with this problem in his *Natural History of Religion* ([1755], in Hume, 1894), where he discussed the thought processes involved in earlier beliefs. He suggested that for a 'barbarous and necessitous animal' such as early man the pressure of need must have been too great to permit the exercise of rational thought. A form of this argument recurred in the nineteenth century in Spencer, and later even in Rivers.

It should be noted that Hume broke fresh ground by looking at 'religion' from the perspective of a detached observer, treating it as a cultural universal. His example was followed by Président Charles de Brosses (1709–77), who had a far more detailed knowledge of 'savage' beliefs and was thus able to explore the topic in greater depth. In his book *Du culte des dieux fétiches* (1760) he propounds the thesis that fetishism of the kind prevalent in West Africa was the earliest form of religion. His views became widely accepted and later formed the – rather meagre – basis for Auguste Comte's first stage of human society.

In some parts of his book de Brosses paints a very unfavourable portrait of primitive humanity, depicted as stupid, weak and living in constant terror, rather like children, though failing to outgrow their irrationality. In that respect he foreshadowed a crude version of nineteenth-century notions of 'primitive mentality'. In other passages, however, his ideas have a strikingly modern ring. Fear, hope and uncertainty in relation to his needs and desires stimulate man to speculate about the causes of future events and lead him to imagine superior beings who can both foresee and determine these events:

> In fact there is a natural tendency for man to conceive of beings similar to himself, and to attribute to external things the qualities he feels in himself. He attributes voluntarily and without reflexion goodness and malice, even to inanimate causes that please or damage him. The habit of personifying either such physical beings or all kinds of moral beings is a metaphor natural to man, with civilized as well as savage nations. . . . In all countries the ignorant populace believes in good faith in spirits, fairies, sprites, satyres, ghosts, etc. Should one therefore be astonished if this same populace, among ignorant and rude people, has come to imagine that there is in certain material objects of their cult a power, some kind of spirit, a Fetich, a Manitou? (1760, p. 215)

De Brosses goes on to describe how such 'projection' of feelings readily becomes generalized to a wide range of objects and situations, 'especially in circumstances where chance, i.e. unforeseen accidents, have much influence'. It is under these conditions that superstition comes to dominate souls. He points out that the mode of thinking of the ancient French was little different from that of savages, referring also to various occupational groups where superstition tends to be prevalent: seamen exposed to unpredictable hazards, and gamblers. Closely similar reasoning may be found in modern discussions of the psychological sources of superstition (Askevis-Leherpeux, 1988; Jahoda, 1969).

De Brosses's insightful analysis of a specific sphere of human thought and emotion was exceptional, though many volumes were published on broad surveys of what was then usually called the 'natural history of man' – a significant terminology, as we shall soon see. Everybody, of course, had to agree that there had been progress in the past, though opinions differed as regards the future. The sceptical Hume did not view progress as inevitable; Helvétius envisaged an alternation of growth and decay. Most were optimistic, and among them Condorcet stood out by virtue of his unshakeable faith in the inevitability of continuous progress.

There was much discussion of the causes of progress and, given the view that human nature remains constant, there were two main contenders, put forward either singly or in combination: either progress is the outcome of external influences, or humans must have a built-in propensity to better themselves. The favourite external factor, already encountered with

Montesquieu, was the physical environment, especially 'climate'. Over the greater part of the next century there was a good deal of debate about this, the most compelling argument adduced against it being the fact that there are striking differences between peoples living under much the same climate. As John Millar wrote:

> How many nations are to be found, whose situation in point of climate is apparently similar, and, yet, whose character and political institutions are entirely opposite ? . . . Can it be conceived that the difference between the climate of France and that of Spain, or between that of Greece and of the neighbouring provinces of the Turkish empire, will account for the different usages and manners of the present inhabitants? ([1771] 1806, p. 11)

Now 'character', 'institutions', and especially 'usages and manners', are aspects of culture in our sense. Millar's view on the causes of progress is a psychological one. He speaks of man's 'inherent human disposition and capacity for improving his condition' and also of 'the similarity of his wants, as well as of the faculties by which these are supplied' (p. 8), which leads to uniform progress. Moreover, he postulates – perhaps somewhat inconsistently – a kind of 'revolution of rising expectations':

> According as men have been successful in these great improvements [in agriculture], and find less difficulty in the attainment of bare necessities, their appetites and desires are more and more awakened and called forth in pursuit of the several conveniencies of life [and so manufacture and commerce arise]. (p. 8)

A similarly psychological approach was taken by Marie-Jean de Condorcet (1743–94) in his *Sketch of a Historical Picture of the Progress of the Human Mind* (1794), written under the shadow of the Terror, just before his death. Under the circumstances, his resolute faith in the future compels admiration. The work begins with a summary of sensationist psychology, closely modelled on Condillac, and he contends that the collective progress of the mind:

> is subject to the same general laws that are observed in the individual development of our faculties, since it is the result of that development, considered at the same time among a great number of individuals united in societies. ([1794] 1966, p. 76)

Condorcet adds further that nature has set no limits to the improvement of human faculties, implying that these are variable; but he does not really explicate the grounds of either statement. The stages are those commonly put forward by both French and Scottish Enlightenment writers – hunting and fishing, pastoralism and animal husbandry, agriculture, commerce and manufacture. Key turning points are said to be – in line with the views of most contemporary authors – the introduction of private property and the invention of writing. In discussing the causes of progressive change, Condorcet also follows the ideas originally put forward by Condillac: at the agricultural stage some surplus is accumulated which gives rise to new 'wants', and these increase in successive periods. Progress in the arts comes when some individuals, by chance, see new possibilities. Invoking 'chance' in accounting for changes was common at the time.

Condorcet's vision thus epitomized the views prevalent at the time, without being highly original. Since he was well versed in mathematics, however, he did make some shrewd observations on the future of the 'moral sciences', suggesting the need to invent a 'social mathematics' to which the calculus of probability opens the way. In thus envisaging a tough-minded scientific approach he was following the example of Helvétius and also that of Pierre Maupertuis (1698–1759) who, in his *Lettre sur le progrès des sciences* (1752), had proposed a programme of research in what he called 'experimental metaphysics'; that programme included topics like sleep and dreams, or the acquisition of language, now considered to be within the mainstream of psychological research.

Incipient Notions of 'Culture'

Given the philosophers' wide range of interests, it would be surprising if they had not been concerned with the kinds of phenomena we now label 'cultural'. This has already been indicated, and I shall now illustrate it in more detail, beginning with Montesquieu:

> Various things govern men: climate, religion, the maxims of government, the examples of things past, the customs and manners; out of all this a resulting general spirit [*esprit général*] is formed. ([1748] 1964, p. 641)

This *esprit général* comes close to what we mean by culture, and in the reference to the effects of 'things past' there is even a hint of its transmission. This was explicitly pinpointed by Anne Robert Turgot (1727–81) who also wrote on 'the successive advances of the human mind':

> Reason, the passions and liberty ceaselessly give rise to new events: all ages are bound up with one another by a succession of causes and effects which link the present state of the world with those that have preceded it. The arbitrary signs of speech and writing, by providing men with the means of securing the possession of their ideas and communicating them to others, have made of all the individual stores of knowledge a common

treasure-house which one generation transmits to another, an inheritance which is always being enlarged by the discoveries of each age. ([1750] 1973, p. 41)

Adam Ferguson (1723–1816) may have gleaned the notion of cultural transmission from Turgot, though this seems unlikely.[5] At any rate, he goes well beyond Turgot by stating very clearly – in his own terminology, naturally – that what distinguishes humans from animals is culture:

> Nature, therefore, we shall presume, having given to every animal its mode of existence, its dispositions and manners of life, has dealt equally with those of the human race; and the natural historian who would collect the properties of this species, may fill up every article now, as well as he could have done in any former age. Yet one property by which man is distinguished, has been sometimes overlooked in the account of his nature, or has only served to mislead our attention. In other classes of animals, the individual advances from infancy to age or maturity; and he attains, in the compass of a single life, to all the perfection his nature can reach: but in the human kind, the species has a progress as well as the individual; they build in every age on the foundations formerly laid; and, in a succession of years, tend to a perfection in the application of their faculties, to which the aid of long experience is required, and to which many generations must have combined their endeavours. ([1767] 1966, pp. 4–5)

Note that Ferguson's position is entirely compatible with the idea of the constancy of human nature: it is not the 'faculties' as such, only their 'application', that is improved. It should also be stressed that Ferguson's comments on culture were *obiter dicta*, and not central to his approach. Like the majority of thinkers then concerned with the development of the human species, he called himself a 'natural historian'. This was not, as is sometimes contended, because eighteenth-century writers were unable to distinguish between 'natural' and 'contingent' history. These highly gifted men were perfectly capable of making that distinction, and often did. They quite deliberately treated humans as part of nature, and consequently subsumed culture under the same category. Far from being illogical, such a view is entirely defensible and by no means unknown at the present time.[6]

Differences between Human Groups and the Image of 'Savage'

There was a tension between the belief in the constancy of human nature and the blatantly obvious fact that there were differences between peoples. Such differences, as we have already seen, were attributed either to physical causes located in the environment, or to such 'moral' causes as type of government, or again to the stage of development reached. Language, often viewed as an embodiment of character, was variously treated as both cause and effect.

A distinction must be drawn between discussions of differences between European nations and those between Europeans and savages. The most systematic examination of the former was undertaken by Hume, in his essay *Of National Characters* ([1742], in Hume, 1894). In a previously cited piece he had maintained that in *most* [original emphasis] respects English and French are closely similar. Accordingly, he begins the essay with a critique of what we would call crude stereotyping, while allowing that there are some genuine national differences. At first declaring himself sceptical of physical causes, he later suggests that peoples in climatic extremes, beyond the polar circles and between the tropics, 'are inferior to the rest of the species, incapable of all the higher attainments of the human mind' ([1742], in Hume, 1894, p. 122); but he did not think that climatic variations within the temperate zone made any difference.

Within that zone it is primarily 'moral' causes that operate. Under this heading Hume includes poverty and hard labour, which 'debase the minds of the common people'. The same effect is produced by 'oppressive governments'. More generally, humans are imitative, and frequent intercourse within a group is likely to create similarities in manners and sentiments. Add to this a common language within a shared political framework, and a national character will emerge over and above individual characters. This also applies to occupational subgroups within a nation who experience similar circumstances; so the character of a soldier will be different from that of a priest.

In the early beginnings of a society, some dispositions will be more frequent than others and thus 'give a tincture to the national character'. Once established, these peculiarities will then be transmitted:

> Whatever it be that forms the manners of one generation, the next must imbibe a deeper tincture of the same dye; men being more susceptible of all impressions during infancy, and retaining these impressions as long as they remain in the world. ([1742], in Hume, 1894, p. 120)

These generalizations are illustrated by a series of anecdotes scattered over a wide range of times and places. The essay fizzles out, rather than concludes, with some curious remarks on the advantages of people in temperate climates: 'their blood not being so inflamed as to render them jealous, and yet being warm enough to make them set a due value on the charms and endowments of the fair sex'!

Apart from airing some of his prejudices, Hume displayed shrewd insights. He regarded it as 'curious' that animals are everywhere subject to physical influences, while humans are not. He came to the conclusion that it is social interactions in a diversity of settings, which have cumulative effects, that outweigh any but the more extreme physical factors. If one reads 'cultural influences' for Hume's 'moral causes', then much of his discussion strikingly anticipates twentieth-century ideas.

Few other writers of the period occupied themselves with detailed consideration of what they – no doubt rightly – saw as relatively minor differences between nations. Usually their eyes were fixed on the broader horizons of the ascent of humankind as a whole, and the contrasts in levels of culture within it. There was some interest in oriental cultures, especially the Chinese, but these were generally seen as peripheral to the main line of progress from 'rude' to 'polite' that culminated in Europe.

One can note a significant difference between the writers of the French and the Scottish Enlightenment. The French were living under an authoritarian regime which they sought to combat, yet they had to be cautious in propagating their ideas, lest they fell foul of the censorship. In fact, many of them spent periods in prison or exile. Hence they were apt to resort to the device of locating their narratives in exotic cultures – as, for instance, in Montesquieu's *Lettres persanes* – or even in outer space, like Voltaire's *Micromégas*. Similarly, the 'savages' – as we shall soon see in more detail – were often used to bring home political lessons.

The Scots, on the other hand, free from such constraints, were able to adopt a more theoretical stance, being genuinely interested in what the 'savage state' was really like. They put a great deal of effort into examining first-hand sources, and viewed them critically. Thus Millar warned against undue reliance on the tales of travellers who might easily either have been deceived, or have intentionally misrepresented the facts to fit in with their preconceptions, so that only the consensus of independent sources could be trusted. However, Millar himself had not much to say in detail about inhabitants of the world who were 'destitute of culture'. By contrast Ferguson, among others, attempted to provide a faithful picture of the culture and psychological characteristics of the North American Indians, considered at the time to be the prototype of 'savagery'. It is noteworthy that he frequently drew on the work of Lafitau (1670–1740), a French Jesuit missionary who had given a brilliantly perceptive account of Indian life that is still an ethnographic classic. Lafitau (1724) was largely ignored by French writers, except for Voltaire, who thought fit to mock him. On the basis of such first-hand sources Ferguson painted a rather sympathetic portrait of 'our species in its rude state', noting that one must 'distinguish mere ignorance from dullness, and the want of arts from want of capacity'. While these people study no science and do not seek to establish general principles, they have a range of very considerable skills:

They can ... trace a wild beast, or the human foot, over many leagues of a pathless forest, and find their way across a woody and uninhabited continent, by means of refined observations, which escape the traveller who has been accustomed to different aids. They steer in slender canoes, across stormy seas, with a dexterity equal to that of the most experienced pilot. They carry a penetrating eye for the thoughts and intentions of those with whom they have to deal; and when they mean to deceive, they cover themselves with arts which the most subtile can seldom elude. They harangue in their public councils with a nervous and figurative elocution; and conduct themselves in the management of their treaties with a perfect discernment of their national interests. (Ferguson, [1767] 1966, p. 89)

Ferguson also records unfavourable features and offers a rounded picture of a cultural level backward in many but by no means all of its aspects; and certainly not lacking either in complexity or in the promotion of adaptive skills. This may be compared to Montesquieu's characterization in his (undated) *Essay sur les causes qui peuvent affecter les esprits et les caractères*:

Those born among a barbarous people have really only ideas relating to their self-preservation; as for all the rest, they live in an eternal night. There, the differences between individuals, from spirit to spirit, are less great: the crudity and dearth of their ideas make them somehow equal ...
A proof that they lack ideas is that their languages are all very sterile; not only have they few words, but they have few modes of conceiving and sensing. The fibres of their brains, being little used to being flexed, have become rigid. (1964, p. 490)

Montesqieu's notion about the poverty of 'savage' languages was not only widespread in his time, but persisted for almost two centuries. The equality that was supposed to prevail among savages was held up as a shining example by some, whilst others pointed out that it was indicative of the absence of a division of labour and thus inimical to progress. Another, even more salient, catchword was 'liberty', with 'savages' often idealized as being free and independent spirits. How far removed this was from any serious consideration of 'savage' peoples may be gauged from the typically sharp and ironic comments by Voltaire ([1756] 1963). In a section entitled 'Savages', he asks whether one means by this term the wretched rustics existing in hovels and surviving on a bare subsistence; the people who have to leave their homesteads to enlist and, for a miserable pittance, go and kill their fellow-men and get themselves killed? In that case, Voltaire says, there are these kinds of savages all over Europe:

One has to agree, especially, that the peoples of Canada and the Kaffirs, which we were pleased to call savages, are infinitely superior to our own. The

Hurons, [list of other peoples concluding with] the Hottentots, have the skills to make themselves everything they need, and our rustics lack those skills. The peoples of Africa and America are free, and our savages do not even have the notion of freedom. ([1756] 1963, vol. 1, pp. 22–3)

The fact that 'savages' were little given to sustained labour was interpreted by some authors as a sign of their degeneracy and stupidity, while for others it indicated their freedom and closeness to nature. The 'savage', whether noble or ignoble, was essentially a negative mirror reflecting what Europeans believed themselves *not* to be. Accordingly, the images of 'savages' displayed a bewildering variety. The *Encyclopédie*, edited by Diderot and d'Alembert, which appeared between 1751 and 1765, provides good examples of this. Its contributors repeatedly proclaimed the unity of mankind, the excellence of living close to nature and the goodness of primitive man. Yet the article entitled 'Savages' states that for the most part they remain ferocious and eat human flesh, that they generally live without laws, government, religion or fixed habitations. Similarly Diderot, in the article on 'The Human Species', reviews a large variety of peoples in most unflattering terms, calling them 'degenerate', 'without either manners or religion', and so on; even the Chinese are described in the main as lazy, superstitious and slavish. Yet later, in another context, Diderot painted an utterly romantic picture of Tahiti in his exhortations to the explorer Bougainville:

Ah, Monsieur de Bougainville, take your vessel away from the shores of these innocent and fortunate Tahitians; they are happy, and you can only destroy their bliss. They follow the instinct of nature, and you are going to erase this august and sacred character. Everything belongs to everybody, and you are going to bring them the harmful distinction between yours and mine; their wives and daughters are in common, and you are going to set up among them the fury of love and jealousy. They are free, and there you are [preparing for them] their future slavery (Diderot, *Voyage autour du monde*, [1772] 1875, p. 203)

Diderot ([1772] 1875) maintained that it was important for future generations not to lose sight of the savages' way of life and manners, since they provide a better perspective on the institutions of civilized society; thus one might say that the ignorance of savages has enlightened the civilized people. There is, no doubt, a great deal of truth in Diderot's comment, which applied to all of Europe since the Renaissance. Similar views came to be expressed by nineteenth-century social evolutionists, who believed that the study of 'savages' was necessary to throw light on the development of humanity. As far as the French philosophers of the Enlightenment are concerned, however, they were, with few exceptions, not really interested either in any particular 'savage' society or in primitive culture as such. Rather, they were apt to use hypothetical 'savages' as weapons in their ideological conflicts.

Towards the latter part of the eighteenth century a group of thinkers emerged who were genuinely concerned with the empirical study of peoples of other cultures for the light this could throw on humans viewed as part of nature. In several respects their ideas were close to a modern positivist conception of social science.

Notes

1. A readily accessible source, providing a concise and illuminating conspectus of eighteenth-century thought, is Hampson (1982); more details about particular countries are provided in Porter and Teich (1981).
2. This might seem somewhat bizarre, but the distinguished nineteenth-century psychologist Hermann Lotze resorted to a rather similar device:

Let us think of an animal body consisting of a largely homogeneous mass, without structure or organisation, yet which contains in one of its parts a mind-substance [*Seele*]. Its homogeneous substance could easily be affected by incoming stimuli which have differential effects for different stimuli, spread through the whole mass and with part of its influence also touch the seat of the mind-substance.

Lotze then goes on trying to show that even such a primitive animal mass, though incapable of spatial orientation, would be able to respond appropriately to environmental contingencies ([1852] 1966, pp. 116–17)

3. For a searching evaluation of the contributions of Condillac and some of his contemporaries, see M. J. Morgan (1977).
4. Kohlberg (1976) was a psychologist concerned with the development of the concept of 'justice' in children. For this purpose he devised a set of stories: the children have to explain why a particular outcome is or is not just.
5. The passage occurs in a relatively obscure piece of Turgot's, and Ferguson does not refer to him, though other French sources are listed in several places.
6. For a discussion of this issue, see MacCormack (1980).

4

The 'Observateurs de l'Homme'

During the latter part of the eighteenth century, not only was a great deal already known about peoples in distant parts of the world, but this knowledge had begun to be systematized and led to ever more searching questions about human nature and its varieties. In France the fall of the *ancien régime* and the Declaration of the Rights of Man engendered a spirit of optimism among the radical intellectual elite – a feeling that everything had become possible, so that science could ensure a rosy future for humanity. This spirit is typified by Condorcet's *Sketch of a Historical Picture of the Progress of the Human Mind* (1794), in which he contemplated the ending of the distinction between advanced and backward races and complete equality among all the peoples of the earth,[1] and also between the sexes; he had a firm belief in the infinite perfectibility of the human mind.

This period saw the emergence of a science of man considered as an integral part of nature, which ranged widely over areas now divided into separate disciplines such as psychology, anthropology, biology or linguistics. As far as psychology was concerned, the lucidity and coherence of Condillac's doctrine had long enabled it to dominate, but its philosophical and speculative character was at variance with the temper of the latter part of the century. It thus came to be modified by two of Condillac's disciples, Destutt de Tracy (1754–1836) and Pierre Cabanis (1757–1808). Tracy invented the term 'ideology' to denote the 'science of ideas', which he claimed was part of zoology:

> One has only an incomplete knowledge of an animal, if one does not know its intellectual faculties. Ideology is part of zoology, and it is with regard to man that it is particularly important and deserves to be dealt with in depth. (Destutt de Tracy, cited in Copans and Jamin, 1978, p. 490)

In fact this claim was rather spurious, since he failed to depart very much from Condillac and viewed the object of study as the analysis of ideas into their constituent sensations. None the less Tracy was deeply involved in contemporary debates; his circle came to be known as the *'idéologues'*[2] – so dubbed disparagingly by Napoleon.

More interesting in the present context is the contribution of Cabanis, a physician, who delivered a series of lectures on the natural history of man at the Institut National (the most prestigious French scientific institution) in 1796/7. These were subsequently published under the title *Rapports du physique et du moral de l'homme* (1802). Abandoning the traditional image of a body subordinated to its soul, he dispensed altogether with the soul. Instead, he substituted a model in which the physical and 'moral' (read 'psychological') aspects of humans are dynamic and interdependent systems – a view remarkably close to our own. He appreciated the key role of the nervous system, adopting and extending the work of the Swiss anatomist Albrecht von Haller (1708–77). The chief remaining link with Condillac was his emphasis on receptivity to sensations from the external world; he showed that this existed even in the foetus. Accordingly, he stressed the importance of environmental influences for human development, both individual and collective. Cabanis's general orientation was physiological, and he treated the physical and 'moral' aspects of humans as part and parcel of a unitary 'organization'. Not surprisingly, when the Revolution was followed by the Reaction, Cabanis was castigated as a dangerous materialist.

The Foundation of the Société

This brief sketch provides only a very partial illustration of the ferment of ideas that characterized the end of the century.[3] It was in such an intellectual climate that the Société des Observateurs de l'Homme was founded by Louis-François Jauffret (1770–1850) in 1799. Adopting as its motto 'Know thyself', it attracted some sixty members, including a veritable galaxy of illustrious names in France, drawn from a diversity of fields, including naturalists, linguists, philosophers, medical men, historians and explorers. It was probably the first interdisciplinary effort on such an ambitious scale, dedicated to the 'physical, moral and intellectual aspects of the science of man'.

Jauffret's first interests were literary, but he soon widened his horizon by studying natural history, a discipline in which he was later appointed to a chair. Leaving Paris during the Terror, he became closely associated with many of the outstanding contemporary figures after his return. This stimulated his interest in studies that were beginning to be called 'anthropological', leading to his initiative in founding the Société. A man of lively curiosity and rigorous scientific spirit, he was one of the first to address the problems of method in the human sciences. These are set out in his introduction to the *Mémoires* of the Société. Unfortunately the major part of them has been lost and what is preserved is reprinted in Copans and Jamin (1978), to which all citations refer. Here Jauffret's Introduction and two accounts of empirical studies will be discussed, one of them a classic of early social science.

Jauffret's Introduction constitutes an outline of his guiding philosophy. He starts by noting that the very name 'Observateurs de l'Homme' indicates the method whereby a more profound understanding of man is to be acquired. The emphasis is to be on the multiplication of factual observations, leaving aside 'vain theories'. The research will involve:

> casting an attentive glance at the physiognomy of the various inhabitants of the earth; it will study the causes that distinguish one people from another, and which alter in various countries the form and primitive colour of the human species. (1978, p. 73)

Jauffret proposes an exploration of the relationship between animal and human nature, continuity being already taken for granted. Equally, ethnic and regional differences between humans ought to be studied. He expresses some cautious reservations on the validity of 'physiognomy', the diagnosis of character from faces, a fashionable doctrine at that time. The interdependence between the physical and moral aspects of man is stressed, with comments suggesting an interpretation that comes close to what we understand by psychosomatic medicine.

Other topics mentioned include the study of the history of various peoples, their customs and migrations – all on a comparative basis. This also covers languages and gestures, especially the signs and gestures of savages believed to be related to those of deaf-mutes. This, no doubt, reflects the influence of Sicard (1742–1822), who had directed a famous institution for deaf-mutes. The establishment of an anthropological museum is also suggested.

Observation should also be the chief method for the study of the faculties of the soul, and in this connection a concrete proposal is put forward for observing the genesis of the faculties from the cradle onwards. When Jauffret seeks to justify this idea, his literary inclinations shine through the florid prose:

> Why should one not find the same charm in following with an attentive eye the development of the first light of the spirit, in keeping a detailed record of the progress of intelligence in a child, in seeing the birth of the faculties one

after the other, as in closely watching the habits and industry of an insect, or observing the blooming of some exotic plant? (1978, p. 80)

Jauffret could not have been aware that such a study had already been pioneered by a German philosopher, Dietrich Tiedemann (1748–1803), who had published his observations on the mental development of an infant (Tiedemann, 1787). Jauffret also mooted an extravagant experiment whereby children would be brought up in social isolation and their development would be observed. It is to be expected, he notes, that a host of problems concerning the origin of language and of ideas could be resolved thereby.

The final peroration strikes a political note, condemning the evils of the *ancien régime* that outraged human dignity, ending as follows:

> May this Society, in whose success one might say Europe is interested today, fulfil in due course the glorious destinies that seem to await it, and merit that one should say of it one day that its foundation served both the advancement of science and the happiness of mankind. (1978, p. 85)

Even this highly condensed summary should convey something of the ferment of ideas generated by the Société, the feeling of liberation with which they were embraced, and the idealistic purposes they were meant to serve.

Empirical Studies

Among the empirical investigations reported, the first concerns a young Chinese, Tchong-A-Sam, who, after some adventures – including capture by privateers – reached France. Although he was by no means the first Chinese to do so, the Société felt that the knowledge for adequate study had previously been lacking, and that he provided an opportunity for learning something about Chinese language and culture.

The first step was to make sure that he was really Chinese, and Cuvier believed that he could confirm this on the basis of skull measurements. The Société did not manage to discover a great deal about Chinese language and writing, but did find common ground in modes of calculation. What they described as the most interesting exercise involved an abacus, used by their subject with great skill:

> But he did not confine himself to answering our questions or to carrying out the calculations we gave him. He also wanted to test our knowledge; he dictated an addition to us and worked it out with the *souan pan* . . . (Copans and Jamin, 1978, p. 122)

As we shall see later, such reversal between observer and observed, indicative of the symmetry of the relationship, also became manifest in the encounters between European explorers and 'savages'. The study was cut short by the government's decision to send Tchong-A-Sam back to the Orient.

Far more important was the case of Victor, the 'Wild Boy' aged about eleven or twelve, found naked and mute in the forest just at the time when the Société came into its stride. His was by no means the first such case, but in previous cases the main task scientists had set themselves was a classificatory one: did these individuals belong to the species *Homo*? In the new intellectual climate, the members of the Société saw this as an opportunity of studying the process of becoming civilized; hence they proposed detailed observations of the unfolding of intelligence in this boy. He was taken to Paris and kept at Sicard's institute for the deaf and dumb, where Jean-Marie Itard (1757–1838), a young and gifted physician at the institute, devoted years of his life to the education of Victor (Itard, [1801] 1932), and presented several reports on his pupil's progress to the Société.

Itard's programme of education was based on Condillac's sensationism combined with some of the physiological ideas of Cabanis. In a sense Victor was an embodiment of Condillac's statue, which has to be awakened and filled with affect and ideas. Other objectives were to teach him language, integrating him into the life of society, and to increase his receptiveness by exposing him to effective stimuli and arousing his affect. Itard's methods may be illustrated by his efforts to 'waken' Victor's sensitivity. Since he appeared quite indifferent to cold, Itard made him lie for hours in a hot bath and dressed him very warmly; and he did in fact become more sensitive to cold. He also used games, such as hiding objects Victor needed, in order to improve attention and memory.

Itard's labours were – at least initially – crowned with some success, and he felt able to draw several wide-ranging conclusions at that stage. He began with the question regarding the extent of intelligence and the nature of the ideas of an adolescent deprived from childhood of all education and isolated from fellow-humans. His confident answer was that such an adolescent's state would be precisely that of Victor – hence he took the view that certain general inferences could be drawn about causes, and proceeded to do so. I shall summarize the gist of his arguments.

In *a pure state of nature*, man is inferior to a great many animals; the moral superiority of humans, usually believed to be *natural*, is in fact only the result of civilization, which leads man to acquire new needs and new sensations. The imitative faculty necessary for learning, especially language, weakens rapidly with age and isolation, which – coupled with other causes – blunt nervous sensibility. Lastly, from the most isolated savage to the most refined urbanite, there is a constant relationship between ideas and needs; so any local circumstances increasing or decreasing needs thereby necessarily widen or narrow the range of knowledge.

What was new about Itard's conclusion was not so much that there can be no true humanity without culture, but his claim that this was a deduction from his observations – a claim that gave rise to considerable debate. One anonymous contemporary writer, cited by Moravia (1977), was particularly perceptive. He pointed out that nothing was known about Victor's origins, so that assertions about his experience or lack of it were bound to be speculative; and to describe him as 'natural man' was therefore highly questionable. Furthermore, in a discussion somewhat reminiscent of modern debates about environmental deprivation, the author argued that the natural environment provides a rich source of stimulation and, as such, might be expected to give rise to some learning. He also criticized what he saw as a conceptual confusion between the 'wildness' of Victor and an alleged 'state of nature', which invalidated Itard's daring inferences. Lastly, he asked whether there was really anything to be learnt from this case beyond the well-known truth that humans need society in order to realize their potential.

While the above shrewd critique was entirely theoretical, an even more telling blow to Itard's conclusions was delivered by the famous alienist Philippe Pinel (1745–1826), commissioned by the Société to investigate Victor. In a closely reasoned memoir (reprinted in Copans and Jamin, 1978) Pinel showed that the 'wild boy' displayed many of the characteristics well known to him from the behaviour of the profoundly mentally handicapped. The precision of his observations is worth illustrating:

> It has been said with good reason that touch is the sense of intelligence, and it is easy to see how imperfect it is in the alleged 'savage' of Aveyron. He is far from consulting this organ in order to judge various bodily forms, and to close his fingers around them in order to feel them better; he shows, on the contrary, a great deal of clumsiness in the way he seizes with the hand various utensils he uses; his fingers remain straightened out, the organ of touch absolutely out of action. Consequently he is very far from making use of this organ for rectifying errors of vision, because he does not seem to distinguish an object painted on to a flat surface from an object standing out in relief, and he also turns away his glance or lets it stray from side to side at the same time as he reaches for an object to grasp it, without any direct intention. Thus one observes in him a kind of dissonance between the exercise of vision and touch, and this is a characteristic I have noted in the hospices, among the children without intelligence. (Copans and Jamin, 1978, pp. 101–2)

Or again, Pinel describes how Victor had witnessed for many months doors being opened with a key, and realized that this has to be done. Yet he was unable to learn in all that time how to turn a key, so that he had to lead someone to the door to let him out. Pinel concluded that Victor, far from being a prototypical 'savage' or 'natural man', was a mental defective whose parents had probably abandoned him as ineducable and who thereafter spent some time roaming in the wild before being found. There is no doubt that Pinel's judgement was correct. In spite of years of unstinting devotion by Itard, after the initial improvement there was no further progress until Victor died, relatively young, in 1828[4].

Thus Itard's expectation that the study of Victor would throw light on the nature of 'savages' and the conditions for the rise of civilization proved illusory, yet at the same time it should be recognized that his work represented a serious attempt at the empirical study of the relationship between culture and psychological functioning. Its failure reinforced the view held by others, that there was no substitute for the direct study of primitive peoples – a task to which the Société also directed its attention.

Degérando's Essay on Methods

An opportunity to study 'savages' directly presented itself when the Société was able to participate in the preparation for an expedition to Australia proposed by Nicolas Baudin (1754–1803), a distinguished explorer and himself an 'Observateur'. Among other objectives, this expedition had been intended to include a study of the physical, moral and intellectual characteristics of the savages of southern Australasia. It was decided that a kind of 'field manual' should be prepared for the scientists who were to study these 'savages', and this task was entrusted to Joseph-Marie Degérando (1772–1842).

While the ostensible purpose of the expedition was strictly scientific, Napoleon, in approving it, was perhaps not unmindful of its potential intelligence value. The main team consisted of botanists, zoologists, mineralogists and geographers, with Péron, representing the sciences of man, being added only at the last moment. The expedition itself, which set out in two ships in 1800, was dogged by ill fortune almost from the start, owing in part to friction between Baudin and several of the scientists, artists and technicians. On reaching Ile de France (Mauritius) ten of the team of twenty-four disembarked. Among the remainder, illness took such a toll that only six returned in 1804, Baudin himself having died before the end of the voyage. Conditions on the ships were deplorable, with very high overall morbidity (three-quarters) and mortality (one-third) rates, due largely to scurvy and dysentery. Thus it must be understood that the scientific team had to conduct their work under very unfavourable circumstances, which makes their achievements all the more creditable.

Here I shall briefly outline subsequent developments. At the time when the remnants of the expedition reached France, the Société also found itself in terminal decline. The Empire had been declared, and the more radical section of the membership objected to Jauffret's request to Napoleon for permission to add 'imperial' to the name. The attempt at rescue by currying favour failed, since Napoleon had become hostile to the radical spirit that inspired the Société. But all that was in the future, and while the expedition was being planned a spirit of excitement and optimism reigned.

It is perhaps surprising that Degérando was chosen to give advice on how to study 'savages', since he himself had never travelled to any exotic lands. Originating from a Royalist background, Degérando spent some time serving in the Republican army until he won a prize from the prestigious Institut for an essay on signs. Its subtitle referred to 'the art of thinking', and it dealt with the influence of what we would call 'symbols' on the formation of ideas, an early indication of his psychological interests. After this success he was called to Paris, joining the ranks of the *idéologues* and becoming a member of the Société. Subsequently he had a distinguished administrative career, becoming readily adapted to the increasingly reactionary political climate of the Empire and the Restoration.

The memoir he wrote for Baudin, which ensured his lasting fame, was entitled *Considerations on the Methods to Follow in the Observation of Savage Peoples.*[5] It is a remarkable document which, as Evans-Pritchard commented in his preface to Moore's translation, often has a remarkably modern ring.

Degérando begins by saying that the science of man is also a natural science, a science of observation. In accordance with the then prevalent notion of progressive development of humanity, he suggests that the 'philosophical traveller' who journeys to the ends of the earth is, by the same token, travelling backwards in time; in other words, we can see ourselves as we once were in the past – an evolutionary idea that persisted in similar form during the nineteenth century and is to be found, for instance, in Comte. Basic human nature is constant, its development governed by natural laws which we can discover by means of the 'comparative method'. Having declared his positivist *credo*, Degérando proceeds to offer detailed practical advice for the empirical study of savages.

At the outset he provides extensive warnings of the possible pitfalls of such an inquiry, beginning with what we would call inadequate sampling. Thus in the past many travellers wanted to judge a nation by a few people, or a character by a few actions; they may have relied merely on the testimony of those savages whom they happened to encounter; the savages may not have understood them properly because they failed to make sufficiently clear what they were asking; or perhaps they were not inclined to tell the truth – or, at least, the whole truth.

He notes the common tendency of observers to judge things by their own alien standards (we now call this ethnocentrism). He also calls attention to the need to be aware of the effects of the observer's presence upon those being observed. Degérando recommends that the observer should fully enter the life of the people he studies, an immersion into the culture that did not become a requirement for anthropologists until the twentieth century:

> The first means of getting to know the savages well is to become in a way like one of them; and it is in learning their language that one becomes their fellow-citizen. (Copans and Jamin, 1978, p. 138)

Given Degérando's special interest, it is not surprising that there is a great deal about language, which overlaps in part with the psychological issues that are the main concern here and will be presented in some detail.[6] It will be evident that the psychological theory underlying his recommendations is a modified version of Condillac's sensationism. Degérando stresses the special problems connected with the study of intellectual and moral aspects. In particular, one ought to guard against premature inferences and keep in mind prejudices that might influence one's judgements.

I shall now outline his salient proposals, organized in the main according to his own categories.

Sensations

The first thing to be observed are the sensations of savage people, looking in detail at their varieties and focusing on the following four questions:

1. What are the senses that among them are most exercised, active and finely discriminating?
2. What are the conditions that might have led to the more marked development of a particular sense modality?
3. What is the extent of development of each of their senses compared with that one encounters normally among ourselves?
4. What is the type of sensation in which they find most pleasure? (p. 149)

There follow some comments on ways to estimate the degree of development of a particular sense modality, including what we would call the threshold as well as speed and accuracy of sensory judgement responses. An example given is the skill in estimating distances. The two most important senses are those of touch and sight. Observers should seek to establish whether innate factors as well as practice contribute to the frequently noted perfection of savage senses. They will also find out if blindness and deafness are more or less common than with Europeans, the effects of such handicaps and the modes of adaptation.

Ideas

'Our ideas are nothing but elaborated sensations' (p. 150), and it is therefore necessary to consider the transformations they undergo. These are of two types: by combination and by abstraction. Savages probably do not have many abstract ideas, since they have not had occasion to make systematic comparisons. Owing to man's need to simplify, however, they will undoubtedly have been led – albeit unknowingly – to form general ideas. In order to ascertain this, one has to start with the easiest abstractions requiring few comparisons. Thus by showing them two trees of different species, one can find out if they have a name for each species and a general term for 'trees'. By showing them together the movement of an animate being and that of a stone, one can learn if they have a name for 'movement' as such. By such means one can both assess the extent to which they are able to generalize and resolve a number of questions like the following:

> Does the savage have any idea of a principle of sentiment and action, located within himself? How does he conceive it? Has he formed abstractions of being and nothingness, of the finite and infinite, of duration and eternity, of the possible and the necessary? Does he have any idea of the *beautiful*, and does he conceive it otherwise than merely what *pleases* him? Does he happen to imagine what he has not seen ? Does he have the idea of a country other than his own, of a universe other than the one he inhabits? Etc. Etc. (p. 150)

Observers cannot hope to deal with such problems by mere questioning, which would probably elicit vague answers. One has to carry out tests involving different kinds of comparisons, and credit savages only with those they have shown themselves capable of executing. When observers discover some general idea they will try to find out how it originated, drawing out, as it were, the savage's intellectual history.

Association of Ideas

'The great law of the association of ideas is one of the principal bases on which the intellectual system of man rests' (p. 151). Hence one should study the facility with which such associations are formed, how solid they are and how rapidly elicited, and also their extent. 'Since needs are so many centres to which associations of ideas are related, it is especially by focusing on needs that the observer will discover how far the associations of ideas can extend' (p. 151).

Opinions and Judgements

Here questions are raised as to whether the savage makes use of analogy, how far he is governed by instinct, and what influence imitation has on his judgements and actions. A series of content-orientated questions follows, dealing with ideas of God, natural phenomena, immortality, and so on.

Faculties

'The faculties are to the understanding what forces are to the body. Both similarly develop through exercise, and can be assessed through their effects' (p. 152). The important faculty to study is *imagination*, since through it all the others develop. One can gauge it by such aspects as promptness in making decisions, ability to find new means of achieving one's ends, and a tendency to describe what one thinks and feels. It is the best single indicator of mental development.

Attention

We should be told of how much attention the savage is capable, the motives directing that faculty and the objects most apt to arouse it. The best way of discovering this is to follow 'the chain of his needs'.

Memory

This depends on attention, since one can remember only what has been noted. Does the savage remember easily what he has seen, heard or felt? How long does the memory trace persist? How far back do his memories go, and in what order are they recalled? What gaps are there? 'To which pivots are the chains they form attached for him, etc.?' (p. 153).

Foresight

'To foresee is to apply the experience of the past. Thus one will note the use the savage is able to make of the experience he has acquired, how far his glance extends to the future, how far he can take advantage of the circumstances in which he finds himself, how he learns to correct his errors . . .' (p. 153).

Reflection

This is the faculty that most clearly characterizes civilized man. It refers to the ability to introspect, become aware of our thoughts and the core of our being: 'It would be interesting to know if the savage possesses at least the beginnings of such a noble power, or if he remains for ever a stranger to himself' (p. 153). One would have to observe if his activity is entirely elicited from the surrounding world, by objects corresponding to his needs, so that in their absence he falls into a kind of vegetative state. The best evidence for the extent of reflection is to be found in language.

Reflective Needs

Once there are complex and abstract ideas, secondary needs not directly tied to immediate existence arise, and one should study their nature and extent. Those mentioned include curiosity, fear or uncertainty, search for variety and strength of emotions and self-control; also 'the idea he might have of his inferiority and of a happier fate than had been his lot' (p. 154).

Varieties

Under this heading some of the earlier cautions about unduly small samples are reiterated, and it is stressed that there must be more diversity among savages than travellers' reports usually indicate. Moreover, one must take into account such factors as age, sex, lifestyle, the organization of society and the particular circumstances prevailing.

The last two headings, although drawn from other parts of the monograph, are of psychological interest.

Imbecility

'Is it true that one never finds any examples of the phenomenon of mental derangement among savages, or is only that such cases are very rare? If any exist, it is important to collect all the circumstances of effects as well as causes, in order to be able to compare them with those we notice with regard to civilized men' (p. 147). Presumably one will find cases of imbecility, since these are nearly always the result of organic defects rather than emotional factors. One will assess the extent of handicaps, any physical signs, the age of onset, and how far such a state attracts notice.

The Moral Education of Children

What is the extent of parental attachment and the nature of interest parents have in their children? How far, in respect of the latter, do supervision and severity extend? Is it the father or the mother who particularly cares for them? Until what age does this care last? Is it the same for all children, or do parents show any preference? How do children learn the language? How do they learn any notions of morality their parents might have? Lastly, how rapidly do they develop the passions and intelligence? (p. 158).

This sketch of Degérando's ideas shows that he anticipated not merely some fundamental methodological issues of anthropological research, but also problems of cultural psychology. The organization of his questions, based on Condillac's doctrines, is obviously old-fashioned. In this connection it might be noted that when he refers to 'faculties' this is not the same concept as that of the Scottish school of faculty psychology, which took faculties to be innate. Rather, these faculties are viewed as emerging from experience and development.

It is remarkable how many of the issues Degérando raised have become material for research. They include comparative studies of sensory acuity (Rivers, 1901), the question how far this is a function of experience (Segall, Campbell and Herskovits, 1966); the problems of self and identity (Marsella, de Vos and Hsu, 1985); memory (Wagner, 1981); the epidemiology of mental illness (Opler, 1959); and all the questions he raised about child training have been prominent in numerous studies of socialization and cognitive development. In one respect his formulations are perhaps still in advance of modern practice, where cognitive and affective/motivational processes tend to be treated in mutual isolation. Degérando constantly referred to the link between cognitive processes and 'passions' as well as 'needs'. He also stressed the insufficiency of mere questioning and mentioned that tests should be conducted, though his suggestions in this sphere were understandably impractical. Like his fellow-*idéologues*, he also went beyond Condillac in proposing the investigation of age and sex differences, as well as stating the need to take account of broad social and other contextual factors.

Degérando's attitude towards 'savages' was in general a tolerant and relatively positive one. While he thought it possible that they might be governed largely by instinct and reacting more than acting, he also felt confident that they were capable of abstraction; many of his nineteenth-century successors flatly denied this. Although he referred to the savages as 'brothers', he was no cultural relativist. Firmly convinced of European superiority, he was anxious to spread the blessings of its civilization, which he thought savages could not achieve without help. The way to bring this about, according to Degérando, was through closer communications and commerce. Contact would bring home to savages European happiness and wealth, thereby inspiring new desires and needs so that they might be led along the path to civilization, which – if well treated – they would follow with gratitude. 'What joy! What conquest, if some hope dawned of exerting a gentle and useful influence on these abandoned peoples . . .' (p. 163). Degérando, humane in his outlook, had no doubts about dispensing the blessings of civilization.

Péron's Experiment

By contrast Péron, one of the actual participants in the expedition, had been convinced before his departure that a price had to be paid for its benefits.[7] François Péron (1775–1810) was the scientist for whose guidance Degérando had written his *Considérations*, though the difficult circumstances of the voyage had made it impossible to apply its lessons to any appreciable extent.

Péron had spent three years at the medical school in Paris and had studied under Cuvier. An unhappy love affair led him to abandon his studies and apply for membership of the expedition. In pursuit of this objective he wrote, at Cuvier's prompting, a paper with the following rather pompous title: 'Observations on anthropology, or the natural history of man, the necessity of furthering the advancement of this science, and the importance of admitting to the fleet of Captain Baudin one or more naturalists specially charged with conducting researches in this field' (reprinted in Copan and Jamin, 1978). He develops this theme at some length, mentioning the importance for medicine of knowing more about the illnesses of savages in hot and cold climates. Moreover, it would, he argues, be useful to find out the reasons for the almost invariably robust health and longevity of savage peoples, which are all the more surprising in view of their rude and often impoverished conditions of life. Their health and vitality are contrasted with what Péron then thought were the numerous ills resulting from civilized urban life. He sings the praises of the savages' '*physical perfection*' [original emphasis], including the acuity of their sense organs and their exceptional physical strength, and contrasts the 'robust majesty of natural man' with the degraded physical state of people in civilized society.

Such ideas were shared by others – notably Itard, who exemplified the influence of civilization with the young 'savage' of Aveyron in his charge: initially unwilling to don any clothing, and completely insensitive to cold, Victor later became unable to endure it and developed repeated heavy colds and sore throats. This kind of notion was related to the doctrine of sensationism, holding that the range of sensations an individual is capable of experiencing determines the extent to which ideas can be generated and combined. By the same token, however, heightened sensibility might also increase a person's vulnerability to illness. On this basis Péron put forward the hypothesis of an inverse relationship between 'moral sensibility' and 'physical perfection'. Savages are lacking in the former, but enjoy the latter to a remarkable degree. There are echoes here of Rousseau's virtues of 'natural man', but in other respects the perspective is totally different: following Degérando, humans are regarded as part of nature; as such, they constitute objects of study by empirical methods – if possible by experiment and measurement.

The asymmetry thereby entailed between the observer as *subject* and the observed as *object* was implicitly questioned by Captain Baudin in a letter about the Tasmanians (cited in Copans and Jamin, 1978, p. 217). He describes an incident in which a group of armed Tasmanians surprised some sailors engaged in cutting wood. They fled in all directions but one, a carpenter, was caught; he was taken to the water, where they stripped him naked and subjected him to a detailed examination, whereafter they freed him quite unharmed. On relating this episode Baudin concluded with the following comment:

> It would perhaps be equally interesting for the history of man to know what the carpenter thought in the circumstances in which he found himself, as to learn the motive that excited the curiosity of the primitives [*naturels*].

A somewhat similar incident in the presence of Péron apparently triggered off an eventual reversal of his previous position. After landing in Maria Island (later Tasmania) with three sailors and one of the expedition's artists, Péron found himself and his companions surrounded by a large group of armed natives. Both sides dropped their weapons as a sign of peaceful intentions, and after some mutual gazing at this first encounter the Tasmanians began to scrutinize the strangers, whose white skin astonished them. They evidently also wanted to find out what was under their clothes, which the Europeans were reluctant to display. Owing to the Tasmanians' insistence, and the difficulty of refusing them in view of their superior numbers, Péron asked the youngest sailor to satisfy their curiosity. At this point the official version of the report glosses over the important details, and the more revealing account subsequently discovered will be quoted:

> Michel suddenly displayed such striking proof of his virility that all of them exclaimed loudly in surprise interspersed with loud bursts of laughter. Such a state of force and vigour in the one among us who appeared least likely to be capable of it surprised them greatly, and they gave the impression of applauding that state, like people for whom it is out of the ordinary. Several showed with a kind of contempt their own soft and flabby organs, they

brandished them with an expression of regret and desire that seemed to indicate that they did not experience it as often as us. No doubt it would be unwise to affirm from such simple appearances the reality of such an important observation. But I feel duty bound not to neglect reporting it here, with the firm intention of going into the matter more thoroughly in due course; I should even add at once that, among the fairly considerable number of natives I have so far seen, I have not been able to find a single one in this state that is fairly common in the civilized man, especially when he is young, healthy and vigorous. (Jamin, 1983, pp. 61–2)

On this slender basis Péron began to speculate about the possibility that sexual desire in savages might be periodic, as in animals, or at least much less frequent than among the civilized. The previous arguments were turned on their heads, and the harsh life of the savage was said to be responsible for his lack of sexual vigour. There follows a florid passage in which the continuity of the pleasures of love is said to be a likely product of civilization!

He regarded another observation as reinforcing this conclusion. Following Degérando's recommendation, Péron used gestures in an attempt to communicate with the natives and thereby learn some of their words. When he tried kissing and caressing, they responded with surprise or even recoil, apparently indicating that they had no terms for such actions. Moreover, he adds that he has never observed such behaviour, whether between the same or different sexes. Further evidence was obtained in what probably constituted the first systematic (albeit flawed) empirical study comparing different peoples. The dynamometer, invented in 1796 by Régnier, was intended to measure the development of physical strength from childhood onwards. Péron took with him instruments for measuring the strength of the back muscles and hands. He made use of them with several different populations in the course of the voyage, but the crucial measures were those of the most primitive of men, the Tasmanians. It is worth noting that these measures were taken *after* the incident with the sailor and the subsequent exploration of the vocabulary of affection. Péron's results are set out in the Table 4.1 below (1 myriagram = 10,000 grams):

Table 4.1 *Péron's measure of bodily strength*

Subjects from	N	hands (kg)	back (myriagrams)
England	14	71.4	23.8
France	17	69.2	22.1
Timor	56	58.7	16.2
New Holland	17	51.8	14.8
van Diemensland	12	50.6	not tested

Thus he found a clear positive correlation between degree of civilization and physical strength – exactly the opposite of what he had expected originally, though conforming to his new ideas about the weakness of savages.

Péron's study is important – not merely because it is probably the first instance of systematic cross-cultural comparison, but also because it continued to be cited throughout most of the nineteenth century. The father of social statistics, Quetelet (1869), looked at the findings critically. He pointed out that Régnier, the inventor of the dynamometer, found the manual strength of Frenchmen to average only 50 kg. Later Ransonnet, a naval officer in command of two frigates and a brig, tested all 345 crew members; he obtained an overall mean of only 46.3 kg, substantially lower than Péron's Tasmanians. Quetelet gave reasons to suppose that Péron had made errors in reading the scales, assuming that such errors had been systematic rather than random or, as seemed possible, biased. He also stressed, in a subsequent passage, the need for caution in view of the great variability of the measure, recommending that one should take the mean of several observations. Yet despite his clear awareness of all the pitfalls, his discussion of Péron concludes as follows:

> Whatever may be the facts [about the conflicting measures], if one takes Péron's values as relative, it seems at least certain that the strength of French sailors was greater than that of the savages; and this result accords with the assertions of a large number of travellers. (1869, pp. 108–9)

A somewhat more critical view was taken by Armand de Quatrefages (1884), who again reproduced Péron's table, with the following comment:

> These figures justify what Péron says about savage life. Quite often it tends to weaken the organism by the very conditions of existence. None the less one should not unduly generalize this conclusion. One knows in particular how much the Polynesians had the better of the Whites. In the experiments of Péron the Europeans, familiar with the use of the instruments and directing their efforts with intelligence, must have made rather better use of the dynamometer than the savages. (1884, p. 325)

This passage is of interest because it is the first reference I have come across to the problem of unfamiliarity with testing devices and the consequent bias.

Returning to Péron: he considered that the measures he had collected provided definite proof of the new theory suggested to him by the incident with the sailor. Savages are not merely uncivilized but – contrary to the old view, which he now ridiculed – they are also physically weaker as a consequence of the harsh conditions of their lives. Thus by civilizing them one would not merely elevate them morally, but also increase their bodily vigour. Thereby scientific support was given to the European civilizing mission which, well-meaning though it sometimes may have been, provided a justification for the destruction of traditional cultures, and colonialism. This was one of the unintended consequences of the Enlightenment belief that humans are best regarded as part of nature, and can thus be studied by the same empirical methods that had proved so successful in understanding the physical universe. Such a view was not universally shared, and had some formidable opponents.

Notes

1. In his *Reflections on Negro Slavery*, he wrote as follows:

   My friends, though I be not of the same colour as yourselves, I have always regarded you as my brothers. Nature has created you with the same spirit, the same reason, the same virtues as the Whites. Here I am speaking only of those in Europe, for as regards the Whites of the colonies, I would not insult you by comparing them with you . . . (cited in Condorcet, 1966, Introduction, pp. 31–2)

2. It will be evident that the connotations of this term are totally different from what is now, often rather vaguely, termed 'ideology'. For an excellent discussion of the '*idéologues*', see Billig (1984).
3. For a detailed and penetrating account of the background to the rise of the scientific approaches to man, see Moravia (1977).
4. It is therefore absurd to describe the Wild Boy as 'the prototypical illiterate', as Pattison does (1982, p. 12).
5. An English translation by Moore (1969) is available, but my citations are based on the original French version reprinted by Copans and Jamin (1978).
6. In summarizing the recommendations I have substituted modern terms where these seem to correspond closely to Degérando's meaning, otherwise retaining his terms. All page references are to the reprint in Copans and Jamin (1978).
7. This presentation owes much to the illuminating account provided by Jamin (1983).

5

The Dissenters

Culture, History and Mind

The challenge to Enlightenment positivism came initially from a few outstanding figures separate in time and space, who therefore did not constitute a coherent movement, yet their intellectual heritage had a profound impact on later thought about the human mind in relation to nature and culture. The three outstanding figures whose doctrines I shall discuss are Rousseau, Vico and Herder. Rousseau and Herder were themselves products of the Enlightenment, but rebelled against it, while Vico was active in Naples during the late seventeenth and early eighteenth centuries, before its full flowering. Their ideas also varied considerably, but they shared the conviction that there is a human order fundamentally different from the natural order.

Since their approaches are so diverse, they do not lend themselves readily to a thematic exposition; I therefore propose to deal with them separately, beginning with Rousseau. This is not in chronological sequence, and the reason is that Rousseau was at the outset most directly enmeshed in the Enlightenment ideas discussed in the previous chapter. Moreover, his views diverge considerably from the rather similar ones of Vico and Herder.

First, a note of caution: the philosophies espoused by these men are highly elaborated, sophisticated, and sometimes rather elusive. Hence there has been – and continues to be – a great deal of debate about the interpretation of their writings, especially those of Rousseau and Vico. In my simplified version of aspects of their thinking, selected on the basis of relevance to the theme of culture and mind, I have tried to avoid controversial issues and to allow them as far as possible to speak for themselves. None the less, the selection itself is bound to reflect my own bias to some extent.

Rousseau

In his early years, Jean-Jacques Rousseau (1712–78)[1] shared the ideas of the Enlightenment, and was castigated by Burke as the apostle of the Age of Reason. Originally friendly with Condillac, Diderot and Voltaire, he later quarrelled with all of them. This hostility was not merely the outcome of intellectual disagreements, though these were real enough; it was also caused by Rousseau's difficult and rather strange character. Personal factors no doubt played a part in his rejection of many fundamental Enlightenment ideas and ideals. He developed a revulsion against a cold rationalism that left out feeling and sentiment, and against a social order he saw as unnatural. According to his own account the change came about in a kind of sudden conversion experience, occasioned by the wording of a prize question set by the Academy of Dijon: 'Has the restoration of the sciences and the arts helped to purify morals?' It came to him in a turbulent flash that the answer was negative, and he poured out his new vision in the prize-winning *Discours sur l'origine de l'inégalité* ([1755] 1964).

In this work Rousseau portrays humans as he believed them to have been originally, in the State of Nature. Solitary animals among other animals, they roamed the forests, nourishing themselves from the fruits of the earth. Their only desires related to basic physical needs – food, a female, and rest (note the male sexist perspective). Their only fears were hunger and pain. Males and females coupled in fortuitous encounters. At the outset the mother suckled the child merely to satisfy her own need, 'then as habit has rendered them dear to her, she feeds them afterwards for theirs' (1964, vol. 3, p. 147). Thus there was no 'parental instinct', but a kind of 'attachment theory' is postulated. There was no language, only the universal 'cry of nature' emitted in pain or distress.

Natural man as seen by Rousseau was strong and healthy, presumably because the weak did not survive. His senses of vision, hearing and smell were very acute (a notion about 'primitives' that persisted until the early twentieth century); but those required for more refined living – touch and taste – were rudimentary. Here and elsewhere Rousseau seeks to support his argument with reference to observations on peoples that are supposed to have remained close to the 'natural' state. Thus he mentions that Hottentots could see with their naked eyes vessels far out to sea quite as well as the Dutch could with the aid of their telescopes.

Natural man, who was entirely non-aggressive, had two pre-rational instincts and feelings: self-preservation, and pity or compassion. Some authors suggest that the inclusion of compassion was probably a reaction against the Hobbesian picture of man; at any rate, as we shall see later, it is not very convincingly justified and hard to reconcile with Rousseau's insistence on the predominant animality of natural man. In his characterization of animals, and the specification of the crucial respect in which even natural man differs from them, one finds strong echoes of Descartes:

> I see in every animal nothing but an ingenious machine, to which nature has given senses so that it can wind itself up independently, and preserve itself, up to a certain point, from everything that tends to destroy or disturb it. I perceive precisely the same things in the human machine, with this difference, that Nature alone does everything in the functioning of the beast, while man participates in his, as a free agent. (1964, vol. 3, p. 141)

This liberty to choose, present already in natural man, also constitutes the root of another of Rousseau's key distinguishing marks: *perfectibility*; though at that stage such properties remain latent. Natural man, whose needs were readily satisfied, existed from moment to moment, without curiosity or foresight over more than the shortest of spans. Here again a supposed example from savage life is cited:

> Such remains today the extent of foresight of the Carib [the name then given to peoples of South America and the West Indies]: in the morning he sells his bed ... and comes crying in the evening to buy it back, not having foreseen that he would need it for the next night. (1964, vol. 3, p. 144)

While the State of Nature was generally solitary, Rousseau does allow for ephemeral groupings prompted by common needs or dangers. It was from these occasions, which require communications prompted by strong emotions, that language gradually emerged. There is a problem here: according to Rousseau there can be no thought without language, yet thought is necessary for inventing language. This dilemma is sidestepped rather than resolved by the suggestion of an interactive process over an extensive time-span. It is only social life, however rudimentary, that allows man to develop his faculties. In a letter to the Archbishop of Paris (cited in Moreau, 1973, p. 21) Rousseau criticizes the then prevalent notion that man's reason is inherent and needs only to be put to work. According to him, reason is one of the slowest faculties to develop; isolated men, preoccupied with procuring the basics for their existence, age and die before emerging from the infancy of reason. Faint glimmers of it, however, begin to develop even in that primitive state, involving the perception of physical characteristics and relationships and such – as yet inchoate – comparative notions as big and small, strong and weak.

The various elements of this nascent mental life are linked in a dialectical circle in which some priority seems to be assigned to the emotions:

It is through [the passions'] activities that our reason becomes perfected. We do not seek to know unless we wish to enjoy, and it is impossible to imagine why he who has neither desires nor fears would take the trouble to reason. The passions, in turn, take their origins from our needs, and their progress from our knowledge; for one cannot desire or fear things unless one has ideas about them, or by simple natural impulses . . . (1964, vol. 3, p. 143)

As man moved from solitary self-sufficiency towards relationships with his fellows, the 'passions' became more differentiated, a theme treated in greater detail in the *Essai sur l'origine des langues*, written before the *Discours*. In this connection Rousseau gives special emphasis to two attributes he calls respectively *amour de soi* and *amour-propre*. These terms are not easily translated: *amour de soi* has the connotations of both self-regard and self-interest, while *amour-propre* probably corresponds to self-seeking or selfish interest. This distinction plays an important role in Rousseau's thought. In the State of Nature there is only *amour de soi*, allied to self-preservation. Pity or compassion, he argues, was given to man in order to counteract *amour de soi* so as to ensure the survival of the species, and especially its weaker members, before any genuine sociality.

The 'social affections' developed later as a consequence of the awakening of the imagination and of reflection, whereby the other came to be recognized as a fellow-human. *Amour de soi*, given to man by God, is legitimate and moral; *amour-propre* is a kind of degenerate form of it that depends upon comparison of self with others; and in much later and more sophisticated societies it manifests itself in vanity, cupidity, and a lack of inner strength:

> Always looking outside himself, [he] only knows how to live according to the opinions of others, and it is, so to say, from their judgement alone that he draws the feeling for his existence. (1964, vol. 3, p. 193)

This is remarkably similar to G.H. Mead's ([1934] 1956) formulation of the genesis of the self: '[the individual] becomes an object to himself only by taking the attitudes of other individuals toward himself . . .' (p. 202); one is also reminded of Cooley's 'looking-glass self', Riesman's 'other-directedness' and Festinger's 'social comparison processes'. The difference, of course, is that Rousseau deplored what he rightly saw as an unavoidable consequence of civilized life.

It will be apparent even from my sketchy account that Rousseau's psychology was subtle and complex, even if not altogether coherent. He had not, of course, set out to produce a psychology – this was merely incidental to a much more general argument about the shortcomings of a civilization that does violence to human nature. He did not suggest that the hypothetical State of Nature, with pre-humans untouched by culture, was a desirable one; his ideal state was one where a certain limited advance had taken place, without going too far. In a famous passage he waxed lyrical about men content in their rustic habitations, clad in skins sown with thorns; they made their own bows and arrows and enjoyed a few crude musical instruments. As long as they could make everything for themselves and did not depend on the labour of others, they were as free, healthy, good and happy as they could be. With the division of labour equality ceased, property began, and it became necessary to toil in slavery and misery.

What Rousseau had done was to trace the hypothetical transformation of humans upwards from a stage where they were almost indistinguishable from animals (which led him to add a footnote suggesting that orang-outangs were perhaps human). It is only at that early stage that they were truly part of nature, their actions dominated by mere affective impulses. With the dawn of reason they entered into what we could call a state of culture and what Rousseau eventually regarded as the degenerate luxury of civilization. Lévi-Strauss (1962a) described this as 'the triple passage (which is in fact only a single one) from animality to humanity, from nature to culture and from affectivity to intellectuality' (p. 144).

Thus Rousseau parted company with the Encyclopaedists and other Enlightenment thinkers, who had argued that society arose from a 'social instinct' with which nature had endowed humans. In their discussions of 'the natural history of man' they necessarily had to take account of culture, but treated it as a kind of natural product. Rousseau established a clear distinction between nature and culture, formulating his own theory about the primitive origin of the human mind and its historical development. It should be noted that he was concerned with culture and mind in general rather than with cultural variations, though he recognized that these had to be considered:

> If one wants to study men, one has to look close to oneself; but to study man, one has to learn to acquire a distant vision; one has to observe differences in order to discover the [common] properties. (cited in Lévi-Strauss, 1962b, pp. 326–7)

The aim of studying the historical development of the human mind was one taken up later by Wundt, while the search for universal features of the mind is being pursued today by cross-cultural psychologists.

It is also worth going back for a moment to one specific aspect of Rousseau's discussion of the gradual emergence of reason. His description of the development of elementary logical operations (though of course he does not call them that) is reminiscent of the relevant passages in Degérando. This is not surprising, since both are derived from Condillac's sensationism. The crucial difference is that Degérando thought of it as progress in the *application* of the reason with which humans are naturally endowed, while Rousseau viewed reason as something developing from the growth of culture. It is also interesting to note that while Rousseau had come to regard Condillac's sensationism as an inadequate account, because the string of association could not explain active human feeling and will, he continued to accept the sequential process of development postulated. The influence of sensationist psychology may be detected in Rousseau's famous pedagogic book *Emile*, where the pupil parallels the statue in moving in stages from the 'concrete' to the 'abstract', from the mere 'sensual' to the 'intellectual'. If this reminds the reader of something, it is more than a coincidence. Piaget was not only associated with the Institut Jean-Jacques Rousseau but, like Lévi-Strauss, had studied Rousseau's thought and referred to him in his earlier work.

The fragments – and they are no more – of Rousseau's thought which I have sketched naturally fail to convey the vast range of his *œuvre*. Philosophers, historians, literary critics, political scientists, anthropologists and others – though few psychologists – have dissected and argued with his writings. He has been characterized as an individualist and a collectivist, an advocate of democracy and of totalitarianism. Rousseau himself, late in life, said that he was 'the historian of human nature'. This is a statement that applies equally well to the next great figure to be discussed.

Vico

Giambattista Vico (1668–1744) was a man remote from the mainstream of Enlightenment thought. At one time he was believed to have been an isolated genius, but more recent research (e.g. Bedani, 1988) has shown that his native Naples had at this time been a centre of lively debate about the relative merits of the 'ancients' and the 'moderns', of the doctrines of the Greek philosophers and the scientific theories of Descartes and Galileo. If these debates appeared somewhat muted, it was owing to the disapproval of the new ideas by the eccelesiastical authorities and the threat of the Inquisition. It is against this background that Vico's work must be viewed.

Originally published in a shorter version (probably owing to ecclesiastical suspicion) in 1725, the third edition of Vico's *The New Science* appeared in 1744 (1948).[2] It is a book whose baroque manner and theological cast contrast sharply with the usually lucid style and rational orientation that characterize the writings of the French and Scottish philosophers. Because the work is difficult to read it was ignored for a long time, even by those who had much in common with Vico. This was true of Herder, whose ideas, as we shall see later, were much closer to Vico's than to the spirit of the Enlightenment; yet when he first looked at *The New Science* he was not impressed, finding it obscure. Vico was not 'discovered' until the nineteenth century – by the historian Jules Michelet (1798–1874), who had been interested in the problem of national characters. He became captivated by Vico and translated *The New Science*, thereby making it available to a wider European readership. So began the first wave of enthusiasm for Vico, the second dating from the aftermath of the Second World War. The range of quite different people who admired Vico – including, for instance, Karl Marx and James Joyce – is astonishing. In the present context, mention might also be made of his influence on Wilhelm Dilthey (1833–1911), whose writings on the methods and status of psychology will be considered in a later chapter; and also on Ernst Cassirer (1874–1945), whose life work, concerned with myths and symbolism, had initially been inspired by Vico.[3]

The fact that Vico, like Rousseau, has been seen as a predecessor by so many different thinkers – often holding incompatible views, be they radicals or conservatives, positivists or anti-positivists – is due in part to the richness and variety of his ideas, but also to ambiguities in their expression. Moreover, predominant interests and biases are likely to govern the selection from the numerous facets of Vico's thesis. Needless to say, this also applies to my own attempt to interpret Vico's ideas on psychology and culture. He dealt with much the same problems as the philosophers of the Enlightenment, so it is not surprising that one can discern some common strands; but the fundamental divergences are more striking.

Among the several different aims Vico set himself, those he seemed to share with the philosophers of the Enlightenment are most relevant here. He wanted to offer a 'history of human ideas', since changes in ideas are linked with changes in customs and values; and also to give an account of 'ideal eternal history'. The second aim could be roughly translated into current terminology by saying that he wanted to establish the principles of social evolution, but with this difference: the framework of 'ideal eternal history' is laid down by Providence and makes for an intelligible ordering of human affairs towards a given goal. In *The New Science* Vico set himself the task of elucidating these principles.

At this stage it is necessary to dispel a possible misunderstanding that is liable to arise from Vico's use of the term 'science' in the title. Vico held a concept of knowledge that is at variance with the modern connotations of 'science'. For him the Newtonian approach to the natural world was concerned merely with external appearances rather than with the essence of things. We can only really grasp, he maintains, what we ourselves have created. Hence we have a true knowledge of mathematics, because we constructed it; and the same applies to 'civil society' – or, as he also significantly called it, 'the world of nations'. By the same token we are in a unique position to reconstruct, historically, the changing character of humans, and in that sense Vico draws a parallel between history and geometry (NS 349). The contrast between his own and Newtonian science is stressed in the following passage:

> But in the night of thick darkness enveloping the earliest antiquity . . . there shines the eternal and never failing light of a truth beyond all question: that the world of civil society has certainly been made by men, and that *its principles are therefore to be found within the modifications of our own human mind.* [emphasis added] Whoever reflects on this cannot but marvel that the philosophers should have bent all their energies to the study of the world of nature, which, since God made it, he alone knows; and that they should have neglected the study of the world of nations, or civil world, which, since men had made it, men could come to know . . . (NS 331)

This is not to say that Vico regarded humanity as being totally outside nature: human affairs are 'natural' in the same sense as the physical world is 'natural'; but we have a special insight into the former and not the latter. It follows – contrary to Enlightenment views – that the methods employed for increasing our knowledge of the physical world, however important and useful they may be for their purpose, cannot help us in understanding the 'world of nations': for its study, a genetic and historical approach is required. Vico viewed history itself as reflecting the collective *active* experience of humans, not just as the quasi-mechanical responses to external influences, as Locke, Condillac and their 'sensationist' followers tended to characterize it.

Vico, like the philosophers of the Enlightenment, also saw human history as a succession of stages, but conceptualized in a totally different manner. At the outset there were only 'stupid, insensate and horrible beasts' (NS 374), much like Rousseau's near-animals in the forests. Thence emerged actual humanity, where three stages are distinguished: the divine, the heroic, and finally the fully 'human'. Vico's stages – unlike, for example those of the Scottish Enlightenment (hunting, pastoral, agricultural and commercial) – had little, if anything, to do with subsistence, but were based on essentially *psychological* features. Even more important is the difference in the perspective within which these stages were located. Enlightenment thinkers theorized about 'humanity' more or less as an undifferentiated whole, while Vico thought of it as 'a world of *nations*'; and his concept of a 'nation' appears to have been very much the same as what we mean by 'culture'. For him the language, morals, customs, myths and rituals of a 'nation' constitute a complex unity of interdependent parts; for this reason it seems justifiable to use the term 'culture' henceforth in this exposition.

All this does not mean, of course – as already indicated – that the Enlightenment philosophers ignored the particularities of nations, or that they were unaware of certain aspects of what we call 'culture', especially its transmission through the generations. But they were usually referring to human culture in general rather than individual cultures, and emphasized continuities. Vico, while acknowledging continuities, was on the whole more interested in varieties and modes of change. Moreover, less optimistic than the Enlightenment philosophers, he envisaged repeated cycles of progress and retrogression for each culture, a notion that had been prevalent in Antiquity.

Vico's reconstruction began with an attempt to trace the transition from 'beastliness' to the first glimmers of humanity:

> Our treatment of [the emergence of humanity] must take its start from the time these creatures begin to think humanly. In their monstrous savagery and unbridled bestial freedom there was no means to tame the former or bridle the latter but the frightful thought of some divinity, the fear of whom is the only powerful means of reducing to duty a liberty gone wild. To discover the way in which this first human thinking arose in the gentile world, we encountered exasperating difficulties which have cost us the research of a good twenty years. [We had] to descend from these human and refined natures of ours to those quite wild and savage natures, which we cannot at all imagine and can comprehend only with great effort. (NS 338)

Thus he sought to explore the mentality of these early and – as he believed – 'giant' proto-humans about to enter the first, 'divine' stage, one of whose main aspects is that of people dominated by their senses, who tend to personify natural phenomena:

> [These early giants] were frightened and astonished by the great effect whose cause they did not know ... And because in such a case the human mind leads it to attribute its own nature to the effect ... they pictured the sky to themselves as a great animated body, which in that aspect they called Jove ... who meant to tell them something by the hiss of his bolts and the clap of his thunder. ... This characteristic still persists in the vulgar, who, when they see a comet ... or some other extraordinary thing in nature ... at once turn curious and anxiously inquire what it means. (NS 377)

These ideas bear a certain resemblance to those of Hume and de Brosses, discussed above. But while de Brosses referred to metaphor in passing as a human universal, Vico maintained that dependence on the use of metaphor varies with stage of culture. During the divine period men are as yet incapable of abstract rational thought, but this is compensated for by their vivid imagination – early men were poets who expressed abstract ideas in concrete form. Neptune, for instance, specified both a trident-carrying divinity and the general category of all the seas. Hence personification was not just the idle fancy of the ignorant, but a means of coming to terms with the world for humans who 'were entirely immersed in the senses, buffeted by the passions, buried in the body' (NS 378). It was with the help of such metaphors, dubbed 'poetic logic' by Vico, that they were able to make sense of and order their experience.

Such a sympathetic view was – except for the case of Rousseau – alien to the philosophers of the Enlightenment, who basically looked down upon 'savages' as irredeemably ignorant and stupid; and this in spite of the fact that they assumed them to have an as yet dormant power of reason. Vico, on the other hand, believed that the fundamental psychological characteristics of peoples varied according to their cultural level. This belief is epitomized in his statement about the three stages: 'Men at first feel without perceiving, then they perceive with a troubled and agitated spirit, finally they reflect with a clear mind' (NS 218).

Vico's next two stages need be sketched only briefly: the second, 'heroic' stage is still barbaric and relatively close to nature, so that language retains abundant metaphor; last comes the 'human' stage, in which full reason is attained and language becomes a set of purely conventional signs. While this constitutes the master scheme based essentially on changing mentalities, it is worth noting an alternative scheme concerning institutions, whose sequential order Vico lists: 'first the forests, after that the huts, then the villages, next the cities, and finally the academies' (NS 239). In view of the fact that he also states that the order of ideas must follow that of institutions, the relationship between the two schemes remains obscure. There is no doubt, however, that his primary emphasis was on psychological changes, repeatedly summarized in several passages:

> Men first feel necessity, then look for utility, next attend to comfort, still later amuse themselves with pleasure, thence grow dissolute in luxury, and finally go mad and waste their substance. (NS 241)

> The nature of peoples is first crude, then severe, then benign, then delicate, finally dissolute. (NS 242)

The idea of eventual degeneration is also found in Rousseau, though he did not espouse a cyclical theory. It is not very clear how Vico envisaged the transition from one stage to the next, though it would seem that he regarded it as part of a general plan by Providence. In this respect the philosophers of the Enlightenment were not much more specific, commonly referring to chance – for example 'various accidental causes' (Millar, 1771, p. 4), sometimes said to be associated with outstanding individuals: 'chance observation of facts by the shrewdest and most experienced man opens up new arts' (Condorcet, 1794, p. 79); progress was also attributed to 'the passions' in the sense that they create new needs to be satisfied. Underlying all this was a notion of the inevitable and lawful progress of reason, which 'in the long run leads them to the good and the true, towards which they are drawn by their natural bent' (Turgot, 1750, p. 70). As we have seen, Vico maintained that mind is not a constant but develops in history jointly with cultural change. These two positions – one regarding 'mind' as on a par with physical nature and at least theoretically capable of being explained by similar laws, the other denying this and instead postulating intimate links between 'mind' and 'culture' – remain, even today, the focus of intense debate.

Vico's effort at historical reconstruction of the minds of early humans resulted in a far more detailed and vivid picture than that offered by most eighteenth-century philosophers. The usual exception was Rousseau, who had reproached Locke for portraying the 'savage' as a modern person in a primitive setting. But even Rousseau relied on imaginative insight and had no method of getting into the minds of his savages. Vico, on the other hand, did have such a method, derived from his insight that language, myths, art, customs, religion – in other words, symbolic systems – are integral parts of a coherent whole characterizing the life of a society: its culture. Hence he felt able to deduce from a study of these elements what the ways of thinking and feeling of past cultures are likely to have been. This approach was also adopted later by the founders of *Völkerpsychologie* and Wundt. Here is an example of Vico's line of reasoning:

> The poetic characters, in which the essence of the fables consists, were born of the need of a nature incapable of abstracting forms and properties from subjects. Consequently they must have been the manner of thinking of entire peoples, who had been placed under this natural necessity in the times of their greatest barbarism. It is an eternal property of the fables always to enlarge the ideas of particulars. (NS 816)

Above all, Vico was probably the first fully to recognize the potentiality of language in this connection: 'Language tells us the history of things signified by words' (NS 354). It is true that most of the philosophers of the Enlightenment were interested in the origins of language and often speculated about its relation to thought, but they did not undertake Vico's kind of historical analysis:

> What was most original and remains most stimulating in Vico's etymologies is his insight that the history of words, like the history of myths, offers valuable evidence of changing values and modes of thought. If in archaic Latin, for example, *fortus*, which is related to *fortis*, 'strong', had the meaning of 'good', this suggests that brute force was more highly prized in early Rome than it

was later, when 'good' was rendered by another term, *bonus*. Thus the history of language provided valuable evidence for the early history of the human race. (Burke, 1985, p. 84)

Moreover, when it came to savages who lived during the 'infancy' of the race, Enlightenment thinkers commented mainly on the supposed poverty of primitive languages. The parallel between the development of an individual and the progress of humanity was a commonplace, but only Vico pursued its logic by seeking to draw inferences on the basis of his observations of child language:

The most sublime labour of poetry is to give sense and passion to insensate things; and it is characteristic of children to take inanimate things in their hands and talk to them in play as if they were living persons. (NS 186)

This philologico-philosophical axiom proves to us that in the world's childhood men were by nature sublime poets. (NS 187)

Children excel in imitation; we observe that they generally amuse themselves by imitating whatever they are able to apprehend. (NS 215)

This axiom shows that the world in its infancy was composed of poetic nations, for poetry is nothing but imitation. (NS 216)

Languages must have begun with monosyllables, as in the present abundance of articulated words into which children are now born they begin with monosyllables in spite of the fact that in them the fibres of the organ necessary to articulate speech are very flexible. (NS 231)

Last of all, the authors of the languages formed the verbs, as we observe children expressing nouns and particles but leaving the verbs to be understood. For nouns awaken ideas which leave firm traces; particles, signifying modifications, do the same; but verbs signify motions, which involve past and future, which are measured from the indivisible present, which even philosophers find very hard to understand ... (NS 453)

Although we now know that such inferences are based on false assumptions, Vico deserves to be credited with a pioneering interest in the language and thought of children more than two centuries before Piaget.

The discussion so far has dealt with the overall pattern of development common to all humanity. Thereby a fundamental difference between the conceptions of the philosophers of the Enlightenment and Vico's has been left out: the former concentrated almost exclusively on the 'progress of humanity' at large, while Vico envisaged a 'world of nations' *each of which* was destined to pass through his several stages. Moreover, Vico treated these 'nations' as separate cultural entities.

The question then arises as to how the differences between nations originated, and here Vico falls back on a view dating back to Antiquity and widely held during the early eighteenth century:

> There remains, however, the very great difficulty: How is it that there are as many different vulgar tongues as there are peoples? To solve it, we must establish this great truth: that, as the peoples have certainly by diversity of climates acquired different natures, from which have sprung as many different customs, so from their different natures and customs as many different languages have arisen. For by virtue of the aforesaid diversity of their natures they have regarded the same utilities or necessities of human life from different points of view, and there have thus arisen so many national customs, for the most part differing from one another; so and not otherwise there have arisen as many different languages as there are nations. (NS 445)

This passage brings out two aspects of Vico's ideas about the relationship between nature and culture. While the main emphasis of *The New Science* is clearly on internal cultural developments, it indicates that external influences are not excluded, though these are not treated in any detail. Secondly, it implies recognition of the fact that there are biological limits to cultural variability. Since this aspect of Vico's thought sometimes tends to be ignored or played down, it is important to note that he stressed it more than once:

> There must in the nature of human institutions be a *mental language common to all nations*, which uniformly grasps the substance of *things feasible in human social life* and expresses it with as many diverse modifications as these things have diverse aspects. A proof of this is afforded by proverbs or maxims of vulgar wisdom, in which substantially the same meanings find as many diverse expressions as there are nations ancient and modern. [emphasis added] (NS 161)

There is thus, perhaps, rather more common ground between Vico and the philosophers of the Enlightenment than is sometimes alleged. None the less, the fact remains that for Vico the cultural changes of the 'nations' were an integral feature of the history of humanity, so that he saw similar processes as occurring over different time periods. The Enlightenment philosophers, on the other hand, described human progress in a simplified, schematic way, as though it had been a linear trend. Their accounts of it were usually divorced from their discussions of variations in the cultural characteristics of 'nations', to which I now turn.

Vico, like the philosophers of the Enlightenment, also refers to the influence of climate; he does not elaborate on the link between 'climate' and variations in people's 'nature', but it seems unlikely that he conceived it as mediated by modes of subsistence. For unlike the Enlightenment philosophers, he ignored economic considerations altogether; this is a weakness in his approach.

Another contrast which may be noted is that Enlightenment thinkers, notably Montesquieu, attributed national differences also to varying forms of government. Vico, however, reversed the direction of causality when he wrote: 'Governments must conform to the nature of the men governed' (NS 246).

In spite of occasional points of contact, it must be said that in relation to the dominant ideas of the Enlightenment Vico, even more than Rousseau, was the odd man out, possessed by a unique vision of the close link between human nature and culture. This led him to reject the physical sciences as models for the study of human nature even before they had become favoured by the Enlightenment. Instead, Vico turned to history – not in order to illustrate a strongly held thesis, but as a *method* of investigating the development of mentalities and their changes in different contexts. Thereby he originated a sociohistorical approach to the study of human nature that was in many respects fundamentally different from speculative empiricism. The whole issue continued to be – and still remains – contentious. But a strong case can be made for the view that Vico's approach was more 'scientific' than the speculations of the philosophers, insightful and intriguing as these often were. About half a century after Vico the German philosopher Herder put forward his thesis about the importance of considering the mentalities of particular peoples and the characteristics of their cultures.

Herder

In his youth, Johann Gottfried Herder (1744–1803) was an ardent disciple of the Enlightenment, but he soon came to question most of its fundamental assumptions. He moved towards a position generally much closer to that of Vico, though he does not seem to have been aware of Vico's writings at the time when he developed his own ideas. In opposition to the prevalent view of the immutability of human nature, Herder stressed its variability, conditioned by historical and environmental factors. The latter, as we have seen, were then usually subsumed under the broad label of 'climate'. Herder went even further than most, using *Klima* as a catch-all covering not only the geographical but also the social and political milieux. Such failure to draw any distinctions badly flawed his environmental theory.

By contrast, Herder's objections to then popular version of faculty psychology are shrewd and pertinent. Enlightenment philosophers had envisaged a hierarchy of separate 'faculties' in quasi-watertight compartments, with 'reason' uppermost and 'passion' as lower and less important. Herder saw the mind as a unitary organic whole:

> We name the powers of thought according to their different relations, imagination and memory, intellect and judgement; we distinguish the impulse of desire from the pure will, and the power of sensation from that of movement. But the most casual reflection tells us that these faculties are not locally separated. . . . The thought processes of our mind are undivided entities, producing in their totality the diverse effects or manifestations which we treat as separate faculties. . . . Every creature is in all its parts one living co-operating whole. (*Ideas about a Philosophy of the History of Mankind* [1785]; cited in Barnard, 1969, p. 19)

While many of Herder's contemporaries regarded man as a rational animal, but none the less essentially an animal, he would have none of this, viewing man as fundamentally different. This comes out very clearly in his prize essay on *The Origin of Language* (1772), in which he opposes Condillac's and Rousseau's theory that language began with animal sounds. Language and thought, indissolubly linked, differentiate man from animals equipped only with instincts. Moreover, language serves not only as a means of communication between living individuals, but also as a mode of transmitting the ideas and feelings of past generations. Thus what Herder calls 'tradition' is not just a static bundle of beliefs and customs, but a *process* in which past and present are fused and which gives a group of people their sense of identity.

The key term Herder applies to such a group – or, better, organic community – is *Volk*. A *Volk* is characterized by a shared language and historical tradition which shape the mentality of its members [*Volksgeist*], not into any permanent mould but in a constant movement of growth and development – or decay. A *Volk* may or may not coincide with a nation-state – it certainly need not do so. This concept is in fact very close to what we mean nowadays by a 'culture', and Herder's somewhat flowery description of the way in which, from infancy onwards, not merely collective ideas but also feelings and images are conveyed is essentially an account of socialization into particular cultures.

The diversity of human languages and cultures is, for Herder, a positive value, something good and 'natural'. In contrast to most philosophers of the Enlightenment, who established scales of 'progress' by which to evaluate different societies as 'high' or 'low', 'barbaric' or 'polished', Herder was a relativist who considered that each culture must be approached, and valued, on its own terms:

> Thus nations change according to place, time and their inner character; each

carries within itself the measure of its perfection, incommensurable with others. (Herder, [1785] 1969, vol. 4, p. 362)

This non-evaluative attitude may also be illustrated by the tone of his discussion of language differences:

> The Caribs have almost two separate languages for men and women, the most common objects such as bed, moon, sun, bow, being denoted differently by either sex – what a wealth of synonyms! Yet these same Caribs know only four names of colours and must refer all others to these – what dearth! The Hurons use two different verbs when alluding to animate or inanimate objects, so that 'to see a stone' and 'to see a man' requires two different expressions to denote 'see'; if this is traced all through nature – what abundance! (*The Origin of Language* [1772]; cited in Barnard, 1969, p. 150)

Herder believed that the languages of primitive peoples contain relatively more emotional than abstract terms; but he did not share the view, fairly common until well into the twentieth century, that 'primitives' are incapable of abstraction:

> Since human reason cannot remain devoid of abstractions, and since no abstractions can be made without language, it follows that the language of every people must contain abstractions. (Ibid; cited in Barnard, 1969, p. 152)

Neither did he share the prevailing complacency about European superiority, envisaging a future where the tables might be turned:

> The more we Europeans find means and tools to subjugate other parts of the world, to cheat and plunder . . . perhaps the triumph will be yours some time! (Herder, *Yet Another Philosophy of History*, [1774] 1969, vol. 2, p. 371)

He also criticizes the assumption of a *general* European superiority applying to every individual European, arguing that not everybody who makes use of an invention thereby has the genius of the inventor (Herder, [1785] 1969, vol. 4, p. 259). This discussion anticipates the closely similar point made in the well-known discussion of African thought by Horton (1970).

It should be apparent even from this brief sketch that Herder's ideas about the relationship between culture-historical development and change and the diversity of human nature foreshadow some of the central themes of Vygotsky's theory. And while some of his followers – not excluding the founders of *Völkerpsychologie* – gave a somewhat mystical flavour to the notion of a *Volk*, and his name has even been invoked in support of racism, Herder himself expressly rejected such an ideology:

Some, for instance, have thought fit to employ the term *races* for four or five divisions, according to regions of origins or complexions. I see no reason for employing this term. Race refers to a difference of origin, which in this case either does not exist or which comprises in each of these regions or complexions the most diverse 'races'. . . . In short, there are neither four or five races, nor exclusive varieties, on this earth. Complexions run into each other; forms follow the genetic[4] character; and in *toto* they are, in the final analysis, but different shades of the same great picture which extends through all ages and all parts of the earth. (Herder [1785] cited in Barnard, 1969, p. 284)

Herder was thus what in the current jargon might be called an 'anti-racist' who envisaged humanity as diverse not in innate characteristics but in cultural acquisitions. Mention should also be made of Herder's general mode of approach, and in particular his conception of holistic empathy for the understanding of cultural characteristics. This notion ran as an underlying thread through the German *Geisteswissenschaften* (Kramer, 1985), as manifest in German ethnology and the work of Dilthey, to be discussed in due course.

More directly, Herder's ideas influenced Humboldt and the founders of *Völkerpsychologie*, but that was only one particular strand in nineteenth-century thought, and certainly not the dominant one. During the nineteenth century human differences were commonly interpreted in terms of biological 'race'. The influence of various biological and social-evolutionary theories on ideas about culture and mind will be examined in Part II.

Notes

1. For general background, see Cassirer (1989); Starobinski (1971).
2. All references will be to *paragraphs*, marked NS.
3. For fuller accounts of the background, see Albano (1986); Berlin (1976); Burke (1985); Vaughan (1972).
4. Herder does not use the term 'genetic' in a biological sense, as is evident from the context, but probably in the sense of 'developmental' in current usage. Thus, for instance, he refers to the process of the transmission of culture as 'spiritual genesis'.

PART II
The Positivist Tradition

To many educated minds there seems to
be something presumptuous and repulsive
in the view that the history of mankind is
part and parcel of the history of nature,
that our thoughts, wills, and actions
accord with laws as definite as those which
govern the motions of waves, the combination of acids and bases, and the
growth of plants and animals. (Tylor,
[1871] 1958, p. 2)

Introductory Overview

W hat I call the 'positivist tradition' includes a considerable diversity of thinkers, often opposed to one another, but sharing the conviction that they were following the path of science. The major issue dividing two broad types of theorists to be discussed was that of 'race', and the intellectual roots of both can be traced back to the Enlightenment.

Before the eighteenth century, the generally accepted idea of the living world was that of the 'Great Chain of Being', a comprehensive hierarchical order instituted by the Creator in which the varieties of living beings are arranged in small gradations, from the simplest animals up to the angels. While, according to the Bible, all humans descended from the original pair (a doctrine known as 'monogenism'), and were regarded as clearly superior to mere animals, the boundary between animals and humans remained somewhat uncertain. It should also be noted that the Chain, being continuous, left no room for the emergence of any new species.

By the eighteenth century the angels had dropped out, and the haphazard clustering of the elements of the Chain came to be replaced by the founder of modern biological taxonomy, Carl Linnaeus, in his *System of Nature* (1735). Although he was a strict monogenist, he took the fateful step of classing the species *Homo* in the same Order as four-footed animals. His contemporary, the great naturalist Georges Buffon (1707–88), was the first to employ the term 'race' in its modern sense of characters fixed by heredity. But Buffon emphasized the unity of the human species, pointing out that races shade into each other. His ideas were in harmony with those of the Enlightenment philosophers, who often cited him. Their most prevalent outlook, which is squarely in the spirit of our own time, is epitomized in the following passage by the Scottish writer William Robertson (1721–93):

A human being, as he comes originally from the hand of nature, is everywhere the same. At his first appearance in the state of infancy, whether it be among the rudest savages, or in the most civilized nation, we can discern no quality which marks any distinction or superiority. The capacity for improvement seems to be the same; and the talents he may afterwards acquire, as well as the virtues he may be rendered capable of exercising, depend, in a great measure, upon the state of society in which he is placed. To this state his mind naturally accommodates itself, and from it receives discipline and culture. (Robertson, [1777] 1808, vol. 2, p. 221)

There were, of course, dissidents among the philosophers, notably Robertson's fellow-Scot Lord Kames (1696–1782), who was probably the first to put forward a full-blown 'racist' approach to history; but he was regarded as something of a crank.

The breakdown of the broad consensus about the uniformity of human nature began later, around the turn of the century. Contributory factors included the rise of physical anthropology concerned with the study of human anatomical differences, the decline of religious authority that made it possible to proclaim multiple human origins ('polygenism'), but especially the advent of the new biology. This is reflected in the life of its chief torch-bearer, Cuvier: in 1770 he had ridiculed the notion of race differences in intelligence associated with skull shapes; by 1817 his theory explained such an association, and he had become convinced of the inferiority of the darker races. For the rest of the nineteenth century, and well into the twentieth, biological race theories remained one of the most powerful intellectual currents. Given the early beginnings of race theories, it is evident that they had no necessary connection with Darwinism; but Darwinian theory could be – and was later – used to bolster them. As far as the problem of the relationship between culture and mind was concerned, the race theorists had a seductively simple solution: mind and culture are jointly determined by inherited racial characteristics; this also accounts for the course of history, in which the superior races come out on top.

In such an intellectual climate, the defenders of the Enlightenment idea of the unity of humankind faced a difficult task. The main strategy open to them was to establish the existence of pan-human cultural similarities, which in turn point to an underlying commonality of mind. Being equally dedicated to the assumption of lawfulness and the necessity for a scientific approach, they found themselves at a disadvantage *vis-à-vis* the race theorists: most of the avid measurers of skulls who obtained hard empirical data were opposed to them, while they themselves had to rely on extracting information from ethnographic reports. None the less, even though positive proof was unattainable, they were able to expose the salient weaknesses in the race theorists' arguments. At least one of them, Bastian, had the advantage of extensive personal experience of people of other races.

The alternative theories they put forward had in common the idea of the parallel evolution of culture and mind, in which biology played little, if any, part. In the case of the earlier writers such as Prichard and Waitz, the theory remained vague and implicit rather than clearly formulated. Later, Spencer and Tylor built it into a subtle and complex theoretical edifice that acquired the label 'social evolutionism'.[1] In essence this constituted an elaboration of the Enlightenment idea that the progress of humanity passed through a series of fixed stages (see Voget, 1967). Initially the theory was modelled on philology and its account of the historical changes in languages, and on geology (a succession of strata) rather than on biology, and 'social evolution' referred strictly to cultural and mental evolution. Subsequently, especially in Spencer's version, Darwinian principles of selection and adaptation were incorporated, thereby moving closer to biological racism, but this did not apply to Tylor's original conception.

The mental aspect of 'social evolution' – evolution of humanity – was conceived by analogy with the development from child to adult. For Tylor in particular, this also meant that the *same* kind of mind grew more sophisticated over historical time. Tylor also introduced the 'comparative method', whose germ may be found in Degérando, who had observed that by travelling to distant places we are also going back in time. Tylor, as will be shown in more detail, systematized this notion and tried to utilize it for identifying successive levels of cultural and mental development, much as geologists deduce a temporal order from the positions of different strata.

This whole scheme was subjected to a radical critique by Franz Boas, who rejected the old assumption of a more or less unilinear line of mental and cultural evolution. While Spencer and Tylor had theorized about human culture and the mind in global terms, Boas maintained that the particular culture and mentality of each people should be studied separately as a coherent unity. Thereby he brought about a transformation in perspective that shaped the modern conception of 'cultures' in the plural.

The new approach developed by Boas was certainly influenced by the fact that he was an active field-worker. On the basis of his experience he took exception to Spencer's characterization of the 'primitive mind', which resembled that of the race theorists. The sources of Spencer's generalizations, like those of most of his contemporaries, consisted of frequently biased and unreliable reports by explorers and travellers. Already in the mid nineteenth century some dissatisfaction with such an approach had begun to be voiced, and plans were made to collect more reliable and systematic information about the culture and psychology of 'exotic' populations. These efforts made little progress until the latter part of the century, when field-work by specialists started to get under way. At the same time Tylor proposed a new method of testing cross-cultural hypotheses on a global scale. This laid the foundations for what was to become, some half-century later, the 'hologeistic' approach based on the Human Relations Area Files, commonly used for testing psychological hypotheses across a world sample of cultures.

During the same period the first attempts were made to verify empirically some of the old stereotypes, especially those concerning the allegedly extraordinary sensory acuity of 'savages'. The most spectacular advance was made when a joint team of trained anthropologists and psychologists, under the leadership of Rivers, embarked on the famous expedition to the Torres Straits. Rivers, under the sway of Spencerian theory, confined himself to studies of sensory capacities; but he tackled this with a rigorous experimental approach, demonstrating the falsity of some hoary beliefs. A few years later Thurnwald, less bound by theoretical preconceptions, carried out exploratory work on the cognitive abilities of 'primitives'. These early researches mark the beginning of 'cross-cultural psychology' as we know it today, dedicated to the scientific study of cultural differences and their determinants, as well as seeking to uncover psychological universals. Such a positivistically orientated approach differs considerably in its methods and objectives from the 'cultural psychology' whose roots will be examined in Part III.

Notes

1. For more detailed and comprehensive treatments of the social evolutionists and their critics see Bowler (1989); Burrow (1966); and especially Stocking (1982, 1987).

6

Biology, Race and Mind

The early nineteenth century saw the beginnings of radical changes in the scientific picture of the world, and of the humans within it. The new geology increasingly showed the biblical time-scale to be untenable. In the earlier years of the eighteenth century the age of the earth had still been estimated in thousands of years, and Buffon had proposed some 85,000. The order of magnitude increased radically during the nineteenth century, though a realistic geological time-scale was not generally accepted until the 1860s. With the rise of the new biology, the notion of the Great Chain of Being, involving a permanent hierarchical order of fine gradations in the organic world, was gradually abandoned.

Early nineteenth-century biology was dominated by Georges Cuvier (1769–1832), dubbed 'the Napoleon of biology'. The purely taxonomic approach of the eighteenth century was replaced by a functional one, and Cuvier tried to show that anatomical structures in both animals and men are related to the organization of their nervous system, and thereby also their psychological characteristics (Figlio, 1976). From this it followed that races with differently shaped skulls would also differ mentally, and Cuvier commented on the resemblance between Negroes and apes – a recurrent nineteenth-century theme. Cuvier, who was also a brilliant palaeontologist, observed the contrasts in animal types found in different strata, which led him to postulate a doctrine known as 'catastrophism'; this entailed separate creations at different periods of geological time. In spite of such views, Cuvier remained an – albeit somewhat inconsistent – monogenist.

His contemporary and rival Jean Baptiste Lamarck (1744–1829) was a remarkable man who did not come to zoology until the age of forty-nine, when the French Convention appointed him to a chair. Lamarck put forward the opposing theory of a continuous evolution, life being generated spontaneously all the time without sudden breaks. He postulated an innate creative force tending towards ever more complex organization of living beings. However, he regarded this main linear trend as being distorted by organisms' needs to adapt to the requirements of their local environments; and that is how, in the commonly cited example, giraffes acquired their long necks.

One of Cuvier's former friends and allies, Etienne Geoffroy St Hilaire (1772–1844), later turned against Cuvier and attacked his 'catastrophe theory' in a famous debate at the French Academy, which Goethe described as the greatest spectacle in the history of the sciences; it also created a sensation in the press and among the educated public. Ostensibly about 'unity of organic life', it also had implications for the issue of monogenism versus polygenism, which by then was becoming increasingly salient. It is important to note that St Hilaire incorporated into his theory Lamarck's second (and, for its originator, less important) idea. Ever since, 'Lamarckism' has come to mean the inheritance of acquired characteristics, and in this sense played a major part in nineteenth-century thought and beyond.

These several tenets of the new biology formed the roots of the numerous 'racial' interpretations of human varieties. There is a considerable literature on theories of race (e.g. Banton, 1987; Haller, 1970; Stepan, 1982) and it is not, of course, possible to summarize it here. However, some indication of the diverse approaches is necessary as a background for appreciating the nature of the powerful tide of opinion against which the advocates of 'psychic unity' had to struggle. This will be given mainly by looking at the ideas of representative figures illustrating some dominant trends.

The Transitional Phase

While polygenism entailed the belief in innate mental as well as physical differences between races, monogenism was by no means tantamount to lack of prejudice. Early in the nineteenth century several writers clung, like Cuvier, at least nominally to monogenism while sharing many of the polygenists' views about the inferiority of non-European races. On the other hand, it would be unreasonable to dub all polygenists in modern terms as prejudiced 'racists'.[1] Reputable scholars of all persuasions – and there were certainly others – deserve to be credited with the fact that they arrived at their conclusions as a result of painstaking studies. An instructive example is the case of Lawrence, a monogenist in the sense that he thought humans had *originally* been created the same. Sir William Lawrence (1783–1867) was a professor of anatomy and a follower of Cuvier. He was also an admirer of Blumenbach, to whom he dedicated his *Lectures* on the natural history of man (1819). Johann Friedrich Blumenbach (1752–1840), known as the father of physical anthropology, was a monogenist who studied anatomical race differences, but he was an egalitarian who referred to 'the good disposition and faculties of our black brethren' (Blumenbach, [1755] 1865, p. 307).

Lawrence, while also declaring himself a monogenist, belonged to a new generation. His proposal – unlike the eighteenth-century style, which was essentially taxonomic – was to study the question of human origins by a comparative functional analysis. He cites Voltaire, who had said that only someone quite blind would doubt that Negroes, Albinos, Lapps, Chinese, and so on are totally different races, but then goes on to reach an apparently different judgement:

> I proceed to consider the circumstance in which the several races of man differ from each other, to compare them to the corresponding differences of animals, and to show that the particular and general results of these inquiries lead us plainly to the conclusion, that the various races of human beings are only to be regarded as varieties of a single species. (1819, p. 271)

Lawrence argues that such varieties have developed in man in the same way as within a given species of domestic animals. But once they have so diverged, the differences in their physical and 'moral' characteristics remain fixed. External factors such as climate or type of government have little or no influence. He goes into considerable detail in presenting his evidence, obviously trying to be scrupulously fair. For instance, one of the reputed features of black women was the pendulousness of their breasts which enabled them to feed infants carried on their back by slinging them over their shoulders. Lawrence quotes a traveller in rural Ireland who told the same story of the 'dugges' of women there. Yet in the end he comes to the conclusion that the non-European 'varieties' are, on average, clearly inferior.

How did Lawrence, who typifies several of the earlier-nineteenth-century writers on race, arrive at his judgement of innate inferiority? One major reason, no doubt, came from the unfavourable images not merely of the 'savages' but also, to a lesser extent, of Eastern cultures conveyed by travel writers. This may also be seen in Lawrence's work, which contains extensive sections on differences in language as well as moral and intellectual qualities. He writes that European observers 'compare [the pronunciation of the Hottentots] to the clucking of a turkey' (pp. 470–1) and reports that the languages of China and surrounding countries 'betray ... all the imperfections of the first attempts at speech. ... They form plurals as children do ...' (pp. 471–2). His summary of the features of what he –rather inconsistently – calls the dark 'races' reveals the revulsion aroused in him by the travellers' tales:

> The distinction of colour between the white and black races is not more striking than the pre-eminence of the former in moral feelings and in mental endowments . . . they indulge, almost universally, in disgusting debauchery and sensuality, and display gross selfishness, indifference to the pains and pleasures of others . . . and an almost entire want of . . . elevated sentiments, manly virtues and moral feelings. The hideous savages of Van Diemen's Land, of New Holland, New Guinea . . . the Negroes of the Congo and some other parts exhibit the most disgusting moral as well as physical portrait of man. (1819, pp. 476–7)

It is noteworthy that this harsh portrait is totally at variance with the views of Blumenbach, whom Lawrence held in such great esteem, and whose reading overlapped considerably with his own.

Such divergences were common, indicating the important fact that the protagonists of sharply contrasting views often based these on much the same evidence, but interpreted it very differently. What Lawrence did share with Blumenbach, however, was a strong opposition to slavery and oppression of the weaker races in general, coupled with the wish to bestow on them the blessings of civilization.[2] In this respect he was more generous than some other nineteenth-century writers who held that 'savages', owing to their innate inferiority, were capable of only very limited progress. The famous traveller Richard Burton (1821–90), for instance, stated:

> The negro, in mass, will not improve beyond a certain point, and that not respectable; he mentally remains a child, and is never capable of a generalisation . . . in Africa, before progress can be general, it appears that the negro must become extinct . . . (Burton, 1864, vol. 2, p. 203)

Given what now seem such preposterous views, attempts were made to explain the supposed mental characteristics of 'savages' by linking them systematically with physical features, notably the size and shape of the skull. This again is reflected in Lawrence's statement that '*The retreating forehead and the depressed vertex* [emphasis added] of the dark varieties of man make me strongly doubt . . . whether they are capable of fathoming the depths of science' (1819, p. 501) The 'retreating forehead' goes back to Cuvier's theory, but the 'depressed vertex' relates to another approach that was gaining ground at the time and in which Lawrence was also interested, namely phrenology. Similarly, in his descriptions Burton employed a phrenological idiom:

> In the negro, the propensities and passions are tolerably well grown, the perceptives and reflectives are of inferior power, and the sentimental or

moral regions remain almost undeveloped. This is apparently the rule of savage and barbarous races ... the upper forehead and the vertex of the cranium are weak, retreating and flattened. (Burton, 1864, vol. 2, p. 198)

Phrenology

Phrenology, dismissively viewed as a pseudo-science, has until recently received rather short shrift in histories of psychology, but it has now come to be recognized as one of the major scientific (Young, 1970) and intellectual (Cooter, 1976) movements of the first half of the nineteenth century. It originated with the Austrian anatomist Franz Joseph Gall (1758–1828) and was later popularized by his disciple and collaborator, Johann Spurzheim (1776–1832) and their prominent Scottish follower, George Combe (1788–1858), after whom the first psychological laboratory in Edinburgh was named.

Gall rejected both Condillac's sensationism and the older philosophical faculty theories. He held that the brain is the organ of the mind and that all propensities, sentiments and faculties are located in separate parts of the brain. Contrary to the views of sensationists, who regarded human dispositions as a function of experience, Gall maintained that they are innate. Dismissing the eighteenth-century 'faculties' of will, imagination and reason as mere philosophical speculation, he claimed that faculties must be empirically derived on the basis of observation.

The notion of cerebral localization as such was an important idea that stimulated later research, but two further assumptions were made: that the size of the part of the brain corresponding to a particular faculty is indicative of the extent of that faculty's development; and further, that the shape of the head usually reflects that relative size. This is reminiscent of Cuvier's view that the shape of the head in both animals and men can reveal the level and complexity of neurological structures. While we now know that these notions are fallacious, they did not appear so at the time. Many prominent contemporary thinkers either believed in phrenology, or at least thought it worthy of serious debate. They included Bain, Comte, Hegel, Spencer and even Broca, distinguished in brain research; Alfred Wallace, the evolutionist, conducted his own studies and remained a firm believer when most other scientists had come to regard phrenology as discredited.

Phrenology was long regarded as a science that could explain human differences of all kinds. According to Spurzheim (1815) the faculties as such have always remained constant, and this proves that they are innate rather than the product of environmental factors like climate or education. What does vary is the *extent* to which any faculty develops and manifests itself. At the same time as stressing innateness, however, phrenologists also maintained that any particular faculty could be improved by education and training; and to that extent one could say that they paid some attention to cultural influences. In fact they were active in promoting reform movements in such spheres as women's education, penology and the treatment of mental illness. The inconsistency between rigid organic determinism and environmental modifiability, while never resolved, was in practice sidestepped by taking one or other position as the particular argument required.

The admission of the influence of environmental factors was mainly confined to *individual* differences within the 'white race'. However, Gall (1819) also wrote about the *Agreement between Dominant Head Form and the Moral and Intellectual Character of Nations*. In this work he did not altogether deny the possible effects of environmental factors of the kind stressed by Enlightenment thinkers; but he dismissed them as being, unlike head shape, incapable of definite proof. Similarly, Spurzheim expressed the view that within nations there are predominant average 'types', overriding individual differences, which he proposed as an important area of study. The suggestion was duly taken up by the then numerous phrenological societies, who began collecting skulls of different nations and races. From some of these, claimed to have been selected on the basis of being as representative as possible, casts were made and sold to the public.

The interest in this comparative aspect is also reflected in the fact that the *Journal of Phrenology* contains many contributions on national and race differences in character. One of the earliest was entitled 'On the coincidence between the natural talents and dispositions of nations, and the development of their brains' (Anonymous, 1825 – probably by George Combe). This article seeks to refute the dominant eighteenth-century belief voiced by the philosopher and exponent of Scottish faculty psychology Dugald Stewart, who is cited as saying that 'the diversity of phenomena exhibited by our *species* is the result *merely* of the different circumstances in which men are placed' (Anonymous, 1825, p. 2) – a clear statement of cultural determinism. Against this it is argued that the Europeans have always displayed a tendency towards moral and intellectual improvement. Asians have shown some improvement, but remain stuck at a level well below that of Europeans:

> The annals of the races who have inhabited [Africa], with few exceptions, exhibit one unbroken scene of moral and intellectual degradation.... The aspect of native America is still more deplorable. (1825, p. 5)

The differences in the national characters of European nations are said to display the same historical continuity. The clinching argument, however, is of course phrenological: nations and races are made up of individuals, whose skulls can be subjected to cranioscopy. Detailed accounts follow, from which some examples will be cited: the Charibs (an American Indian tribe) are, among all the races studied, most deficient in the 'reflecting organs', their 'animal propensities' greatly preponderating, and Brazilian Indians are not much better.

The general strategy adopted by phrenologists for the study of exotic peoples was to begin by scanning the available literature describing them, and subsequently to read the characters portrayed into the skulls. Here is an example:

> Considering Mr. Malden's pledge as affording a good prospect that we should see the Sandwich Island and Otaheite head when Blonde [the leader of an expedition] returned, we were led during the interval to attend more minutely to what we possess, in the writings of navigators and missionaries, on the character of this interesting race. (Anonymous, 1826)

They then tended almost invariably to find full confirmation of the travellers' tales in their readings of the skulls (see also Combe, 1842; Davey, 1847). Occasionally one comes across what purports to be a 'blind' reading, as in the case of a Hottentot killed by some farmers after stealing horses (Anonymous, 1834). His alleged 'dying confession' was compared with the inferred character and said to confirm it 'in its most striking features'; but for a number of reasons the case does not stand up to critical scrutiny.

Yet in spite of what now appears to be its absurdity, the phrenological approach to ethnic and national group differences has to be taken seriously, as indeed it was by numerous notable figures at the time as well as the person in the street. Through phrenology negative stereotypes of the 'inferior races', stamped with the scientific seal of approval, were widely disseminated. Although its scientific status declined sharply around the middle of the century, its popular appeal persisted unabated and continued to influence opinion. It also contributed substantially to physical anthropologists' preoccupation with measurements of the skull.

Craniology and the Gospel of Race

One of the best-known 'craniologists', concerned with the study of skulls, was Samuel George Morton (1799–1851), an American who studied medicine at Edinburgh; there he most probably encountered the phrenologist Combe. At any rate, in his *Crania Americana* (1839) he expressed his belief in the fundamental principles of phrenology, noting that the cranial features of the [American] Indians correspond closely to their mental characteristics. Subsequently Morton's interests shifted to the measurement of the capacity of the skull, then widely believed to correlate closely with mental capacity. Morton thereby 'proved' the inferiority of Negroes and Indians.

The idea that cranial capacity, indicative of the volume and weight of the brain, could serve as a measure of intelligence had been given added plausibility by Cuvier's new biology. Coupled with the then prevalent notion that the skulls and brains of 'savages' resemble those of the primates, this resulted in a plethora of comparative craniological studies throughout the nineteenth century. It cannot be said that all these studies were truly objective, and the early American School in particular was enlisted in the defence of slavery.[3]

It would be mistaken, however, to imagine that such crude bias was the rule. Among the notable supporters of the relationship between brain size and intelligence was the great Paul Broca (1824–80), one of the founders of the Société d'Anthropologie de Paris, who was a polygenist. Numerous studies by physical anthropologists purported to establish differences between Negro and white brains; probably one of the last of this kind, conducted early in the twentieth century at Johns Hopkins University, was later shown to have been fraudulent.[4]

The view that 'savages' had smaller brains and were closer to the apes remained scientifically respectable for most of the nineteenth century, persisting at the popular level well into the twentieth.[5] This, of course, is not to deny that critical voices were raised. One of the earliest was that of the German anatomist Friedrich Tiedemann (1781–1861) who, in 1837, published a monograph comparing the Negro brain with that of the European and the orang-outang. The first part reports a painstaking histological analysis, leading to the conclusion that the Negro brain is essentially indistinguishable from that of the European and differs from that of the orang-outang in the same ways. The second part, entitled 'Some remarks on the mental capacities of Negroes', surveys reports concerning intellectual achievements and moral qualities, concluding that the attribution of inferiority is unjustified.

Tiedemann's careful study was summarily dismissed by the German-Swiss naturalist Carl Vogt (1817–95) in his *Lectures on Man* (1864). Confessing that he did not possess a Negro brain, he relied on a drawing of the brain of a Hottentot woman examined by Cuvier, and on that basis he found 'a remarkable resemblance between the ape and the lower human type' (1864, p. 183). One is tempted to quote at some length from Vogt, because of his extravagant absurdities. Thus a full page is devoted to the ape-like character of the foot of the Negro which is said to be ugly, and he cites a writer who claimed that it 'produces a disagreeable impression'.

While Vogt was rather more extreme than most, he was only one of the writers, often with medical or other scientific training, who spread the racist gospel. In Britain the polygenist Charles Hamilton Smith published *The Natural History of the Human Species* (1848), in which he maintained that there had always been three fundamentally distinct human types: the Caucasian, the Mongolian and the Negro. In support of his claim of the last two's lesser mental capacities, he referred to Morton's work in America.

Even more important was the notorious Robert Knox (1791–1862), whose career as a professor of anatomy at Edinburgh University was wrecked over the Burke and Hare murders, undertaken to supply the medical faculty with corpses for dissection. Knox began lecturing on race in various parts of the country, propagating polygenist views – later published (Knox, 1862) – which had considerable influence not only on the general public but also on scientific opinion. He proclaimed himself a follower of Cuvier and Geoffroy St Hilaire, giving their theories his own particular twist. Although Knox was an anatomist, he was concerned mainly with differences in intelligence between races, which he regarded as greater than physical differences. However, his use of the term 'intelligence' included such aspects as religion and literature, thus – oddly enough – corresponding more to what we now mean by 'culture'. For Knox, various European groups like Saxons or Celts also constituted 'races', whose biological inheritance conditioned their history. As far as non-European races are concerned, his comments were highly unflattering. Nearly all, according to him, lacked the capacity for civilization because their mental development had been arrested at an earlier stage. The dark races in particular are psychologically inferior, and extinction is likely to be their ultimate fate.

One of Knox's keenest adherents was James Hunt (1833–69), who had broken away from the relatively liberal Ethnological Society to form the rival Anthropological Society of London. A skilled publicist for his extravagant racial theories, he made no original contribution and his book *On the Negro's Place in Nature* (1863a) is full of borrowed gems like the following: 'The typical Negro, unrestrained by moral laws, spends his days in sloth and his nights in debauchery' (p. 47). He gave an address to the Society on the same topic (Hunt, 1863b) in which he summarized his views:

Everywhere we see the European as the conqueror and the dominant race; and no amount of education will ever alter the decrees of Nature's laws. . . . First . . . there is as good reason for classifying the Negro as a distinct species from the European as there is for making the ass a distinct species from the zebra; second, . . . the Negro is inferior intellectually to the European; third, . . . the analogies are far more numerous between the Negro and the ape, than between the European and the ape. (p. 387)

In Germany, some of the formulations of the doctrines of race consisted of a quaint combination of Romantic *Naturphilosophie* and 'race science'. Karl Gustav Carus (1789–1869) contrasted the dark 'night races' with the light 'day races'; only the latter are capable of intellectual achievements. As proof he adduced the supposed fact that the jaws of the 'night races' resemble those of animals more closely [*tierähnlich*] and, as usual, also cited Morton.

In France, the book by Joseph Arthur Gobineau (1816–82) on *The Inequality of Human Races* made little impact upon its publication during the mid 1850s; but it subsequently exerted a powerful influence. Gobineau's doctrine claimed that civilization was entirely the product of an 'Aryan' super-race, an aristocratic elite of natural rulers who are – or at least ought to be – the wielders of power. The racists who later based themselves on Gobineau usually either misunderstood or deliberately distorted his arguments – notably the Nazis, who equated 'Aryan' with 'German'. In fact Gobineau was a racist but not a nationalist, despising narrow patriotism as unworthy of the elect. Success went to his head, and in a later edition he made the absurd claim that Darwin had appropriated his ideas without acknowledgement.

Darwin, Darwinians and Race

During the second half of the nineteenth century, many of the advocates of the innate and permanent inferiority of the 'lower races' welcomed Darwin's theory of evolution as providing scientific evidence for their views. In order to show why this was quite unjustified, I shall briefly outline Darwin's own position and that of some of his followers. At the same time this will help to distinguish, in due course, Darwin's *biological* from *social* evolutionary theories.

Darwin himself was a monogenist who put forward several reasons why all humans should be regarded as a single species. He noted, for example, that no character is both distinctive of a particular race and constant; also that there is no sharp dividing line, so that races 'graduate into each other'. His main interest was to establish a continuity between animals and humans, so when considering 'mental powers' he did not specifically compare human races, but 'man and the lower animals'. The comparisons he did make were between various kinds of 'savages' and civilized peoples, and these tend to be peripheral to the main line of his discussions.

At the same time it must be admitted that he was certainly not free of the preconceptions of his period. While expressing occasional scepticism about some of the more extravagant reports about 'savages', he did accept others.

Here is an example drawn from a section on 'Self-consciousness and mental individuality':

> But how can we feel sure that an old dog with an excellent memory and some power of imagination, as shewn by his dreams, never reflects on his past pleasures or pains in the chase? On the other hand, as Büchner has remarked, how little can the hard-worked wife of a degraded Australian savage, who uses very few abstract words, and cannot count above four, exert her self-consciousness, or reflect on the nature of her own existence. (Darwin, [1874] 1901, pp. 127–8)

Or again, Darwin expounded his theory of language as derived originally from imitation on the grounds that the imitation of the sound of a predator would be a useful warning signal. In seeking to support this argument he bracketed together 'monkeys, microcephalous idiots, and . . . the barbarous races of mankind' as all having a strong tendency to imitate whatever they hear. Here I might mention in passing that as far as I have been able to ascertain, Darwin made almost no reference to anything that might be regarded as cultural influences, except perhaps in connection with language. He suggested that the acquisition of language makes it possible to express the wishes of the community, and this collective voice then becomes a guide to action for individual members.

Generally, Darwin's main concern was to show how intelligence could have developed as a result of natural selection. The comparisons he made were between peoples at different levels of cultural attainment rather than between 'races'; and in this his ideas were much closer to those of the social evolutionists, whose ideas will be examined in the next chapter, than to those of the race theorists. It is true, of course, that Darwin repeatedly stressed the intellectual distance dividing a Newton or a Shakespeare from 'the lowest savages', but he also pointed to continuous gradations of intellectual ability, which implied at least the possibility that the mental faculties of 'savages' would in future rise to similar heights.

In addition to his published work, Darwin made some notes on comparative psychology, but did not wish to pursue that line himself. He gave the notes to a young friend, George John Romanes (1848–94), who was especially interested in psychological aspects of evolution. Romanes maintained that there is no difference between 'brute' and human psychology, and that the study of evolution would go a long way towards 'bridging the psychological distance which separates the gorilla from the gentleman' (1888, p. 439). One might imagine from this phrasing that he held liberal views on the question of 'race', but this was not so. Romanes, unlike Darwin, drew sharp distinctions between different races and suggested that the uncivilized, even if exposed to Western culture and education, would be capable of only very slow and limited progress.

One can discern some ambivalence in the writings of several of the Darwinian evolutionists. The logic of their theory entails that even the most 'primitive savages' may in time become the equals of highly civilized Europeans, yet they tend to betray a feeling of incredulity, a reluctance to accept that conclusion. I shall illustrate this with the striking case of Armand de Quatrefages (1810–92), an anthropologist of the school of Broca. He had come to abandon the master's polygenism, and one of his earlier books defended the unity of the human species. In a later work, Quatrefages (1887) discussed the problem of the intellectual characters of what he regarded as the main racial groups: white, yellow and black. There is an interesting passage acknowledging the importance of cultural influences:

> The state of society, obviously related to the intellectual faculties, points essentially towards the *local development* [emphasis added] of these faculties;[6] but there are really no such things as racial characters. (1887, p. 236)

Quatrefages cites the fact that some whites have been arrested at the stage of subsistence by fishing, thus remaining in effect 'savages', while many African peoples have reached the higher stage of agriculture. Moreover, he argues, some peoples believed to have been incapable of civilization have provided striking proof to the contrary. After the expression of such liberal ideas one is surprised to find them followed immediately by a sharp attack on 'Negrophile philanthropists' who support the equality of all races: 'some are different but equal, others superior or inferior'. Yet – Quatrefages adds at once – things can, of course, change: we ourselves were still savages when the Egyptians were in their temples.

Biology without Culture

This chapter has surveyed one of the most powerful currents of nineteenth-century thought – and beyond. Race theorists espoused the view that the advance of civilization depends on intelligence, which in turn is a function of a racially inherited brain. Hence the permanent inferiority of the 'barbarous peoples' is part of the natural order of things. Such a chain of causation leaves little, if any, room for cultural influences. In principle such a restriction need not apply to Darwinian evolutionary theory, but in practice few nineteenth-century biological evolutionists had much to say about culture.

The theories of race as an ineluctable fate, permanently dividing humankind into groups of unequal mental capacity, were widely accepted; but they did not remain unchallenged. As we shall see in the next chapter, the arguments of those opposing them rested largely on cultural similarities as evidence of fundamental psychic unity.

Notes

1. There was also a great deal of terminological confusion about the use of such labels as 'race', 'species' or 'variety', which cross-cut the monogeny–polygeny distinction.
2. This was a common stance even among the most rabid polygenists, and may have had more to do with 'social desirability' than with conviction.
3. An example is the American writer J.C. Nott, who in 1842 had penned an emotive diatribe against the 'negro race'. The then Secretary of State in Washington became embarrassed by British and French appeals against slavery, and found that the hitherto adequate biblical argument of Noah's curse on the alleged descendants of Ham no longer cut any ice. Hence he decided to obtain some 'scientific' proof and called in Nott, who duly obliged.
4. A brilliant critical discussion of these general issues is provided by Gould (1981).
5. During the colonial period it was not uncommon for Europeans to refer to indigenous peoples as 'monkeys', which was greatly resented. As late as the 1950s an African workforce went on strike because a European foreman had called someone 'a black monkey' (see Jahoda, 1961).
6. This is reminiscent of Harris and Heelas's (1979) thesis of 'local constructionism'.

7

'Psychic Unity' and Social Evolution

In the history of ideas, one must beware of anachronistically imposing one's own categories in interpreting and evaluating theories of the past. Thus readers might be tempted to equate nineteenth-century race theorists with modern 'racists', and their opponents with 'anti-racists'. At the very least this would be a gross oversimplification. It is true that there were some figures, like James Hunt, whom the cap would fit, but others were genuine and honest seekers after scientific truth. Viewed through contemporary eyes, the case for 'race' as an explanation of human differences was a strong one. Some of the prominent race theories were being put forward by scientists with great reputations, and on the basis of empirical studies. Moreover, these theories provided a convincing interpretation of the vast distance then observed between the civilized European and the 'naked savage' – a distance that is hard to imagine at the end of the twentieth century.

Supporters of more egalitarian ideas, therefore, had to attack entrenched positions in accordance with what was then the conventional wisdom. It would also be quite wrong to imagine that they were anti-racists of a late-twentieth-century kind. Most of them shared many ideas and values with their opponents, above all a cultural chauvinism that saw European civilization (often as embodied in their own nationality) as the unique peak reached by the 'ascent of man' and as the standard against which everything else was to be measured. With few exceptions, the critics of race theories were not cultural relativists but maintained only that all races have more or less the same intellectual *potential*, which might be realized at some future period.

Among those who did not share the view of absolute and permanent racial inferiority, one can distinguish several approaches. One was that of Tiedemann, already mentioned, who constituted a rare exception among the scientific 'craniologists'. Tiedemann attributed blacks' lack of intellectual achievement to what might be called 'cultural deprivation', citing exceptions that proved their potential. Several of the early opponents of race theories were connected with the anti-slavery movement (and it should be mentioned that generally the race theorists approved of its aims). While many of the anti-slavery writers mainly expressed their abhorrence of this inhuman practice without entering into any theoretical debate, some in both France and Britain did so. Forichon and Maupied (1844), for instance, argued that human intelligence, unlike animal instinct, is not fixed but constitutes a faculty dependent on external conditions: 'You people with your conceit of superiority, which you owe to your fortunate circumstances, it ill behoves you to write . . . that the Negroes are not your equals' (p. 113). While expressions of opinion of this kind were not lacking, they cannot be regarded as coherent theoretical statements. These were formulated by thinkers who have been grouped under the rather vague umbrella term 'social evolutionists'. While they differed considerably in their ideas, they were opposed to the biological race theorists and mostly shared the conviction that the human mind is basically similar in all peoples, variations in its manifestations being a function of culture and history. The tenets of some of their major representatives will now be reviewed.

Critiques of the Dominant Ethos: Prichard and Waitz

Both these men – one English and the other German – defended what in essence had been the Enlightenment concept of a universal human nature. James Cowles Prichard (1786–1848) was a contemporary of the anti-egalitarian monogenist Lawrence, whose views were discussed in the previous chapter. In terms of their background the two men had much in common, but they developed sharply contrasting outlooks. Prichard became dedicated to the idea of the unity of mankind, a dedication which he shared with his father. His most important work was *The Natural History of Man* (1843), in which he attacks the prevailing theories.

His approach – later followed also by Waitz – was twofold. First, he sought to discredit the supposed concordance between skull shape and mental capacity. In this connection it should be recalled that one of the main arguments of the race theorists had been that certain races, as collectives, had few or no cultural achievements to their credit. The form of Prichard's refutation was basically the same as that long employed to discredit rigid climatic determinism: he showed that populations with similar skull shapes varied widely in cultural levels, in both time and space.

The second leg of his approach concerned social institutions and psychological characteristics. Being acutely aware of the preconceptions he would have to overcome, Prichard met them head-on in the opening part of the section entitled 'Comparison of human races with respect to mental endowment':

If now it should appear . . . that one common mind, or psychical nature, belongs to the whole human family, a very strong argument would thence arise, on the ground of analogy, for their community of species and origin . . . but can it be maintained that such is really the fact? On first adverting to this inquiry, most persons would be likely to adopt the negative side of the question; for what greater contrasts can be imagined than those which present themselves when we compare in their actual state the different races of mankind? Let us imagine, for a moment, a stranger from another planet to visit our globe, and to contemplate and compare the manners of its inhabitants, and let him first visit some brilliant spectacle in one of the highly civilized countries of Europe, – the coronation of a monarch . . . let the same person be carried into a hamlet in negroland, in the hour when the sable race recreate themselves with dancing and barbarous music . . . let him be placed near the solitary den of the Bushman, where the lean and hungry savage crouches in silence like a beast of prey, watching with fixed eyes the birds which enter his pitfall, or the insects and reptiles which chance bring within his grasp, – let the traveller be carried into the midst of an Australian forest, where the squalid companions of kangaroos may be seen crawling in procession in imitation of quadrupeds, – can it be supposed that such a person would conclude the various groupes [sic] of beings whom he had surveyed to be of one nature, one tribe, or the offspring of the same original stock? ([1843] 1848, pp. 487–8)

In order to persuade his readers to accept such a counter-intuitive view, Prichard enjoined them to adopt a historical perspective and allow for the vast changes human groups underwent as a result of external circumstances. While this made for enormous variety, one could also discern crucial elements common to all humans: above all language, but also the use of fire, artificial clothing, the domestication of animals, funeral rites and the belief in some supernatural powers.

Prichard also surveyed a wide range of the ethnographic literature available to him in order to gain information about the psychological dispositions of what he regarded as a representative sample of humanity. This led him to conclude that 'the same inward and mental nature is to be recognized in all the races of man' ([1843] 1848, p. 546). It is worth noting that the ethnographic material was, of course, much the same as that used by his opponents, only seen through another kind of intellectual filter.

Prichard's writings were influential, and he was instrumental in the foundation of the Ethnological Society. In 1839 he had read a paper to the

British Association on 'The extinction of native races'; this created so much interest that a committee was set up for the purpose of preparing a questionnaire designed to help anyone who was in contact with 'native races' to collect relevant information; and the Society was formed initially as a repository for such information. This questionnaire, to be discussed in more detail in the next chapter, continued to be published in modified form until the mid twentieth century.

Prichard's attempted demonstration, on the basis of ethnographic materials, of similarities betweem human institutions and mental characteristics had not as such been psychological in intent; rather he marshalled all this evidence in order to establish, against the polygenists, the 'unity of the human species'. This was also one of the main aims of the work of Waitz, whose range and depth considerably exceeded his predecessor's; and it was Waitz who coined the famous phrase about 'the psychic unity of mankind'.

Theodor Waitz (1821–64) was a scholar with a background in Herbartian psychology, though he later became critical of certain aspects of Herbartian doctrines. In 1849 he published a *Textbook of Psychology as a Natural Science*, in which – contrary to the impression given by the title – he presented psychology as not only scientific but also closely linked with the humanities. He shared Herbart's belief that psychology should not ignore the social nature of humans and an interest in applying psychology to pedagogy. Thereby Waitz was led to search for common human features manifested in social life to serve as a firmer basis for pedagogy. Accordingly, he spent some six years studying the ethnographic literature and became absorbed in the problems of the then emerging discipline of anthropology, whose scope he also sought to define. His *magnum opus* was the *Anthropologie der Naturvölker*, whose first volume appeared in 1859; it was then translated and published in 1863 under the title *Introduction to Anthropology*. Five more volumes dealing with all then known primitive peoples appeared later, the last three posthumously. Here we shall be concerned mainly with the second part of the introductory volume, entitled *Psychological Investigations*. Here Waitz set himself the task of rebutting the polygenists, who maintained that the lower races, owing to their permanent mental inferiority, were incapable of civilization; in addition, he sought to specify the conditions that make for advances in civilization.

At the outset he conceded, as had Prichard before him, that the popularity of the views put forward by the race theorists was perhaps not surprising, given the descriptions of:

> the thoughtless Negro, the restless nomadic American, the cannibal south-sea islander. The primitive man stands in such striking contrast to the civilized man, that the latter in his vanity considers the former as specifically different [i.e. of a different species]; that he himself once occupied a similar position, he does not seem to take into any serious consideration. (p. 260)

One of the main reasons for this attitude, Waitz suggests, is that the question of the unity of the species has been dealt with by naturalists who did not concern themselves with psychological issues. They simply took it for granted that psychological characteristics are associated with physical ones. Waitz then proceeds to demolish this assumption by showing in some detail the inconsistencies in the copious published data then available about cranial capacity,[1] and also the fact that intra-group variations tend to be generally ignored. He concludes: 'We are thus compelled to renounce the doctrine that the capacity of the cranium indicates the amount of mental endowment' (p. 268). He makes it clear that he is not claiming actual but only potential equality, given further development under favourable circumstances:

> Here the question is not either to prove or to refute that *at present*, e.g. an individual Negro, or the Negro race generally, is capable of the same intellectual performance as an European civilized people; for nations are as much dependent on the historical basis of their vital development as individuals. (p. 266)

Thus nothing can be inferred merely from current performance. Waitz then resorts to a sophisticated argument still prevalent in twentieth-century nature–nurture debates: comparing intra-group with inter-group variability, at the same or different times. He was not, of course, in a position to do this quantitatively, but in later sections he sought to demonstrate a high degree of variability that throws doubt on the assumption of fixed and permanent differences in potential.

As Prichard had done before him, Waitz proceeded to examine what all men, including the 'so-called savages' (a significant qualification) have in common, and what especially distinguishes them from animals. The obvious answer is language: 'even the most barbarous nations possess a language with a more or less regular grammatical structure' (p. 273). This common element, permitting all humans to express their thoughts, is far more important than any physical differences and establishes the 'psychic unity of mankind'. Wherever travellers go, they find essentially the same modes of psychological functioning, the same human nature – and here the contemporary stereotypes break though – 'even in the most ape-like Negro' (p. 274). This is in utter contrast to animals, whose inner life we can never penetrate:

> But in the presence of human beings we are never in the same dilemma. However great the difference between their mental culture and ours, we may, if time and opportunity are favourable, learn to understand all their actions, and we are thus justified in assuming in the human species, *only differences in culture*. (p. 274 [emphasis added])

One should not be deceived here into imagining that Waitz used the italicized phrase in its twentieth-century sense; rather, he was referring to level of culture or degree of civilization.

Waitz reviews other specifically human features, including the desire for ornamentation, some form of collective or individual property rights, religion, and attachment to one's country and people. Here he returns to the key role of language in a passage that appears to reveal the influence of Herder:

> It is chiefly language which separates and unites mankind, by impressing the national character upon the individual, and the peculiar mode of thinking and feeling belonging to his stock, drawing thus closer the bonds which unite the individuals as a whole. (p. 277)

In pursuit of his project, Waitz goes on to ask what the truly primitive or natural state of man – no longer existing – could have been like. He comments that Enlightenment writers had regarded such early humans as peaceful children of nature in contrast to the corruption of the civilized; that view had changed so radically that many of his (i.e. Waitz's) contemporaries saw 'natural man' as little better than an ape. Two possible avenues for exploring the character of man in his primitive state are considered, the first being the human child; but he rapidly concludes that this could not lead anywhere. There remain the 'so-called' savages, discussed at great length with reference to ethnographic material. Their dominant traits are said to be indolence and thoughtlessness:

> Indolence and thoughtlessness, to an incredible degree, are characteristic of perfectly uneducated human beings, and it requires but little knowledge of the lower classes, even in Europe, to perceive that indolence is enjoyment to man in his natural state . . . (p. 290)

Neither the so-called savages, nor the lower classes in Europe, display any spontaneous wish for intellectual progress if their basic material desires are satisfied, and they have little thought for the future. The difference between primitives and civilized is by no means an absolute one, and traces of the earlier dispositions can always be found. There is also evidence that the mental level of populations is by no means uniform and can also fluctuate:

> even now, there are communities in Ireland, and even in the heart of France, the civilization of which is scarcely higher than that of many Negro tribes, and . . . a comparison of the free Negro population in the larger cities of the United States, especially of New York and Philadelphia, with that of the above-mentioned Irish districts, turns to the advantage of the free Negroes. (p. 307)

Thus it is a mistake to attribute differences in levels of civilization directly to differences in mental endowment. Since people have no built-in drive for intellectual progress, external influences must be involved; and in a later section Waitz deals at great length with a range of ecological and historical factors. In any case, given the great antiquity of the earth (which had been established in Waitz's time by geologists), a mere few thousand years of advance in civilization is too short a period to judge the relative capacity of all mankind; hence he judged the available facts to be entirely consistent with what he called 'the theory of the psychic unity of the human species' (p. 321). This is not to say that he believed all peoples to be the same; for just as there are great within-group differences there may be, he thought, also some between groups: the reported failure of attempts to educate some savage children convinced him, as it was later to convince Tylor, that there is probably no absolute equality. Yet the whole tenor of his carefully balanced argument is that any race differences in ability are relatively minor, and as such cannot be used to explain differences in levels of culture.

It should be said that Waitz was well in advance of his time with his grasp of what we would call the sociocultural foundations of mind and knowledge. In his discussion of these topics he rejected the Idealist conception, fashionable in the Germany of his time, of mind having the inherent property of lifting itself up by its own bootstraps. Instead, he put forward ideas anticipating, to some extent, those of thinkers like Wundt or Vygotsky:

> There can be no doubt that it is man's thought which produces and preserves civilization; this thought, however, does not originate by itself, nor is it the function of *one* mind, but is the combined activity of all individuals living together, produced by surrounding media, and nourished and matured by the historical events which befall them. (1863, p. 380)

In my opinion, Waitz's contribution has been generally underestimated. He rates barely a mention in most histories of either psychology or anthropology, and the coining of the phrase 'psychic unity' is often wrongly attributed to Bastian.

Bastian and 'Elementary Ideas'

Adolf Bastian (1826–1905) was the son of a wealthy Bremen merchant who attended the universities of Berlin, Heidelberg, Prague, Jena and Würzburg. He began by studying jurisprudence and natural sciences, eventually qualifying in medicine in 1850. While at Würzburg he began a lifelong friendship with Rudolf Virchow (1821–1902), the renowned physiologist and pathologist also noted for his work in physical anthropology. Bastian also attended lectures by Lazarus, one of the founders of *Völkerpsychologie*, for whom he had a high regard. This wide range of erudition, spanning the humanities and natural sciences, informed his writings; at the same time, it led to a tension in his thinking between the heritage of the Romantic Movement and German positivism that was never fully resolved.

Bastian was a complicated man, and evaluations of his work vary so widely that one might be forgiven for wondering whether they relate to the same person. Harris (1968), for instance, dismisses him as a 'cultural idealist', and Kramer (1977) portrays him as a confused loner, unable to come to terms with any culture, including his own. On the other hand, Bastian has been fortunate in his recent biographer (Koepping, 1983), who attributes to him a remarkable vision of the science of man that eventually reached its fruition in the present century.

Among the reasons for these divergent judgements is certainly one of Bastian's characteristics on which all biographers agree, and which anyone (who reads German) can personally confirm: while his travel accounts are lively, Bastian's theoretical writings suffer from a style which the American historian of anthropology Robert Lowie described as 'inconceivably crabbed'. Native German-speakers have complained no less strongly about the difficulty of reading his work.[2] His output was vast, and in his later years his writings became increasingly obscure and repetitive.

There is no doubt that Bastian was distinguished from most other writers of his time, who usually relied on secondary sources, by the fact that he gained first-hand experience of a wide variety of world cultures. Shortly after completing his studies, he enrolled as a ship's doctor on a voyage to Australia and New Zealand; from there he went to South America, spending most time in Peru; and then on to Mexico and California, crossing the Pacific again to China, Indonesia and India; the next stage took him overland by caravan to the Near East, and then by boat to South Africa, returning along the West Coast; from there he went to Lisbon, and after spending time in Russia, Turkey and several European countries, he arrived back in Bremen after eight years. This was only the first of his numerous travels – he rarely stayed in Germany for more than a few years – and he died in Trinidad on his last journey.

Unlike the majority of travellers, who reported about the geography of the places they visited and the physical character of the peoples and their artefacts, Bastian was mainly interested in people's ideas and beliefs; though not, according to some, in the people themselves. He tried to learn some of their languages, but attained no real mastery of any of them. When little time was available he seems to have obtained his information from resident Europeans rather than indigenous informants, but he usually made the best of any opportunities that offered themselves. Thus on his second journey, to Asia, which began in 1861 and lasted for five years, he found himself detained in Burma and forced to act as the king's physician for a year. He made good use of this time, studying Buddhism with a native priest in Mandalay. A man of restless energy, he brimmed over with ideas which he was often unable to organize with sufficient clarity.

Bastian's industriousness may be gauged from the fact that his first major three-volume work was published in 1860, an incredibly short time after his return from eight years of crisscrossing the globe. It was called *Der Mensch in der Geschichte* (*Man in History*) and subtitled 'Towards the foundation of a psychological *Weltanschauung*'. The three volumes deal, respectively, with 'Psychology as a natural science', 'Psychology and mythology' and 'Political psychology'. The last of these follows Herbart's terminology and concerns what we would call 'social psychology'; as such it is not a prominent strand in Bastian's later work. The titles of the two other volumes, however, epitomize the dual facets of his approach: he wanted to use ethnographic material in order to establish a scientific basis for psychology by documenting both the fundamental commonalities of the human psyche and its variations, and to discover the laws governing its transformation in time and place. A substantial part of his intellectual heritage can be traced back to the tradition of Herder, especially the latter's emphasis on the collective consciousness of particular peoples, and his cultural relativism. On the other hand, his training in natural science led him not merely to collect empirical data but also to seek to assimilate psychological and ethnographic phenomena to prevailing biological and even physicalist conceptions. This is apparent from numerous analogies to be found in his works, for example:

> The same necessity of organic growth, which in indissoluble interaction with the environment produces cells in plants, elicits ideas in man and predisposes them towards further unfolding. (Bastian, 1868a, p. XII)

This notion of 'ideas' is a crucial one in Bastian's scheme, richer and more subtle than the rather curt treatment of many expositors might suggest. In *Man in History* he first introduced the paired terms *Elementargedanken* ('elementary ideas') and *Völkergedanken* ('folk ideas'). Bastian was impressed by fundamental similarities he discerned among all the various peoples he visited on his travels, and this led him to postulate that certain 'elementary ideas' must be shared by all humankind. However, the differences were equally obvious and must be accounted for. Bastian attributed them to adaptations to the contrasting geographical environments in which people find themselves and to historical changes, including migration and contact.

Bastian has often been criticized for giving no concrete examples of 'elementary ideas', but this objection misses the point. The existence of such 'ideas' can only be inferred, not observed, since they have invariably become overlaid by the operation of the factors he adduced. Even what were then increasingly called in Germany *Naturvölker* ('natural peoples'), rather than *Wilde* ('savages') were, according to Bastian, closer to nature only in the sense that they had relatively less control over it; but they also had a history, and he saw no way of getting back to origins. Thus all one can collect are 'folk ideas', but that is an important task for ethnology and will in turn provide a basis for comparative psychology:

> A comparative psychology can only be established on the basis of ethnology, which traces in the various ethnic groups [*Volkskreisen*] the genetic development of mental products [*Gedankenschöpfungen*] and explains their local colouring in terms of geographical or historical contexts. (1868a, p. XI)

The ultimate aim, therefore, was to arrive inductively at the developmental laws governing the transformation of 'ideas'. It will be evident from this that Bastian's conception of 'psychology' was very different from what we understand by this term: he was not really concerned with *individual* psychology at all, only with *collective* mental phenomena. For the same reason he regarded Fechner's work, which he knew and respected, as irrelevant for his purpose. The development that interested him was essentially historical in character, and he thought (probably inspired by the Belgian pioneer statistician Quetelet) that it might be captured by a statistical study of the distribution of 'ideas':

> Our science needs a *Gedankenstatistik* [statistic of ideas], a statistic that comprehends simultaneously the organic growth of mind and the lawful transformations of its products. (1860, vol. 1, p. 429)

He goes on to say that understanding must be based on the smallest elements, which in mental life are 'ideas'; one should classify them and analyze their relationships so as to bring out the overall pattern at a higher level, just as physiology rests on data provided by physics and chemistry. In a broad sense Bastian's aim could be said to have been realized by more recent work like Osgood, May and Miron's (1975) cross-cultural study of meaning, which found basic similarities – *Elementargedanken* – as well as differences. Whether this really corresponds to Bastian's notion is difficult to tell, since there is a certain lack of clarity as to what kinds of higher-order units he had in mind, and what exactly he meant by 'ideas'. Occasionally he seems to use the term in the sense of 'thoughts', but most of the time the context does not fit such an interpretation.

In order to elucidate this issue, let us go back once again to Bastian's ethnographic material, on which the arguments are based. This consists, in the manner later followed by Wundt, of religious beliefs and practices, myths, legal and political forms, customs, artefacts, and so on. Thus as a totality, the material on which Bastian based his comparisons corresponds to what we now call 'culture'; moreover, we also recognize that culture is a mental product. It therefore seems reasonable to conclude that Bastian's concept of 'folk ideas' has a good deal in common with what we mean by 'culture'.

There is yet another aspect of the meaning of 'ideas' connected with the notion of 'psychic unity'. Waitz had previously used the expression in opposition to the claim of biologically determined psychological differences between ethnic groups; but he had certainly not held the view that 'savages' and the civilized are in any way on the same level. Bastian was much more radical in proposing that 'elementary ideas' are common to all humankind. It is not just that he thereby wanted to indicate the presence of certain cultural universals: in this context it would seem that by 'ideas' he meant 'thought processes'. He was denying any differences in this respect between 'primitives' and 'civilized', and considered that the products of the thinking of both should be treated in the same way. It is difficult for us to appreciate how scandalous such a view appeared at the time. Happel, a one-time opponent and later supporter, described this vividly:

> I experienced it as a kind of affront to find him placing side by side, without qualification, the thoughts and sayings of the greatest minds [*Geistesheroen*] of our 'civilized' world with similar-sounding remarks of, say, an Indian chief or an African fetish-priest . . . (Happel, 1887, p. 1)

Bastian, a faithful follower of Herder's cultural relativism, declared that Europeans had been accustomed to look down on other cultures, labouring under the delusion that theirs is some kind of ideal. In reality it is only one of many, and a minority one at that, among a wide range of cultures in different times and places. Bastian believed that the collective mentality of cultural groups is – especially in its earlier stages – enshrined in their religion and mythology; hence much of his descriptive writing was devoted to these themes. Such a mentality develops through social interaction, and particularly linguistic intercourse, and he stressed the link between language and culture:

> The language of a people is the expression of the developmental process, the audible expression of the cellular mental formations which undergo a growth process in history; language therefore gives us surprising insights into the impulses of thought, it allows us access to the deepest emotions of the national character . . . (Bastian, 1869, p. 1; cited in Koepping, 1983, p. 43)

The phrase 'cellular mental formations' reveals the biological conceptions which underlay much of Bastian's thought. This also emerges from his views concerning the development of higher forms of culture. One of his arguments, already put forward during the Enlightenment, was that humans are predisposed to build on the mental capital accumulated by preceding generations; but he believed that this also has bodily effects. Moreover, he thought that there is a certain inertia such that mere external influences like education do not by themselves produce any permanent changes:

> As a result of teaching the forehead may be enlarged by the awakening of previously dormant mental powers, and the face of an African schoolchild may gain in its expression of intelligence; but these partial modifications remain none the less under the dominant control of the former type, to which they rapidly revert, possibly even already in the next generation when this grows up under less favourable conditions . . .
>
> History shows us the causal factors in those cases where out of the ethnological roots of primitive races a historical civilization [*Kulturvolk*] developed: such an event always involves the combination of two causes, namely sexual crossings and exchanges of ideas. Their interaction yields a product that each in isolation would have been incapable of generating. (1868b, p. 22)

There are thus, according to my own reading, two different facets of Bastian's theoretical writings that are never adequately reconciled. He was opposed to polygenism; this comes out very clearly in his dispute over this issue. Ernst Haeckel (1834–1919) had suggested that the major races of mankind had descended respectively from the different kinds of primates: orang-outangs, gorillas and chimpanzees. In an open letter published in 1874 Bastian indignantly tried to refute this, in large part on the grounds that it would be incompatible with the *Elementargedanken* shared by all humans. On the other hand, he regarded miscegenation (and not just the contact of different peoples) as essential for cultural advance. Bastian also shared the then prevalent ethnocentrism, as when he stated that the ideal of a normal person is to be sought not in 'the fragmented characters of primitive peoples [*Naturvölker*], but in 'the national type of civilized states in the vanguard of development' (1868b, p. 61). At the same time it must be recognized that Bastian, perhaps more directly than either Prichard or Waitz, stressed the importance of culture in transforming the mentality of different peoples over historical periods.

There has been some discussion as to whether or not Bastian was an evolutionist (see Koepping, 1983, p. 52), which hinges on what one understands by this term. He clearly held that there had been a psychological development of humanity, though not in the eighteenth-century sense of simple linear progress. On the other hand, he sided with

Virchow against Darwinism, so that his evolutionary ideas are distinct from those of social evolutionists like Spencer or Tylor, who readily accepted Darwinism as entirely compatible with their own schemes. In other respects Bastian's ideas had a good deal in common with those of Tylor, a much clearer and more systematic expositor.

Social Evolutionists: Spencer and Tylor

Social evolutionism was in a direct line of descent from the Enlightenment 'natural history of man', and evolutionary theories of various kinds were common during the half-century before Darwin. One was the theory put forward by Herbert Spencer (1820–1903), mentioned above. This idea was not new, and Darwin's achievement was that he not only applied it systematically and supported it with massive evidence, but above all also put forward the process of natural selection capable of explaining it. Spencer had first encountered the theory of biological evolution in 1840 when reading Lyell's *Principles of Geology*, which criticized Lamarckism, but for Spencer it was a revelation, and he became a Lamarckist. He elaborated a social theory which treated society as an organic entity, developing in the course of history from homogeneity to heterogeneity. After Darwin had published his *Origin of Species* in 1859, Spencer also incorporated natural selection into his theories. There are so many different themes in his voluminous writings that it is hard to disentangle his various ideas (see Peel, 1971), and I shall concentrate on his representation of the 'primitive mind'. His conceptions were important because, as we shall see in the next chapter, they influenced several early empirical studies.

In some of his most general statements, Spencer expressed the relationship between culture and mind in similar terms to those used recently by Cole and his associates. Thus he refers to 'the reciprocal relations between the characters of men and the characters of the societies they form', to 'the interdependence of individual nature and social structure', and to 'mental development as a process of adaptation to social conditions, which are continually remoulding the mind, and are again remoulded by it' (Spencer, 1876a, p. 20). The resemblance, however, is merely superficial, since Spencer envisaged a Lamarckian process whereby adaptations to the environment are genetically transmitted to offspring. The nature of the environment is thus crucial in such a scheme, and in his *Principles of Sociology* Spencer declares that it is only in highly organized societies that people can gain and assimilate the kinds of experiences through which 'the powers of thought' develop.

Since Spencer viewed the environments of savages as relatively simple, adaptations were limited and their progress was slow, though it followed the same evolutionary track. Spencer also adopted a notion of some craniologists, according to which a lack of the necessary stimulation results in relatively smaller brains, which also holds such people back. Altogether, he took a rather dim view of the chances of progress of the 'lower races'.

Spencer's description of the mind of the savage was based on these theoretical preconceptions, set out in his *Principles of Sociology* (1876b, vol. 1). The mind of the savage initially shows rapid development, but this ceases early in life. Thus he lacks a true ability to think or speculate and, contrary to what is sometimes believed, the need for understanding his surroundings 'does not occur to him'. Spencer supports his claims with anecdotes drawn from the ethnographic literature, and to show savages' lack of interest in theoretical speculation he cites the following from the explorer Mungo Park: 'Park asked Negroes if the sun in the morning is the same sun as that which disappeared at night, and they considered the question very childish' (p. 100). One wonders how Spencer himself would have responded if faced with this question! Again, he goes on at some length about the 'imitativeness' of savages, already mentioned in connection with Darwin:

> Among the partially civilized races we find imitativeness a marked trait. Everyone has heard of the ludicrous ways in which Negroes, when they have opportunities, dress and swagger in grotesque mimicry of the whites . . . and this peculiarity, common to the lowest human types – this tendency to 'ape' others, as we significantly call it – implies a small departure from the brute type of mind. It shows a mental action which is, from moment to moment, chiefly determined by surrounding incidents. (1876b, pp. 92, 94)

Spencer adhered to the old belief that savages have extremely acute senses, and are closer to animals inasmuch as their mental life tends to be dominated by immediate perception. He went on to enunciate a kind of 'law of the conservation of mental energies', which became influential:

> For in virtue of the *general antagonism* [emphasis added] between the activities of the simpler faculties and the activities of the more complex faculties, it results that this dominance of lower intellectual life hinders the higher intellectual life. In proportion as the mental energies go out in restless and multitudinous perception, they cannot go out in calm deliberate thought. (1876b, p. 89)

It will be clear from all this that Spencer's social evolutionism, while emphasizing a reciprocal relationship between culture and mind, took on a rather different tinge when it came to his treatment of the psychology of 'savages'. There his characterizations were closer to the race theorists than to Bastian, Waitz or Tylor. Yet it must be recognized that Spencer's 'law of

mental energy' stood almost alone at the time as a relatively precise and –
at least superficially – plausible formulation of the workings of the primitive
mind. As such, it later served as the theoretical basis for some empirical
work.

Tylor's original brand of social evolutionism (see Leopold, 1980) shared
with Spencer's the application of the 'comparative method' (I shall say
more about this later). Their psychological views, however, were radically
divergent. Spencer believed, from the way he saw 'savages', that 'early
human nature differed from later human nature'. Edward Burnett Tylor
(1832–1917) was an inheritor of the Enlightenment tradition of a basically
unchanging human nature. His theory of the evolution of culture depended
on the notion of progressively changing ideas rather than on any struggle
for survival. Unlike Spencer, who regarded 'savages' as incapable of
reflection and speculation, Tylor's theory of magic and religion presup-
posed an essentially rational questioning on the part of 'savages' about the
world and their place in it. Even though Tylor was inclined to accept what
he called the 'trite comparison' between savages and children, this did not
mean that he believed totally different mental processes were involved:

> In later years, and among highly educated people, the mental process which
> goes on in a child playing with wooden soldiers and horses, though it never
> disappears, must be sought for in the midst of more complex phenomena.
> (Tylor, 1865, p. 109)

There are occasional psychological gems to be found in his writings –
Chapter VI of *Primitive Culture*, for example, contains a cross-cultural
analysis of words denoting human relationships and their connection with
'baby language'. In his later years Tylor became persuaded that genetic
race differences in the complexity of the convolutions of the brain set limits
to the progress of some races,[3] but this did not substantially alter his
conception of cultural evolution.

Tylor's general aim was to study the historical development of human
civilization or culture – and it is significant that he treated these terms as
synonymous. He was not concerned with particular cultures and never
seems to have used the plural of the word. Like his Enlightenment
predecessors, Tylor regarded humans as an integral part of nature and, as
such, subject to essentially the same kinds of laws; his views are forcefully
expressed in the epigraph at the beginning of this part. The stress on
scientific rigour was not really matched by a correspondingly rigorous
method. Later in his life he did invent a new quantitative method, which
will be discussed in the next chapter. During most of his life, however, he
employed an approach dating back to Comte that was widely current at the
time, though it was particularly associated with his name and that of James

Frazer as its most notable exponents. This approach came to be known as 'the comparative method' for the study of historical development. It rested on the postulate that social institutions and material artefacts constitute a regular series in historical development, though they proceed at differing rates over time. This uniformity – far more important than what Tylor called relatively superficial differences of race and language – resulted from the universal features of a common human nature.

The essence of the method consists first of a taxonomic procedure: cultural materials of any kind, be they concerned with kinship, religion, material objects or whatever, are arranged in a series from simple to complex – the latter being, of course, invariably drawn from European civilization as the apex. A temporal dimension is then introduced, based on the often fragmentary evidence available; given the evolutionary presupposition, it usually turns out that the simplest is also the earliest. In this way the analysis focuses not on specific cultures but on universal aspects of 'culture' in the singular; these might consist of the evolution of *the* kinship system or of tools in general.

One of the key features of this kind of analysis is the identification of similarities, allocated to the same position within the series. Such similarity, as Tylor fully recognized, might have been due to 'diffusion' – the transmission of ideas, beliefs and skills through culture contacts. However, when this appeared unlikely owing to spatial and/or temporal separation, the similarity was interpreted as the uniform response of the human mind to the same problem. For instance, ancient Swiss lake habitations were very similar to those of nineteenth-century Maoris, and were taken to show that the same evolutionary path was being followed by both peoples, though the Maoris were well behind. The assumption underlying the whole scheme was that of 'psychic unity': faced with similar challenges, all human minds will respond in a closely similar way. Moreover, we should be able to understand the minds of primitive peoples by putting ourselves imaginatively in their place.

The weaknesses of the comparative method were attacked by Franz Boas (1858–1942), who had come to America from Germany, where he had been influenced by the writings of Lazarus and Steinthal on *Völkerpsychologie*, and those of Bastian. First of all, he pointed out that similarity does not necessarily imply an identical cause, showing with examples how the same outcome could result from combinations of quite diverse historical, environmental and psychological factors; hence classifications and inferences based on mere superficial similarities are unjustified. Furthermore, he objected to specific traits or complexes being torn out of their particular cultural contexts and, as it were, lumped together indiscriminately. Unlike Boas himself, hardly any of the cultural evolutionists had done any field-work, so they lacked the 'feel' of cultures as more or less coherent wholes. On the basis of his field experience, Boas also criticized Spencer's crude image of 'primitive mentality'.

Boas was instrumental in changing the intellectual climate towards thinking about 'cultures' in the plural. This did not mean, however, that he jettisoned altogether the concept of 'psychic unity', but he no longer regarded it as a simple explanatory principle. In his book on *The Mind of Primitive Man* (1911) Boas stressed the effects of particular cultural contexts on mind and behaviour; this later inspired his students, notably Ruth Benedict and Margaret Mead.

As we shall see in the next chapter, a modified form of the comparative method, coupled with the principle of 'psychic unity', is still with us today. Furthermore, as Wertsch points out (1991), the kind of reasoning represented by the comparative method still sometimes insinuates itself nowadays when implicit comparisons are being made between the modes of thought of children and 'primitives'.

Notes

1. In addition to relevant tables, Waitz produced various quaint bits of information. Thus according to some studies, the cranial capacity of Englishmen is 9 cubic inches greater than that of Irishmen; but the difference between the latter and Negroes is only 4 cubic inches. Waitz suggests that the heads of American Indians, then regarded as very low on the intellectual scale, must be larger than the head of the average Frenchman: the hats made in Paris for the Indians during the war of liberation were all too small!

2. An Austrian who wrote his doctoral thesis on Bastian lamented his 'almost unbelievably confusing modes of expression. With some assiduity one can read at most two or three of his shorter pieces in succession; thereafter one's strength fails' (Eisenstädter, 1912, p. 11).

3. The change is apparent in the following passage of his text on anthropology:

In measuring the minds of the lower races, a good test is how far their children are able to take a civilized education. The account generally given by European teachers who have had the children of lower races in their schools is that, though these often learn as well as the white child up to about twelve years old, they then fall off, and are left behind by the children of the ruling race. This fits with what anatomy teaches of the less [*sic*] development of the brain in the Australian and African than in European. It agrees also with what the history of civilization teaches, that up to a certain point savages and barbarians are like what our ancestors were and our peasants still are ... (Tylor, [1881] 1930, vol. 1, p. 58)

8

Towards Cross-cultural Psychology

S ince it was first coined a century and a half ago, the connotations of the phrase 'psychic unity' have undergone a considerable change. The passionate disputes about the single or multiple origins of 'races' to which the concept was originally closely tied are now forgotten. By a subtle transformation, 'psychic unity' is now associated with the idea, once shared by both parties to the dispute, that humans are part of nature and as such subject to general laws. This is an article of faith of the positivist tradition in psychology and neighbouring fields.

Within the narrower context of the relationship between psychology and culture, this tradition has, in the course of the twentieth century, split into at least two distinct strands. One of these, the so-called 'hologeistic' or 'holocultural' approach, remains rigidly wedded to strictly universalist aims. The other, now known as 'cross-cultural psychology' combines universalist objectives with an interest in the ways cultural influences produce human differences. Since the 'hologeistic' approach is more salient in psychological anthropology than in psychology, its antecedents will be dealt with relatively briefly at the outset.

Tylor's Pioneering Study of 'Adhesions'

Tylor's evolutionary scheme was for the most part entirely theoretical in character, with a single important exception. It was inspired partly by the work of the Belgian statistician Quetelet, and partly by Bastian's suggestions for a *Gedankenstatistik* (a statistic of ideas). These sources led Tylor to attempt a quantitative application of the 'comparative method'. In 1888 he read a paper to a meeting of the Anthropological Institute, chaired by Galton, which was published a year later under the title 'On a method of investigating the development of institutions' (Tylor, 1889). In the introduction he argued that if anthropology was to become accepted as a reputable scientific discipline, it had to adopt stricter methods. His aim, he stated, was 'to show that the development of institutions may be investigated on a basis of tabulation and classification' (p. 245). He proceeded to demonstrate this in relation to the topic of marriage and descent. Examining the rules and practices of some 350 cultures around the world ('from insignificant savage hordes to great cultured nations'), he classified and tabulated them so that resemblances and differences became apparent. The next step was to try to find what he called 'adhesions' and we now call correlations, showing which customs clustered together: '*From the recurrence or absence of these customs it will be our business to infer their dependence on causes acting over the whole range of mankind*' (p. 246). This sentence (emphasis added) epitomizes the objective of what is now called the 'holocultural method'.

In order to illustrate Tylor's approach, the issue he began with will be considered – namely, 'avoidance': 'a quaint and somewhat comic custom as to the barbaric etiquette between husbands and their wives' relatives, and *vice versa*: they may not look at one another, much less speak, and they even avoid mentioning one another's names' (p. 246). Although the custom might appear odd to us, Tylor emphasized that it cannot be just a matter of 'local fancy', since from among a total of 350 societies for which he had data it appeared no fewer than 66 times. Scanning his material, he noted that the custom seemed to be related to modes of residence after marriage: 'Thus there is a well marked preponderance indicating that ceremonial avoidance by the husband of the wife's family is in some way connected with his living with them' (p. 247). He set out to demonstrate this by cross-tabulating[1] patterns of avoidance and types of residence. Tylor then computed the expected co-occurrence of elements of the two sets and compared these with observed values. If the observed exceeded the expected values, this was taken as evidence of an association, from which the operation of a causal influence could be inferred.[2]

Tylor then went on to address the question of the probable causal link. His suggested answer as regards avoidance practices, in the course of which he affirmed the uniformity of human nature across space and time, was as follows:

> As the husband has intruded himself among a family which is not his own, and into a house where he has no right, it seems not difficult to understand their marking the difference between him and themselves by treating him formally as a stranger. So like is the working of the human mind in all stages of civilization, that our own language conveys in a familiar idiom the same train of thought; in describing the already mentioned case of the Assineboin marrying and taking up his abode with his wife's parents who pretend not to

see him when he comes in, we have only to say that they don't *recognize* him, and we shall have condensed the whole proceeding into a single word. (p. 248)

Tylor went on to warn that a plausible reason might not be the real one. The problem of a lack of direct relationship between correlation and causation, which still bedevils holocultural studies, had not escaped his notice. After dealing with a whole series of social institutions such as naming practices, the couvade, exogamy, and so on in a similar manner, he concluded with an appeal for an international research effort before too many tribes became extinct or radically changed.

After the address the president, Galton, complimented Tylor but also drew attention to an assumption underlying his statistical method – namely, that the various customs studied are *independent*. Since there is much 'borrowing' between neighbouring cultures, the extent of such independence must be ascertained, an issue that has become known as 'Galton's problem'; and in fact the solutions arrived at are essentially elaborations of that put forward originally by Galton: the consideration of geographical propinquity (see, for instance, Naroll *et al.*, 1980). In the modern exposition by Naroll and others of the 'holocultural' method, it is described as '. . . a means for the empirical testing of theories that attempt to explain some general characteristics of human culture' (p. 480); and it should be added that shared psychological features are commonly postulated as underlying such commonalities.[3] Another author states: 'A sizeable number of holocultural studies have involved ordering data along evolutionary lines' (Bourguignon, 1979, p. 81). In spite of a somewhat ingenuous disclaimer that the term 'evolutionary' was not meant in the classical sense of historical reconstruction, one cannot help feeling that such phrasing closely echoes Tylor's thought a century earlier.

Psychological Concerns Reflected in Observation Checklists

The data for Tylor's statistics, like those used by Prichard, Waitz or Spencer, had to be laboriously culled from a wide range of publications authored by travellers, missionaries and others in contact with 'primitives'. Field anthropology as a professional specialism lay far in the future, though a few gifted amateurs, like Lewis Henry Morgan, collected some of their own material. Moreover, for nineteenth-century theorists of culture and society it was generally inconceivable, as it had been for the Observateurs de l'Homme, that such problems could be studied whilst ignoring human psychology.

It is not surprising, therefore, that this interest should to some extent have been manifest in the first – and not very successful – attempts to create a more systematic database. These were made in 1851, when a subcommittee of the British Association for the Advancement of Science was given the task of drawing up *A Manual of Ethnological Inquiry* containing a series of questions designed to assist in 'studying the varieties of man'. These were first published two years later (British Association, 1853) with the aim 'to induce Consuls, political and other residents and travellers, to obtain precise knowledge in reply to them . . .' (pp. 243–4)

In this first version, among a total of 103 questions, only a few could be regarded as psychological. They relate mainly to the sensory acuity of the people observed, and their modes of child-rearing – Degérando had gone into much greater psychological detail. In 1874, however, the *Manual* was succeeded by the first edition of *Notes and Queries in Anthropology*, which contained a special section by John Beddoe (1826–1911), surgeon and anthropologist, on 'psychology':

> Under this head may be included inquiries respecting the degree of quickness of perception, the power of reasoning, learning and generalizing, of fixing the attention, of memory, of perseverance, exhibited by the tribes or races observed. It would not be possible to lay down precise tests for the use of the investigator.
>
> The power of forming abstract ideas seems to be extremely limited in the lowest races. The faculty of attention is apt to be easily wearied. The memory may be keen with regard to particular classes of objects, but in other respects almost a blank. The power of drawing a map of the neighbouring country varies immensely, and may be tested with advantage. (The Esqimaux seem to equal or surpass Europeans on this point.) (Beddoe, 1874, p. 25)

In his first paragraph Beddoe raises a series of issues but is unable to make any suggestions as to how the psychological characteristics mentioned might be assessed. In his second he tells the potential investigators what they are going to find, expressing views based partly on contemporary theoretical notions (e.g. Spencer) and partly on hoary stereotypes; the only comment based on actual observation, to which Galton also referred, is that on Eskimos.

The section on psychology contains other parts dealing, for instance, with the effects of culture contact. It concludes with detailed questions, mostly based on a set drawn up by Galton (see Jahoda, 1980). There is no indication that the psychological section in the first and subsequent editions ever elicited much, if any, relevant information. All it did was to testify to anthropological interest in the psychological characteristics of non-Western peoples and in the extent to which these are determined by cultural influences.

When Beddoe mentioned 'quickness of perception' he was referring to the reports, dating back at least to the eighteenth century, of the supposed exceptional sensory acuity of 'savages'. The same topic was also raised in a parallel set of instructions for travellers prepared in France by Paul Broca (1879).[4]

Sensory Acuity of 'Savages' and Reaction Time of 'Lower Races'

The latter part of the nineteenth century saw the beginning of increasingly lively debates about the validity of reports which often attributed quasi-miraculous sensory capacities to 'savages'. Such notions related especially to vision, but were also referred to in connection with hearing and smell.

As regards vision, examples of the supposedly outstanding acuity of 'savages' were cited in the course of a debate in the pages of *Nature* (e.g. XXXI, 1885). Lord Rayleigh, a sceptic, wrote:

> It has always appeared to me that the superiority of the savage is a question of attention and practice in the *interpretation* of minute indications ...
> (p. 340)

Others accepted that superiority as a fact, attributing it to evolutionary factors. Thus Carter (p. 387) thought that town life had had a negative evolutionary impact, leading to 'degradation'. Guppy (pp. 503–4) reported that he had tested Solomon Islanders and found them clearly superior; he also added various anecdotes of a kind that had a hoary ancestry, such as the islanders' supposed ability to see ships on the horizon long before Europeans could.

Roberts (pp. 552–3) criticized Guppy's test results, showing that they were not really different from those of an English sample. As regards the anecdotes, he had this to say:

> it is obvious that the question cannot be decided by general questions, nor by comparisons with sight the value of which we are ignorant. Travellers naturally record cases in which their own sight (which they believe to be good, but which may be very bad) is outstripped by savages, but do not encumber their pages with negative evidence of the kind.

The above quotes indicate that a number of rather scattered observational studies had begun at that time. Such studies were usually carried out by ethnologists or colonial medical officers in the field, but it was also common to take advantage of the presence in Europe of troupes of exotic peoples brought there for the amusement and instruction of the European natives. At any rate, what all these had in common was a concentration on a quite limited issue; moreover, the methods employed – when they were specified, which was by no means always the case – were often inadequate.

After an interest in reaction time had begun during the 1860s, the view was also put forward that it varied according to 'race'.[5] One curious study on this topic is worth a brief mention, since it illustrates the influence of evolutionary ideas. Meade Bache (1895), an American psychologist basing himself mainly on Spencer, elaborated a set of highly convoluted biological arguments whose gist amounts to the claim that the nervous system of the 'higher' races is more differentiated and its functioning is less automatic. According to Bache it follows that, contrary to the prevailing view, the 'lower' races should be quicker in making simple responses: 'The automatic man is the educated slave of the brain' and 'the reflective man should be the slower being' (pp. 478–9). Bache claimed to have confirmed his conclusion by (in fact highly questionable) reaction-time experiments, and was thereby also able to account for the fact that blacks make better boxers!

Rivers and the Cambridge Expedition

Reaction time was also one of the topics investigated by the Cambridge Anthropological Expedition to the Torres Straits in 1898. They found few clear ethnic differences, and in any case the ranking of ethnic groups varied with the sensory modality tested. The Cambridge Expedition marked a turning point, a culmination as well as a new departure. Firmly anchored in the tradition epitomized by Pike (1870), who stated that 'without psychology there is no anthropology' (p. xi), its organizer, the anthropologist Alfred Haddon (1901), reiterated the view that no investigation of a people is complete if its psychology is ignored. Previously such psychology had been of the do-it-yourself variety; it had been taken for granted that anybody collecting ethnographic material would be competent to cover these aspects. Haddon took the – then unusual – step of inviting William Halse Rivers (1864–1922), an experimental psychologist and colleague of his at Cambridge, to take part in the expedition. Rivers in turn recruited two other psychologists (William McDougall and C.S. Myers) and a young physician interested in psychology (C.G. Seligman). Thus, for the first time, trained psychological specialists formed part of a team making up an anthropological expedition. Yet the ethnographers and psychologists worked in parallel rather than together, and their respective reports are in separate volumes, with no attempts at unification.[6] Their work in the field took up most of the problems previously either discussed only speculatively, or studied empirically in what had often been a haphazard and inadequate manner. The team made an attempt to cover systematically a wide range of mainly sensory functions, including hearing, smell, taste, cutaneous sensations, muscular sense and reaction times.

The most fruitful work was done by Rivers (1901) himself, who took responsibility for various aspects of vision. Thus he was able to explode the old myth of the fantastic visual acuity of 'savages'; he took up the issue of colour perception and naming, putting forward a hypothesis that retinal pigmentation produced a diminished sensitivity to blue, which was taken up again some seventy years later (Bornstein, 1973; Jahoda, 1971; Pollack and Silvar, 1967). Rivers demonstrated that there is no general difference in susceptibility to visual illusions between Europeans and 'primitives', but that the direction of ethnic differences is a function of illusion type; he suggested that differences in susceptibility are probably a function of differential experiences. This view was later taken up, elaborated, and tested on a wide scale by Segall, Campbell and Herskovits (1966), whose work stimulated a spate of cross-cultural research on visual illusions (for a survey, see Deregowski, 1980).

There would be little point in trying to summarize all the rich material available in the original Report of the Cambridge Expedition, which is still eminently worth reading. Rivers was a careful and sophisticated experimenter, who developed novel approaches and had a better insight into some of the pitfalls of cross-cultural research than is displayed in some of the current field manuals. Yet their work was trenchantly criticized by Titchener (1916), who took the view that research of this kind is bound to be inadequate and therefore of limited value. Although the issue cannot be pursued here in detail, two aspects of Titchener's comments are worth noting. Near the beginning of his article he writes that Rivers's report reminds us:

> time and again, that human nature is much the same the world over. The old lady on Murray Island who, 'by association of some kind,' gave her own and her friends' names when she was asked to name a set of colored papers, have we not met her . . . in our summer sessions? (p. 206)

In addition to this affirmation of 'psychic unity', the burden of Titchener's arguments in the body of his article amounts to the claim that cross-cultural research presents so many difficulties that it cannot lead to any firm conclusions. While his reservations about what was then a quite novel approach are understandable, it is regrettable that one can find almost exactly the same type of objections still being raised nowadays: 'the outcome of a cross-cultural replication is likely either to show that culture is unimportant for the phenomenon or to produce an uninterpretable result' (Messick, 1988, p. 43). It cannot be denied that cross-cultural studies often present special problems of interpretation, owing to the complexity of the factors involved; hence complete control is usually not feasible, so that one has to rely on 'quasi-experiments' based on naturally occurring variations. But methods have been devised for dealing with such problems (see Cook and Campbell, 1979). In any case, there is now a solid body of cross-cultural findings that refutes Messick's sweeping statement (see Berry *et al.*, 1992).

Rivers was undoubtedly the founding father of modern cross-cultural psychology, but in some important respects his ideas at that period were nineteenth-century ones. This facet of his approach is rather easy to miss, since in his report Rivers confined himself largely to describing the experimental procedures and results. Only from a few passages can the implicit theoretical assumptions be gleaned. The clearest is the one below, in which Rivers begins by stating that 'the savage' is an extremely close observer of nature, aware of all the minute details of the flora and fauna; then he continues as follows:

> Minute distinctions of this sort are only possible if attention is predominantly devoted to objects of sense, and I think there can be little doubt that such exclusive attention is a distinct hindrance to higher mental development. We know that the growth of intellect depends on material which is furnished by the senses, and it therefore at first sight may appear strange that elaboration of the sensory side of mental life should be a hindrance to intellectual development. But on further consideration I think there is nothing unnatural in such a fact. If too much energy is expended on the sensory foundations, it is natural that the intellectual superstructure should suffer. (Rivers, 1901, pp. 44–5)

Now this line of argument follows precisely that of some of the social evolutionists, notably Spencer (see pp. 110–11 above). It also helps to explain why Rivers was content to confine his studies to sensory and perceptual aspects of behaviour. At that time, of course, there were few methods of investigating higher mental processes, but this did not trouble him, as he did not think that such processes played an important part in the mental life of what he then called 'savages'. Subsequently Rivers himself came to repudiate his earlier views: 'I have been able to detect no essential difference between Melanesian or Toda and those with whom I have been accustomed to mix in the life of our own society' (Rivers, 1926, p. 53); and he explained that he had then been under the sway of the 'crude evolutionary doctrines of the time' – which refers, of course, to the theories of Spencer and Tylor.

A few years after Rivers had completed his studies on Murray Island another researcher, Thurnwald, went into the field with fewer preconceived ideas. He should be credited with having explored the relationship between psychology and culture in greater depth than Rivers. Since his contribution has been largely ignored in the relevant literature, I shall treat it here in greater detail.

Thurnwald on Ethno-psychology, Culture and Cognition

In 1906 Richard Thurnwald (1869–1954), an anthropologist with a deep interest in psychological issues, was planning to leave for a field trip to New Guinea and the Western Solomon Islands. He turned to Carl Stumpf (1848–1936) with a request for some guidelines on possible ethno-psychological[7] field research. Stumpf, who at that time held a prestigious chair at Berlin, was a prominent scholar; both Köhler and Koffka were among his students. But since he had never been concerned with the psychological study of *Naturvölker*, he passed the question on to colleagues attending the Second Congress of Experimental Psychology in Würzburg. The outcome was a collection of ideas about problems in various areas of psychology that might usefully be studied in 'primitive' cultures. Thurnwald was able to make use of some of these ideas in the course of his field-work from 1906 to 1909. After his return the *Institut für angewandte* [*applied*] *Psychologie* pursued the matter, eventually publishing a monograph supplement entitled *Proposals for the Psychological Study of Primitive Peoples* (Stern and Lipmann, 1912), to which Thurnwald made a substantial contribution. Thurnwald's own field report on his 'ethno-psychological' studies appeared a year later (Thurnwald, 1913).

The following discussion of Thurnwald's ideas draws on both these publications, beginning with his field monograph. Internal evidence suggests that he had not been aware of Rivers's studies before going into the field. While this was a disadvantage in so far as he was unable to benefit from Rivers's experience, it was an advantage in that it left him free to break fresh ground; and he did not feel obliged to confine himself to mere sensory capacities. In his introduction Thurnwald makes it clear that his psychological studies constituted only a minor sideline in comparison with his major ethnographic concerns. Hence only some 'tentative fragments' are offered, more in the spirit of exploring methods and raising problems than in the hope that real answers could be given. It is important to keep this modest disavowal in mind when evaluating Thurnwald's ethno-psychological explorations. The details of his studies are somewhat beyond the scope of the present discussion; but since they are of interest, and not readily available in English, a summary is appended.

The introduction to Thurnwald's monograph is rather sparse, stating only that there are two main lines of psychological research: directed either at universals or at human differences, his own being of the latter kind. He does not specifically discuss the determinants of such differences, but indicates in passing that cultural influences are probably paramount:

> With regard to the people we study we have to keep in mind that their whole type of intellect is conditioned by the cosmology [*Weltbild*] of their cultural tradition. It depends upon 1. what a person has seen and learnt in his life in general and 2. how he assimilates [*verarbeitet*] the experiences gained. (Thurnwald, 1913, pp. 3–4)

The last part of the report, following the accounts of the experiments, is in the ethnographic mode. While also dealing to a considerable extent with psychological characteristics, it is based essentially on inferences from observations. Numerous concrete examples are given, but there is hardly any reference back to the experimental findings. This applies, for instance, to the extensive discussion of people's modes of thought, in which magical beliefs are said to be salient: 'What we call superstition and magic is for these people a kind of law' (1913, p. 113); it is notion similar to that of Tylor and Frazer, though Thurnwald does not mention them. At the same time he did not share to the same extent the then common disdain for the supposed 'illogicality' of primitives:

> One cannot maintain in these cases that it is a matter of a lack of logic. It is not the logic that is lacking, which is exactly the same as our own; but the components manipulated by the logic are different. (1913, p. 113)

This conclusion is evidently derived from ethnographic observation rather than from the ethno-psychological studies. One discerns here a similar split between ethnography and psychology as that already noted with reference to the Cambridge Expedition, though it was of course intra- rather than interpersonal.

In his introduction to the 'proposals' edited by Stern and Lipmann (1912), entitled 'Problems of ethno-psychological research', Thurnwald made an effort to bridge the gap. Ethnology, he argues, which deals with cultural complexes and the transmission of culture, is bound to remain superficial and schematic unless it also concerns itself with the psychological processes of the people who are the carriers of culture. It is insufficient to do this indirectly, by looking at the artefacts of different peoples such as arrows, fish-nets, ornaments, and so on that are collected for museums, and try to infer from them the mentality [*Geist*] of those who have constructed them.[8] Thurnwald's liberal outlook, unusual for his time, is indicated by the fact that he questions the use of terms like 'savages', '*Naturvölker*' or 'primitives' by those without personal knowledge: one can use the term 'savages', he suggests, as long as one realizes that it also fits some Europeans, especially in the tropics!

The contrast between *Naturvölker* and *Kulturvölker* indicates that the former are at a lower level of culture, but then what is 'culture'? Thurnwald answers this question very differently from Tylor: it refers to 'the mastery and exploitation of the environment for the purpose of easing and promotion of the life of human individuals, of groups and the species as a whole' (1912, p. 5). While different cultures may excel more in one domain than in another, an overall assessment does allow a determination of cultural level. Thurnwald repeatedly used the metaphor of 'a tree of culture' where the blossoms are at different heights. As was common at the time, he often shifted between the present-day meaning of 'culture' as a human universal, and 'culture' in the sense of 'extent of civilization'.

The optimal criterion for determining cultural level is the prevalent mode of thought, exemplified in magical ideas, respect for property, blood feuds, notions of chivalry, and so on: 'Here is it not a question of "*Elementargedanken*" [referring to Bastian], but of "elementary modes of thought"' (1912, p. 10). At the individual level it would be important to determine the frequency of particular abilities and characters within different ethnic types.

Thurnwald then proposed what he called a 'social chemistry', which corresponds to what we understand by social psychology: the psychological processes involved in inter-group relations and their cultural variations. Such studies, he contended, would be easier in the less complex societies. In fact, such cultural studies would be a means of understanding the deepest psychological processes in humanity at large – an idea that echoes Degérando.

Thurnwald briefly reviewed past approaches such as those of Herder, Lazarus and Steinthal, and Bastian. He described their psychology as old-fashioned and considered them too wide-ranging in their aims. What is needed, he contended, are intensive studies of particular peoples. He then went on to discuss matters of method, starting with questionnaires, which were gaining popularity at the time. Criticizing their frequent naivety, he pointed out that they often assume a degree of theoretical sophistication on the part of the respondents that is usually unwarranted. What questionnaires should try to elicit are straightforward descriptive accounts on various topics.

Another method discussed is what was then known as the 'psychographic' method and is now called psychometry, for the testing movement was already under way at that time. Thurnwald stated that one might imagine that the best approach would be to investigate all ethnic groups by means of the same tests, thereby gaining measures on the same scale. He recognized, however, the problem now known as 'equivalence', discussing in some detail a range of probable sources of uncontrolled variation. He also suggested psychological comparisons of ethnic groups with social strata of 'modern European peoples', seemingly unaware that here equivalence becomes an even more tricky issue.

In addition to group comparisons Thurnwald proposed the intensive study of 'typical' individuals, though without explaining how 'typicality' is to be established. With regard to intelligence, which he saw as a key aspect, he made the shrewd remark that 'The best intelligence test is in general to ask what someone has really achieved in his life' (1912, p. 20). The typical individual, Thurnwald contended, will manifest in concrete form the sum of features we describe in the abstract as 'culture'. This anticipates a key notion of the 'culture-and-personality' school that flourished from the 1930s to the 1950s (see Barnouw, 1973; Bock, 1980).

The study of the individual can also employ experiments, though for ethno-psychological purposes the psychophysical ones are of limited value. Rather, one is interested in the phenomena of the higher mental processes. It is well known, said Thurnwald in this context, that the outcome of an experiment may be influenced by the personality of the experimenter; this presents a difficulty when comparing the results of different experimenters. Then he gives a number of practical hints and warnings about the problems facing the psychological researcher in the field. Some of these are reminiscent of Degérando, while others reflect the changes that have taken place. Thus one might have to carry out the experiment in a jungle clearing or a hut, very different from a laboratory setting. Apparatus must be simple and light, and one must remember that electricity will not be available. Communication with the subjects may be hard unless one commands their language – if not, one should choose experiments that are minimally dependent on verbal instructions. One cannot be careful enough in the use of interpreters, preferably choosing Europeans who have spent a lot of time in the country. One needs a great deal of patience and should do extensive piloting, selecting also, for control purposes, subjects who are particularly intelligent or the opposite. Above all one must remember that one is dealing with people who have had no schooling, though comparisons with subjects who have attended mission schools may be valuable. The object of the studies should be not only the demonstration of differences from Europeans, but also the ascertainment of inter-ethnic contrasts.

In due course, the goal to be aimed at goes beyond mere differences towards causal interpretations. The ultimate objective is the intensive comparative study of different peoples with a view to establishing the relative causal contributions of a series of factors such as the psychophysiological, the physical environment, what Thurnwald called the 'inner' group dynamics (presumably meaning the social relations within a community), and external social influences.

As explained at the outset, Thurnwald made an effort towards an integration of ethnological and psychological approaches. He struggled to order numerous ideas drawn from both disciplines, and if he did not always succeed, it must be remembered that he was writing at a time when both anthropology and psychology were undergoing rapid transition, which made his task very hard. For instance, he mentioned the then quite novel method of correlation as a valuable tool, but was evidently rather uncertain about how it might be applied.

Thurnwald, unlike Rivers, was not an experienced experimental psycho-logist, and his studies were mainly descriptive; nor did he put forward hypotheses that could later be tested. On the other hand, while Rivers had confined himself to the senses, Thurnwald at least tried to focus on the higher mental processes that later became a major objective of cross-cultural research. Above all, as an anthropologist he was deeply concerned with the influence of culture on mental processes. Rivers, blinded to this issue by his adherence to evolutionary theory, had totally ignored it. In this and other respects Thurnwald was far ahead of his time. The fact that his writings are available only in German prevented them reaching a wider audience. Yet in terms of ideas his contribution was arguably no less significant than the well-known one of Rivers, and deserves to be rescued from oblivion.

Rivers and Thurnwald mark the end of what one might dub the 'prehistory' of the positivistic tradition of thought about psychology and culture, concerned with general laws and the causes of differences. A largely fallow half-century followed, with only sporadic signs of interest in the area; an example would be the writings of Bartlett (1932) about cultural influences on memory; it is certainly no coincidence that Bartlett had been a student of Rivers. The revival did not come until the 1960s when cross-cultural psychology in the modern style began to emerge as a special field, burgeoning thereafter. Less than two decades later, enough material had accumulated to fill a six-volume *Handbook* (Triandis [ed.], 1980).

Appendix: Thurnwald's Ethno-psychological Studies

Outlines of the main studies reported in Thurnwald (1913) are given below, excepting only his comments on an extensive collection of drawings that do not lend themselves to summary.

(a) Handedness

A dynamometer was employed with a view to establishing the frequency of three types: right-handed, left-handed and ambidextrous. Thurnwald is careful to note that performance depends not merely on strength, but also on skill; however, he failed to pursue the implications of this fact. He notes the existence of indigenous norms regarding hand use, which mostly favour the right.

In this and all following experiments, full data for each individual tested are given; numbers of subjects are usually small; no details of sampling are provided. In the present case 25 people were tested: 12 were right-handed, 4 left-handed and 9 ambidextrous. It should also be noted that they came from no fewer than eight different tribes, thus constituting a highly heterogeneous sample. In categorizing individuals Thurnwald relied on (often quite small) mean differences, ignoring the – in some cases extensive – cross-overs of the curves for the two hands.

(b) Colour Vision

This was tested with Holmgren's wools, one of the methods also used by Rivers. Without mentioning how many subjects were tested, Thurnwald states that he found in general no anomalies, with the exception of one 'suspicious' case and another where the instructions had apparently not been grasped.

(c) Colour Nomenclature

At the outset, Thurnwald mentions the 'well-known' fact that there is no close relationship between colour discrimination and naming. Subjects were asked to name the bundles of wools and to put together those which for them had the same name. A further task was that of selecting from a bundle the thread that corresponded most closely to a vernacular colour term; elsewhere, subjects were told to pick colours out of the bundles and name them.

The whole approach was frankly exploratory, as different groups were given different instructions; moreover, it is not clear in what language these instructions were conveyed – most probably pidgin – and thus if they were adequately understood. The only generally valid finding to emerge was that colours are usually contextualized: 'Colour as such is mostly not meaningful enough to become isolated from the other characteristics of an object' (pp. 14–15). In other words, as Rivers had noted, colours are most commonly designated by the names of objects.

(d) Attention and Memory

Here again, Holmgren's wools were pressed into service first. Five bundles, consisting of saturated yellow, green, white, red and blue, were placed on a table in that order, and covered with a cloth. Subjects, who had previous familiarity with the wools, were asked to remember the colour sequence. The bundles were then exposed for a minute, then re-covered for another minute, after which the subjects had to attempt to reproduce the sequence, which took them twenty to forty seconds. Only a single subject performed faultlessly; one is not told out of how many, but from the subsequent account of errors one can infer that the total was six. Given this small number, Thurnwald's analysis of error-types is not really meaningful – except, perhaps, for the fact that green was never correctly placed, while blue was misplaced only once. This is rather intriguing, since for his subjects there was no word for 'blue', but many contextualized terms to denote 'green'. Thurnwald's conclusion that blue captures the attention most and green least is not very informative.

Another series of experiments used picture postcards that varied in two respects: white-and-black versus coloured, and the longer side forming the base versus upright. Various combinations of displays, mostly of nine (3 × 3) cards, were employed. Details are not important, since presumably only the same six subjects were involved. As in the previous experiment, the sequence had to be recalled, though exposure duration was initially reduced to five seconds – the shortest that yielded any results. As a modification Thurnwald tried to discover the length of exposure with which the subjects were most comfortable, when they felt that they had accurately memorized the sequence of picture cards. This instruction was conveyed as follows: 'Suppose you look him finish you speek [*sic*] him me' (p. 17). If that is a fair example of the procedure, the subjects must have been very bright indeed to understand what was required! At any rate, this led to a fifteen-second exposure.

Thurnwald reports that there was great confusion when the orientation of the cards was mixed. When one takes into account the fact that the pictorial representations mostly made little sense to the subjects, this is not really surprising. What Thurnwald found most striking in the reproduction of sets with the *same* orientation was the tendency for subjects to ignore the (for him) very salient symmetrical pattern. This issue of symmetry is one that has recently been extensively studied (see Deregowski, 1980), with rather different conclusions.

In the last of this series, three-dimensional geometric objects were used in the following arrangement:

Cylinder	Cube	Pyramid
Egg	Cone	Sphere
Three-sided pyramid	Six-sided prism	Four-sided prism

These were exposed for one minute, subjects then being asked to reproduce the array. Cylinder, egg, sphere and four-sided prism were always correctly placed. Thurnwald comments that the first two are both round, and that the other two were located at the top left and bottom right corners respectively.

(e) Suggestion

For this the same materials were again pressed into service, beginning with Holmgren's wools. The task immediately followed the previous one with the wools, but the account of the procedure is not entirely clear. Essentially it entailed a challenge as to whether the sequence had been correctly reproduced ('He put him right all the same?') and the question was whether the subject would change his response. The main outcome was once again the appearance of blue–green confusions.

A similar follow-up with the picture postcards yielded no coherent results. The lack of attention to orientation, coupled with inability to understand the scenes represented, are once again mentioned.

(f) Counting

In these experiments matches or twigs were used in order to ascertain what quantities could be assessed at a glance and to analyze the modes of calculation. For this purpose the pieces were placed on a table in a single heap or in several distinct groups, and covered before exposure. The task was to name the quantity of items on the table as quickly as possible. The duration between exposure and answer was recorded with a stopwatch; the grouping carried out by subjects when counting with their fingers was also recorded. Altogether three subjects were intensively studied, with very full details of their responses. Two of them had some mission education, one was completely unschooled; here only some extracts from the record of the unschooled subject will be presented:

Table 8.1 *Performance of the unschooled subject*

Number of sticks	Duration	Response	Comments
5	(9 secs)	5	
10	(10 secs)	9	(prompt: correct?)
10	(5 secs)	10	
15	(15 secs)	12	'plenty too much'

The following groups are presented: 5, 5, 5, 4, 5, 5 (= 29)

counts   5 (at once)
           + 5 + 5 [= 10 (rapidly)] = 15
           + 4 = 19
           [+ 5 (split into 1 + 4)]
counts   19   + 1 = 20
           + 4 = 24
           + 5 = 29

In the same way, full details of all calculations by the three subjects are provided. Certain common tendencies are noted – for example, the tendency to split numbers in order to arrive at tens – and Thurnwald adds that such a procedure is also employed by Chinese and Japanese with the abacus. It seems that no more than four sticks were ever apprehended simultaneously as a number. For instance, if a group of five sticks was presented, they were either counted individually or split into smaller groups. Without any details, it is mentioned that this corresponds to the indigenous numbering system. It is also noted that where it was possible to reach equal subgroups, the correct result was obtained much more rapidly than when they had to be unequal. Thurnwald also observes wryly that the calculations were no great joy for the subjects, who much preferred the other 'games'.

This counting experiment is noteworthy, since it anticipates the recent interest in what has come to be known as 'everyday cognition' (Rogoff and Lave, 1984). Thus a study by Carraher *et al.* (1985) of the computational strategies used by Brazilian child street-traders resembles in some respects the work of Thurnwald.

(g) Associations

1. Through pictures and geometric figures   Six subjects, all from the Methodist Mission, were presented individually with a series of stimuli and asked, in the vernacular, 'What does this resemble?' A semicircle bounded by a straight line elicited the following responses: a harp, a (European) boat, a carrier basket, a bow, a pig and the moon. Two straight lines intersecting at right angles were described as a cross by four of the subjects, one interpreting it as the letter 't'. The mission influence was therefore very noticeable – together, no doubt, with the context of being tested by a European. Thurnwald's comments on the responses are not very illuminating – he says, for instance, that one should not assume that different ethnic groups would give the same kinds of answers.

2. Word associations   For this, a then standard word list (Sommer's) was used, the experienced Methodist missionary acting as interpreter. As might be expected, considerable translation difficulties were encountered; for instance, there was no single equivalent for 'red': one vernacular term denoted red-brown earth, while another referred to blood; the context-bound nature of colour terms had been noted earlier by Rivers. It is evident that these problems proved insuperable in the case of many terms. Full details, including reaction time in seconds, are provided for two subjects, and more limited information for another one. Thurnwald himself made no use of the reaction times, but one can see that intended vernacular equivalents for some terms, such as 'broad', must have created difficulties for the subjects, as the duration was some three times the overall mean. In all likelihood there was considerable ambiguity, as Thurnwald himself cites as sources of error the *pronunciation* of the stimulus word and its range of meaning. Nevertheless, he gave it as his view that 'these experiments on the mechanisms of thinking of the natives are particularly valuable' (p. 38), yet without specifying. In fact, although he was evidently not aware of it, the material does contain some clues that can be culled from his summary of response types:

(i) Mere repetition or circumlocution;
(ii) A property is applied to a particular object, e.g. 'bright' = the village; or alternatively the property of an object is named, e.g. 'the tree' = bears fruit, or 'the house' = one sleeps in it.

If one assumes that the informants interpreted their task as something like a request for a definition, which is perhaps not unreasonable, then the responses may be compared to those obtained by Luria (1976) during the 1930s from unschooled people in Uzbekistan, Soviet Central Asia. There too, the predominant modes of response were either repetition or what we now call a *functional* definition.

Notes

1. This is not strictly correct: in fact he employed a combination of graphic and numerical presentations, like an elaborated Venn diagram.
2. At that time, of course, there were no significance tests.
3. The salience of psychological topics may be seen in a content analysis of hologeistic studies between 1898 and 1975 (Schaefer, 1977). The most frequent theme was 'social structure' (p. 108), followed closely by 'life cycle and psychological concerns' (p. 97).
4. In other respects this manual was totally different, since French anthropology at that time was mainly physical. Hence it concentrated almost exclusively on anatomical features, but some quite bizarre matters are also mentioned – for example, a request to check the report that Hottentots never yawn!
5. The third edition of Myers's *Textbook of Experimental Psychology* (1925) still mentions such race differences.
6. This was symptomatic of the emerging split between the two disciplines that came to be reflected in the subsequent life-careers of the participants: of the four psychologists two, McDougall and Myers, later abandoned their anthropological interests to become distinguished psychologists; the other two, Rivers and Seligman, moved away from psychology into anthropology.
7. By 'ethno-psychology' Thurnwald meant roughly what is now called cross-cultural psychology; it should not be confused with the current meaning of 'ethnopsychology', which refers to the study of indigenous psychologies.
8. Thurnwald was referring here to the theories of Friedrich Ratzel (1844–1904), a geographer, and especially Fritz Gräbner (1877–1934), who was not a field-worker either but a museum specialist given to that kind of speculation. In general Thurnwald was critical of extreme diffusionism, which held that the probability of independent invention in several places is low, if not negligible: 'As everybody knows, people can from time to time have their own brain-waves!' (1912, p. 7).

PART III
German Idealism and
Völkerpsychologie

In the year 1860 I conceived the idea of
adding a kind of superstructure to experimental psychology, which by the nature
of its aims and methods has to confine
itself to the facts of individual mental life.
Although this superstructure is bound to
rest on the foundation of these facts, it
has to go beyond them and take its
departure from the phenomena of human
social life. Soon this began to appear to
me as the higher task of psychology, and
truly its proper completion. (Wundt,
1920a, p. 201)

Introductory Overview

While Enlightenment ideas spread throughout Europe, the Romantic counter-movement was centred on Germany and connected with the profound changes occurring there during the nineteenth century. In the early part of that century Germany consisted of thirty-nine separate states, loosely associated in a confederation whose dominant element was the Prussian monarchy. The bourgeois revolution of 1848, which aimed at German national unity based on democratic institutions, was defeated, and unification under the leadership of Prussia was imposed from above by Bismarck in 1871. Throughout this period national unity and national identity remained salient themes, not merely in politics but also in various spheres of intellectual activity.

The term *Volksgeist* introduced by Herder, and also the terms 'nation' and 'national', acquired a powerful emotional charge,[1] especially during the period of Romantic idealism that lasted until the 1830s. This is typified in the writings of Georg Wilhelm Friedrich Hegel (1770–1831), who regarded the *Volksgeist* as embodied in the person of the absolute national ruler. Hegel's philosophy of history is a dialectical one whereby each epoch is characterized by a nation that plays its part in the preordained succession of stages of the 'World Spirit' before disappearing from the scene. According to Hegel, there were three great stages: Asian despotisms, Graeco-Roman civilization and, as its apogee, Germano-Christian civilization. In this grand scheme the 'uncultured' peoples of the world played no part whatsoever, and neither Hegel nor most other German philosophers displayed much interest in the 'non-civilized'.

If one views the German intellectual scene as a whole, the debate between the proponents of biological doctrines and the supporters of 'psychic unity' (discussed in Part II, Chapter 2) was only one among many, and not even a particularly salient one. So-called 'vulgar materialists' clashed with the proponents of idealism as well as with theologians. Natural science rapidly gained in prestige, and classical humanistic studies began to feel increasingly threatened. Among the latter was philology, whose representatives defensively widened its scope from what had been a narrow concentration on linguistic issues to include the cultures of the language-bearers. Moreover, they broadened out from an almost exclusive concentration on Greek and Roman texts towards the study of 'primitive' languages. Among all these diverse and overlapping trends, the problem of the nature of the human mind constituted a focal element. Can human psychology be fully accounted for in terms of its physiological basis? This is what scientists like Ernst Haeckel believed. In his 'monistic' epistemology, cognition was a natural process mediated by the brain rather than – as he disdainfully put it – a 'transcendental miracle'. Such views were dubbed 'vulgar materialism' by the Idealist philosophers, who maintained that the mind is a totally separate entity. The splits along these lines did not closely follow the boundaries of disciplines, since philosophers and natural scientists were to be found in both camps, as will be illustrated later by the example of Fechner.

The two founders of the original version of *Völkerpsychologie*, Lazarus and Steinthal, reached maturity in the midst of such intellectual ferment. Among the influences shaping their work was Hegel, but two others were even more important: Herbart and Humboldt. Herbartian doctrine, curiously enough, appealed to a wide range of ideologies – the materialists because of Herbart's quasi-mechanical account of mental processes and mathematical speculations, and the idealists because of his notion of the soul, including the proposition that concepts persist in the immortal soul after death. Philologists' interest in issues of psychology and culture is particularly evident in the work of Wilhelm von Humboldt, who wrote extensively on the relationship between language, thought and the mentality of peoples. Together with Herbart he provided the major inspiration for Lazarus and Steinthal. *Völkerpsychologie* is often translated as 'folk-psychology' (see p. 184 below), but this fails to convey the peculiar flavour of the German word, which I shall therefore retain.

The grand scheme of a *Völkerpsychologie* dreamt up by Lazarus and Steinthal was coloured by the prevailing ethos and tended to glorify the 'national spirit'. Their somewhat vague and excessively ambitious programme never had any serious prospect of realization, yet it may be seen as a first attempt to create an independent social and cultural psychology. Their ideas attracted the interest of Dilthey and Wundt, who both, in rather different ways, sought to pursue the problems that had been raised. Both men became involved in the debate, vigorously renewed during the latter part of the nineteenth century, about the relationship between the natural sciences and the *Geisteswissenschaften*. Here also I shall continue to use the German expression, for which there is no exact translation; *Wissenschaft* is roughly equivalent to 'discipline'; *Geist* means 'spirit' or 'mind'. The term broadly encompasses the fields of what we call humanities and social studies.

The main aim that neo-Kantian philosophers such as Windelband or his follower Rickert set themselves was one of showing that the kind of knowledge embodied in humanistic fields such as history is at least equal in certainty to that of the natural sciences. The preliminary task for that purpose was one of description and demarcation of different types of knowledge. In this context psychology came to occupy a key position in the discussion, since with the emergence of its physiological and experimental branches psychology had come to straddle the great divide. Rickert wrestled at great length with the issue of the relationship between nature and *Kultur* and its bearing on the status of psychology. Another participant in the debate who opposed the neo-Kantians, the positivist historian Lamprecht, advocated a social psychology as the scientific basis of history long before social psychology had become established as a distinct specialism. One of the issues raised at that time – and frequently discussed ever since – is whether psychology is a nomothetic (i.e. generalizing) or an ideographic (i.e. concerned with particular phenomena) discipline.

In order to avoid any misunderstanding, I should stress that in this whole affair psychology had become a kind of pawn in a struggle concerned not only with some fundamental philosophical issues but also with the status of the humanistic and social disciplines. Focusing, as I do, on psychology tends to convey a somewhat distorted picture, but has the advantage of showing how considerations of culture unavoidably obtruded themselves. This is most clearly apparent in the ideas of both Dilthey and Wundt, which had the most powerful and lasting impact.

Dilthey had abandoned his early hopes for the kind of *Völkerpsychologie* put forward by Lazarus and Steinthal, while retaining their basic tenet that collective mentality exerts a powerful effect on individuals. In contrast with many of his German peers, Dilthey was thoroughly familiar with the writings of the empiricists. John Stuart Mill, for instance, in his *Logic*, had considered the scientific status of psychology and even proposed an 'ethology' or science of national character (see Jahoda, 1980). Dilthey took issue with Mill as well as with Comte and Spencer rather than simply ignoring them. At the same time he was not dogmatically anti-empiricist, conceding the legitimacy of a scientific experimental psychology devoted to the explanation of physiologically based psychological processes. Yet he argued that these failed to account for the varied and enormously rich range of human experience, which could be grasped only by the kind of insight he termed *Verstehen*. Human experience, he maintained, is a product of particular cultural and historical settings and, as such, impossible to capture within the laboratories of experimental psychology; it therefore requires a different method. The approach he advocated was that of 'hermeneutics', a term that will be explained more fully in due course. Here it will be enough to say that it constitutes a newer version of an ancient interpretative method. Despised for nearly a century while the ideal of a scientific psychology modelled on physics held sway, it has re-emerged and is being powerfully advocated by an increasingly vociferous band of rebels against the mainstream.[2]

The threads leading from Dilthey to the modern exponents, being subtle, complex and often indirectly relayed through philosophers like Husserl and Heidegger, cannot be traced here in detail. Gadamer's *Truth and Method* (1965) examined the hermeneutic approach in depth; this in turn led Habermas to adopt it as an ideological weapon against positivism. Habermas was one of the younger members of the so-called 'Frankfurt School', which included Horkheimer, Marcuse and Adorno, well known for his work on the 'authoritarian personality'. The following quotation from Adorno is squarely in the tradition of Dilthey, even employing Dilthey's by then rather outmoded terminology:

> It appeared to me, and I am still persuaded today, that in the cultural sphere what is regarded by the psychology of perception as a mere 'stimulus' is, in fact, qualitatively determined, a matter of 'objective spirit' and knowable in its objectivity. (T.W. Adorno, cited in Rickman, 1979, p. 172)

Dilthey's emphasis on the salient role of cultural factors – what he often called the 'socio-historical reality', implied a marginalization of experimental psychology. By contrast Wundt, though he was always interested in *Völkerpsychologie*, began by treating it as more or less an adjunct to truly scientific physiological psychology. His early orientation was biological, and he was receptive to Darwinian ideas (see Farr, 1980). Only gradually did he come to regard *Völkerpsychologie*, to which he devoted more and more of his energy with advancing years, as an integral part of psychology, complementary to its experimental aspect. This change arose from his growing conviction of the limitations of the experimental method, which he believed to be incapable of dealing with the higher mental processes. In his view, these could be studied only by looking at historical development in its sociocultural context. Wundt regarded the progressive emergence of the higher mental processes as the cumulative product of social interactions. Moreover, these created – in a manner Wundt failed to specify – a *Volksseele* (literally 'soul of the people') or collective mentality, which he sought to differentiate from the similar concept that had been put forward by Lazarus and Steinthal. Supposedly superior to and yet dependent upon individuals, its logical status remained rather obscure. The burden of Wundt's message, expressed in modern terminology, was that complex psychological processes are dependent on culture. In fact he toyed at one stage with the notion of changing the name of his *Völkerpsychologie* to *Kulturpsychologie*.

Wundt's hopes of establishing *Völkerpsychologie* as an integral part of psychology were not fulfilled, and only a few of his students carried on the tradition for a while. It was unlucky for him that Titchener, who promoted his version of Wundt's teachings in America, seems to have found *Völkerpsychologie* an embarrassment, and so played it down. Wundt's own theoretical writings on it were not translated, and even in the original German they are scattered across a range of different publications. It is no wonder, therefore, that it soon fell into undeserved oblivion. Only with the growing recognition of the importance of culture for psychological functioning over the past decade or so has Wundt's contribution come to be recalled. Yet although lip-service is now frequently paid to Wundt, his complex and difficult ideas in this sphere are commonly misrepresented.

Notes

1. During World War II expressions like 'national butter', used in Britain, would have been inconceivable in Germany.
2. I use this term to refer to the positivist-empiricist orientation dominant in much of twentieth-century academic psychology.

9

The Beginnings of Völkerpsychologie

Intellectual Ancestors:
Herbart and Humboldt

On the morning of 22 October 1850, Gustav Theodor Fechner (1801–87) was lying in bed, thinking of how the bane of materialism might be overcome. A vision came to him of a unified world of thought, spirit and matter, brought about by the mystery of numbers. It was this vision which showed him the path that led to psychophysics. His outlook was totally at variance with the twentieth-century image of the tough-minded scientist, and his character illustrates some of the complex cross-currents of his period. Fechner, a professor of physics, was captivated by the *Naturphilosophie*[1] then much in vogue in Germany. This was a rather hazy and mushy kind of philosophy that strove to find spiritual meaning in every aspect of the natural order, and Fechner gave it his own particular twist by equating organization and rule-governed system with life and possession of soul; accordingly, he viewed not only humans but plants, animals, stars and the universe as a whole as having life and soul. One of Fechner's early works was the *Little Book of Life after Death* (1836); in a later book on Persian dualism, the *Zend-Avesta* (1851), he mentioned that he had recently found a simple mathematical relation between the material and the spiritual world. For us this seems a strange way of referring to the formula that sensation increases according to the logarithm of the stimulus!

Fechner had nothing directly to do with the origins of *Völkerpsychologie*, and my reason for mentioning him is merely to exemplify a certain style of thinking common in his time – a style more difficult for us to grasp adequately than the more analytical eighteenth-century type. It was characterized by a grand, all-embracing vision epitomized by Hegel's ideas about the 'Absolute Spirit', and shared to some extent by the founders of *Völkerpsychologie*. It would be a mistake, however, to imagine that those dedicated to a Romantic and mystical vision were mere idle dreamers. Fechner considered that his philosophy was in complete harmony with his empirical work on psychophysics. Similarly Herbart, whose psychology provided one of the main theoretical pillars of the early version of *Völkerpsychologie*, was actively interested in the application of his ideas to pedagogy. On the other hand, he was deeply concerned with an issue that is now forgotten, but at the time preoccupied many thinkers, including Lazarus: the relationship between soul [*Seele*] and mind or spirit [*Geist*].

Johann Friedrich Herbart (1776–1841) was a successor to Kant's chair at Königsberg. Kant himself had been sceptical about the possibility of any rational or empirical psychology, a view challenged by Herbart. None the less, Herbart's system was essentially metaphysical, and this is why it was later criticized by Wundt. For Herbart, the underlying unity of all mental activity was the soul, itself unknown and unknowable except through its indirect manifestations. These consist of sets of ideas not linked (as maintained by the British School) through 'laws of association', but subject to a set of forces capable of being described mathematically. Herbart's calculus, however, unlike Fechner's, could not be linked to any empirical facts and constituted a quasi-mystical attempt to represent the manifestations of the soul. He also believed that his postulated psychological laws (dismissively dubbed later his 'mechanics of the soul') continue to operate after death, when a rearrangement of concepts takes place.

If that were all, it would be difficult to account for the considerable impact of Herbartian doctrines. On the positive side, he took over and modified Leibniz's concept of 'apperception', combining it with his notion of ideas as active forces struggling for access to consciousness. The dominant forces constitute an 'apperceptive mass', open to congruent ideas but presenting obstacles to others. This notion had obvious pedagogical implications, which Herbart pursued extensively:

> The deepest impressions are given to a man's character through his external deeds when they belong to his vocation or his daily occupation. Here we see in the clearest manner both the conflict and the cooperation that exist in the dominant masses of concepts that belong to the series which is actually passing through his mind . . .
>
> One of the most important directions for the practical educator and teacher is that he observe as accurately as possible how the concept series ought to proceed among his pupils, and how they can and actually do proceed. (Herbart, [1816] 1901, p. 95)

The concept of 'apperception' was thus directly related to practical life. It was adopted by Lazarus and Steinthal, elaborated by Wundt, and still remains part of the psychological vocabulary.

What perhaps most directly inspired Lazarus was Herbart's stress on what we would call the sociocultural nature of man: 'Psychology will remain one-sided as long as it considers man standing alone' ([1816] 1901, p. 190). He even proposed a 'psychology of politics', a kind of social psychology, and recommended that attention should also be paid to the history of humankind. Herbart warned against undue concentration on the unrepresentative 'cultured' person: the beginnings of mental life should be studied in animals, savages and children. He speculated about the consequences of educating a young (Maori) New Zealander in Europe: given that a certain system of ideas had already been implanted, he would neither become completely European, nor remain entirely Maori (Herbart, [1821] 1890). In this and similar passages one finds the germs of some of the ideas that later found expression in *Völkerpsychologie*.

Yet in spite of these sociocultural interests, Herbart rejected any notion of a 'folk-soul'. In the introduction to his *Psychologie als Wissenschaft* [*Psychology as Science*] (1824) he insisted that the real, the only, fact is the individual. The general can be derived from the individual only by abstraction, and our main task is therefore to gain an adequate understanding of the individual. Subsequently Lazarus struggled with the problem as to whether or not the *Volksgeist* might be some kind of supra-individual entity, but he remained faithful to the Herbartian view. Later Wundt also discussed the issue at length, strongly criticizing Lazarus and Steinthal for following Herbart. Yet his own position on this tricky question was so hedged in with reservations as to remain unclear.

Herbart, while denying the existence of a 'folk-soul', proposed a parallel between the interplay of ideas in a person's 'soul' and the interactions of individuals within a collectivity:

> In every social whole the individual persons are related to one another in almost the same way as the concepts in the soul of the individual if the social ties are sufficiently close to secure the mutual influence completely. Conflicting interests take the place of the opposition among concepts. ([1816] 1901, p. 190)

This key passage provided Lazarus with the fundamental hypothesis for the new field he sought to open up. It amounts to the notion that one ought to be able to treat collective events in society as closely analogous to the processes going on within individual minds. As Lazarus was to write later, almost exactly echoing Herbart:

> in the collective mind [*Gesamtgeist*] ... the individual minds behave in just the same way as the particular concepts, or mental elements in general, behave within the individual mind. (1865, p. 9)

Lazarus then went on to link what he called the 'collective mind' with the national state. In so doing he was following an aspect of Hegel's esoteric teaching about the 'objective spirit' [*objectiver Geist*], by which he understood custom, morality and law as found in the family, society and the state. Hegel had viewed the history of humanity as an immanent logical process of the 'World Spirit' [*Weltgeist*], and the 'objective spirits' or *Volksgeister* embodied in particular nation-states as mere expressions of that spirit and of its stage of development. Lazarus adopted the concept of 'objective spirit', stripping it of some of its metaphysical overtones, and sometimes called it 'collective spirit' [*Gesamtgeist*]. Thus although Lazarus and Steinthal were overtly critical of Hegel's philosophy of history, they did not altogether escape from his intellectual clutches. Herbart, by contrast, was a freely acknowledged master, as was Humboldt, to whose teaching I shall now turn.

Wilhelm von Humboldt's (1767–1835) formative years coincided with the transformation of philology. Far from treating language as a kind of dead body ready for dissection, the new approach saw it as an activity that cannot be divorced from its wider cultural context. Humboldt often used the term *Geist*, or spirit, of a people in much the same sense as the modern term 'culture'. German philology, however, was not the only important influence on Humboldt's thought. In 1798 he went to Paris and, in the salons of Madame Helvétius and others, came into contact with all the leading *idéologues*, including Cabanis, Destutt de Tracy and Degérando. At that time Degérando was a member of the National Institute's section on 'analysis of sensations and ideas', and Humboldt established a warm relationship with him. Thus Humboldt came to adopt some of the ideals of the French Enlightenment, which he combined with an approach to the idea of the *Volk* similar to that of Herder. From Paris he went to Spain, where he undertook a study of the Basque language, setting the stage for his later career, which embraced not merely philology but education [*Bildung*], historical work and political theory.

In Humboldt's approach philology was allied to psychology, and a pervasive theme in his work was the relationship between the languages, thoughts and mentalities of peoples. For an understanding of the way he conceptualized these relationships, a brief excursion into his wider philosophical position is necessary. For Humboldt, the basis of all reality is a primeval force [*Urkraft*], unitary and universal. All that is individual is a manifestation of this force, and there is a hierarchy of individualities: from the individual person to the *Volk*, and thence to humanity at large. Different nations are imperfect embodiments of the Whole, progressively ameliorating each other by their contacts in the march towards a more perfect humanity. Thus Humboldt coupled the Enlightenment optimism about continuous progress with the Romantic notion of the *Volksgeist*.

The element that unites the three different levels of the hierarchy is language, identified with the spirit of humanity as a whole as well as being the main principle of individuation. Language is neither of supernatural origin, nor created by individuals; it is the *Volk* that actively constructs its language by the interaction of its component individuals. A particular individual is not a closed system but the product of past generations and all the influences that surround him or her, and integrated into the larger unit of the *Volk* or nation. It is this relationship, mediated largely by language, that is central to much of Humboldt's discussion.

Humboldt's dominant interest is epitomized in the title of his most important work, *The Diversity of Human Language-Structure and Its Influence on the Mental Development of Mankind* ([1836] 1988). While he was concerned with the effects of variations in language and culture on mentality, he also had a profound conviction of the 'governing principle of universal humanity'. Accordingly, he did not subscribe to Herder's cultural relativism, rejoicing that civilization was being transported to the remotest parts of the earth. None the less he did not look down on 'savages', as most of his contemporaries – and later also Lazarus and Steinthal – were apt to do:

> Even in his earliest circumstances, man transcends the *present* moment, and does not remain sunk in mere sensuous enjoyment. Among the roughest tribes we find a love of adornment, dancing, music and song, and beyond that forebodings of a world to come, the hopes and anxieties founded on this, and traditions and tales which commonly go back to the origin of man and of his abode. ([1836] 1988, p. 30)

Not unlike Piaget, but perhaps somewhat inconsistently for someone who also claimed that there can be no thought without language, Humboldt held that concepts must exist before words. Hence, in contrast to many other writers – not excluding some of his followers, such as Lazarus and Steinthal – he did not think it was justifiable to assess the range of concepts possessed by a people at a given epoch by means of its vocabulary. A large number of concepts, Humboldt maintained, can be expressed indirectly, perhaps through metaphors unknown to us. He affirmed that one finds abstract concepts in the languages of 'uncultivated nations', and gave a number of examples. He also emphasized the richness and multitude of expressions in the languages of 'so-called savages'.

Humboldt had a great deal to say on the relationship between language and thought, holding not only that language is indispensable for thought but also that social processes are an essential prerequisite for adequate cognitive functioning: 'man understands himself only when he has tested the intelligibility of his words on others' (1836, p. 53).

People who share a language develop 'a similar subjectivity', so that each particular language has built into it a certain *Weltanschauung*. Hence learning a foreign language should open up new mental perspectives. Yet this does not mean that language is a straitjacket within which particular populations remain confined:

> every language has the flexibility to take everything within itself and then again to give it expression. It can never, and under no circumstances, become an absolute barrier for man. (1836, p. 305)

The same applies to the relationship between languages and the intellectual wealth of nations. Humboldt argued that the advantage a particular language might have depends on the mental energy devoted to it. If a language is less perfect, this merely indicates a lesser drive directed at it and does not permit any inferences about intellectual level.

Several of Humboldt's ideas had been put forward by some of his predecessors. For instance, his view that metaphors capture 'the youthful sensibility of earlier ages' is reminiscent of Vico; or again, the notion that the character of a people finds expression in its language may be found in Condillac. But none of his predecessors offered such a systematic survey, based on intensive studies not merely of Indo-Germanic languages but those of a wide range of non-European peoples. Humboldt's postulate of a close link between language and modes of thought, and his belief that the effectiveness of thought is enhanced when there is a correspondence between it and the logical categories of grammar, anticipated in essence what later became known as the Sapir–Whorf hypothesis.

Humboldt has frequently been credited in the literature – mistakenly, in my opinion – with coining the term *Völkerpsychologie*.[2] This is not surprising, since his theories anticipated some of the essential elements of what it was later to become. Lazarus and Steinthal took over from Humboldt the notion of the dependence of thought upon language, and also the view that language is primary among the forces that hold a *Volk* together. On the other hand, in contrast to Humboldt's tolerant cosmopolitanism, their writing is suffused by the pan-German nationalism typical of their period.

The Founders: Lazarus and Steinthal

'We have named a field of study that as such does not yet exist' (Lazarus, 1851, p. 112). Thus Lazarus began his article entitled 'On the concept and posssibility of a *Völkerpsychologie*'. He defined its task as that of determining the psychological nature of the *Völksgeist* and its process. Furthermore, the laws governing its inner, spiritual [*geistige*] or ideal activity must be discovered, as expressed in life, art and science – in its culture, as we would put it. The lawful origins, development and eventual decline of the particularities of a *Volk* should also be studied.

A consideration of Lazarus's background helps us to understand how he arrived at this idea. Moritz Lazarus (1824–1903) was born in Filehne, a small German-Polish town in the province of Posen. He was the son of a merchant, lawyer and member of the rabbinical college. The diversity of the population in his home town (Germans, Poles and Jews) led him even in childhood to ponder the question: why are people so different? He recalled a wooden post, marking the division between two parts of the town: on one side there was 'German civilization', on the other 'Polish disorder' [*polnische Wirtschaft*]: clean and tidy versus dirty and messy. This image haunted him, stimulating an early interest in national differences. On the other hand, however, he also thought of a *Humanitätsgesellschaft*, a society open to all nations and religions (Leicht, 1904, p. 10). This kind of duality runs through his mature writings. He went to the *Gymnasium* in Braunschweig, where his German teacher was a Herbartian. He was particularly impressed by a passage in Herbart to the effect that an empirical psychology separated from the history of mankind is bound to remain incomplete. It is also noteworthy that in the course of his secondary-school career he wrote an essay on German national pride, in which he already touched upon the relationship between the individual and the community. In 1845 he began to study theology in Berlin, abandoning this field for a mixture of physiology, other natural sciences, and philosophy. It was there that he first met Steinthal and communicated to him his enthusiasm for the project. In 1860 he became Professor of *Völkerpsychologie* in Bern – the first chair of psychology anywhere.

From this brief sketch it is evident that a fascination with national differences began early in Lazarus's life. He read widely in the field, but – as he said in that seminal article – the various approaches to the study of the character of peoples, such as the philosophy of history, or naive climatic determinism, fell short of what was needed. This led him to formulate the proposal for a new science, a project that took further shape in collaboration with his close friend, Steinthal.

Hajim Steinthal (1823–99) studied philosophy, philology and theology, mainly in Berlin. Specializing in Chinese, he was due to make a voyage to China that would have jeopardized his partnership with Lazarus. In the event he decided against it, visiting only London and Paris. For Steinthal language was central to psychology, the study of different languages being, in his view, the key to the understanding of the 'souls' of the peoples who are their speakers. These views were, of course, derived from Humboldt, whom he fervently admired and whose work he sought to continue. In

1858 Steinthal published a book on the origin of language, in which he reiterated and expanded Humboldt's message, spelling out the influence of language on the mental [*geistig*] development of man and the formation of his representations. Such development, he maintained, is governed by the laws of individual and *Völkerpsychologie*, though the only concrete example was Herbart's teaching on apperception. The intimate connection between language and thought is stressed throughout: language, while not identical with thought, is its essential precondition – language is the 'organ of thought': 'It is through the eyes that the soul sees, and through language that it thinks' (1858, p. 120).

After Lazarus had published his initial proposal, Steinthal enthusiastically took up the idea. During the winter semester 1856–7 he announced a course at the University of Berlin on 'The connection between language and national spirit'. While Lazarus had introduced Steinthal to Herbartian psychology, it was Steinthal who persuaded Lazarus that language is of key importance for the study of the *Volksgeist* of particular peoples.

Given the direction of Steinthal's interests, it is not surprising that when he joined Lazarus in the promotion of the new field, a distinct shift of emphasis resulted. They launched a *Zeitschrift* (journal) intended as a forum for scholars sympathetic to their ideas, whose leading article was entitled 'Introductory thoughts on *Völkerpsychologie* as an invitation to a journal for *Völkerpsychologie* and *Sprachwissenschaft*' (Lazarus and Steinthal, 1860). The addition of *Sprachwissenschaft* (philology) was significant: although a considerable part of the article consists essentially of an extended restatement of Lazarus's position, much of the new material relates broadly to the area we would call 'language and culture'.

While this joint programmatic article remains the *locus classicus*, the ideas were further elaborated – but not fundamentally altered – in subsequent contributions by the founders to the *Zeitschrift*. Lazarus and Steinthal were wrestling with complex ideas, which they expounded in the prolix style that was the fashion among nineteenth-century German scholars. My outline of the salient aspects of their teaching draws on these various sources.[3]

The *Völkerpsychologie* of Lazarus and Steinthal

1. *What is the* Volksgeist?

The notion of the '*Volksgeist*', they wrote, is in the (mid-nineteenth-century) air, being referred to by historians, ethnologists, philosophers and jurists. In spite of such common usage there has been no rigorous analysis of the concept, and it remains exceedingly vague. The most appropriate discipline for clarifying it is psychology, which has always dealt with the individual '*Geist*' (spirit/mind); a logical extension, the object of *Völkerpsychologie*, is to study collective mental phenomena.

The question to be tackled at the outset concerns the very existence of the *Volksgeist*, since there are those who believe that society is nothing apart from the individuals composing it. Now admittedly the *Volksgeist* cannot be regarded as a substantive entity in the same way as the individual *Geist*, yet the whole is greater than the sum of its parts. Society has a logical, temporal and psychological priority over the individual, powerfully influencing individual development and producing a certain mentality characteristic of a particular people. The *Volksgeist* promotes unity and harmony of collective psychological functioning. It may be defined as 'the inner activity common to all individuals' (Lazarus and Steinthal, 1860, p. 29).

The *Volksgeist* is governed by the same basic psychological processes as the individual mind, only they are more complex and extended. There are also many other parallels between the individual *Geist* and the *Volksgeist*. For instance, the collective sentiment of nationality in a people corresponds to the sense of personality in the individual. Or again, just as the psychological well-being of an individual depends on the health of the body, so the state of the *Volksgeist* depends on the health of the 'body politic' – that is, the state. The restriction of consciousness at any one moment to a small fraction of the total mental content corresponds to the preoccupation of the *Volksgeist* at any one time with a particular set of events such as the Crusades or the Reformation; a moment for the individual is perhaps a decade for the *Volk* – it is simply a question of scale.

The unity of the *Volksgeist* is reflected in a feeling of being at one with the community. In part this is the outcome of sense of shared background and fate; but the primary factor is a common language, the creation *par excellence* of the national genius. Language is the instrument mediating social relations; it unites all individuals and unifies their psychic contents. Hence in order to reconstruct the national characteristics and the *Weltanschauung* of peoples of the past, the preferred method must be that of the philologist.

The *Volksgeist*, or 'objective spirit', exists in two different modes: one is intrapsychic and consists of thoughts, sentiments and dispositions; the other represents its material embodiment in books, works of art, monuments, industrial products, means of transport and exchange, weapons of war, and toys. Between these two the 'objective spirit' also manifests itself in all kinds of institutions, be they educational, administrative or whatever. Thus the *Volksgeist* is part of the individual – not, of course, as an organism, but as a historical being living in society; moreover, the *Volksgeist*, being all-pervasive, also surrounds the individual in material or organizational form.

All this would seem to imply complete uniformity, which is obviously not possible. One has to eliminate first children, who are not yet developed; then also idiots and the retarded, who cannot develop; and finally exceptional persons of genius. The *Volksgeist* in its pure form is to be found among the average members of a society.

The *Volksgeist* is the 'objective spirit' of a *Volk*, but what is a *Volk?* Although language is a prime source of the unity of the people, it cannot be used as a criterion, since the outer boundaries of a language are as hard to pin down as those of a *Volk*. In fact, there can be no objective criterion: 'the concept of a *Volk* rests on the subjective views of the members about themselves, their shared identity and feeling of belonging together' (Lazarus and Steinthal, 1960, p. 35). I might add here that after much subsequent debate on the issue this view has come to be generally accepted, usually without awareness that Lazarus and Steinthal had shrewdly anticipated it; one might add, though, that the 'subjective' position is not without its difficulties (LeVine and Campbell, 1972).

2. *The Elements of the* Volksgeist *and its Development*

First and foremost, there is language. Language displays the range of concepts available to a people – which, among savages, is severely restricted – and reveals the depth or shallowness of their thinking.

Another important element is mythology, not to be confused with religion. Among primitives mythology constitutes a general mode of apprehension, and the whole outlook of the popular mind is mythological in character. Mythology permits the study of the processes of apperception and blending [*Verschmelzung*] of impressions in the broadest perspective. The transformations of myths over centuries mirror the development of the *Volksgeist* and show its abundant creativity. So comparative mythology is one of the most powerful tools for the study of the *Volksgeist*.

While myths concern mainly the intellectual side of the *Volksgeist*, religion manifests all aspects of theoretical and practical activity, ideals and purposes, and emotional life. In it one finds the germs of poetry and other arts, so that comparative literature is also necessary for apprehending the *Volksgeist*. Above all, styles of architecture are the most illuminating expressions of the *Volksgeist* – a curious claim that is not further justified.

In addition to these intellectual, aesthetic and emotional elements, one must not forget the practical ones. The repetition of an action in the pursuit of a given end results first in habit and then in custom; customary behaviour therefore arises unintentionally, and is then transmitted through the generations. Its origin being forgotten, it tends to be attributed to gods or heroes and gains an authoritative grip on the individual. At a later stage some customs may be dropped and others codified in law. The attainment of literacy is a watershed, when peoples become truly civilized; and one of the first uses of writing was in recording laws.

There is an interaction between what we would call ecology and modes of subsistence (in this connection the potato in Ireland is cited) and mental functioning: 'Everything the *Geist* has created reacts back on it . . . the character of man is formed in his actions' (Lazarus and Steinthal, 1860, p. 58). At the lowest level of culture the way of life is dictated solely by nature, as among miserable fisherfolk; hunting peoples are more lively, but lack *Geist*; in pastoral peoples the *Geist* dreams, and these dreams are often poetic; but agriculture marks the beginning of civilization. This development is accompanied by changes in the position of women, the cornerstone of all types of social relationships – not merely the concept of marriage, but also the relationship between fathers and children and that between adult males. The kind of education received by the young is universally connected with the *Volksgeist*, and in turn influences the development of the *Volk*.

3. The Two Parts of Völkerpsychologie *and Its Relationship to Other Disciplines*

The task of *Völkerpsychologie* is a dual one: both general and specific. The former is *völkergeschichtlich* (folk-historical): 'Just as the biography of the individual person rests on laws of individual psychology, so does history – the biography of humanity – receive its rational foundation from *Völkerpsychologie*' (Lazarus and Steinthal, 1860, p. 19). It is completely abstract and general, unconcerned with the variations of peoples in space and time; one might say that it treats humanity at large as a *Volk*. It addresses the question of how the processes whereby the elementary forms of individual consciousness come to be combined into the total complex of forces that constitutes the *Volksgeist*. In other words, it concentrates on the study of the laws governing the growth of the *Volksgeist* in general.

The second part, named 'psychological ethnology', descends from abstract humanity at large to the concrete level and is concerned with the variety of actually existing *Volksgeister* and their development. It is essentially descriptive, dealing with the life processes of particular peoples studied by means of 'observation, ordering and comparison of phenomena'. In terms of research strategy, psychological ethnology has to precede folk-historical psychology, for the laws of the latter must be derived inductively from the material assembled by the former. This material is virtually all-embracing: language, writing, myth, religion, custom, law, political constitution, arts, sciences, trade, and all institutions of public life – all is grist to their mill.

* * *

Given the vastness of the scope envisaged, it is necessary to consider the potential contributions of other disciplines and their relationship to *Völkerpsychologie*. First of all there is, of course, individual psychology; this is incomplete without *Völkerpsychologie*, but its laws are relevant. Since the state is the embodiment of the *Volksgeist*, politics is to *Völkerpsychologie* what physiology is to individual psychology. Anthropology, though it sometimes deals with national characters, focuses generally on phenomena inter-mediate between physiology and psychology, for instance the effects of climate; but these factors do not adequately explain the peculiarities of the 'ethnic *Geist*' of different peoples. Ethnology is even less useful, being, in effect, a branch of zoology that treats humans as part of animal nature (this refers to the then prevalent 'craniology'). History is little more than a descriptive account of events; it is important as the major supplier of source material, but needs to be supplemented by *Völkerpsychologie*, which alone can explain the laws underlying historical change. Much the same applies to the philosophy of history, ostensibly sharing the aims of *Völkerpsychologie* but lacking adequate means of achieving them and thus being confined to mere speculation. Generally, therefore, all these disciplines are largely descriptive, and it will be the function of *Völkerpsychologie* to provide explanations.

The relationship between *Völkerpsychologie* and the natural sciences is more problematic. Among the latter one finds a similar duality of descriptive versus experimental/explanatory. Fields like mineralogy, botany and zoology are observational and descriptive; physics and chemistry are concerned with the general laws according to which 'these forms of reality come into being and fade away, seek the *Urelemente* [basic elements] and fundamental forces of nature' (Lazarus and Steinthal, 1860, p. 19). In the same way, individual psychology shows the mechanical lawfulness of certain processes, or the invariance of concepts like those of space, time, and so on. Now in so far as *Völkerpsychologie* also attempts to discover general laws, it resembles the natural sciences. There is, however, a significant difference in the nature of the phenomena being investigated. Natural phenomena, including those of individual psychology, remain constant, while the *Geist* that constitutes the object of *Völkerpsychologie* progresses and is continuously being enriched. The conclusion must be that *Völkerpsychologie* is a *tertium quid*, intermediate between the humanities and the natural sciences.

'Volksgeist', 'Culture', and the Contribution of Lazarus and Steinthal

In an earlier chapter I commented on the similarity between Herder's notion of the '*Volksgeist*' and the modern concept of 'culture'. How far does the same apply to the Lazarus/Steinthal version? One way of approaching this is by substituting 'culture' for every occurrence of '*Volksgeist*' and seeing if the result still makes sense in our terms. On trying this out – not very systematically, it must be admitted – my impression is that Herder usually came rather closer to anticipating our concept than Lazarus and Steinthal. The reason is, paradoxically, that Herder's notion of the *Volksgeist* was more simple and theoretically unambitious, while Lazarus and Steinthal attempted a more thorough and systematic analysis on the basis of Herbartian psychology. As a result they came up against – and failed to resolve – some conceptual problems also encountered by later writers dealing with the elusive notion of 'culture'.

The major problem concerns the relationship between individuals and their culture. Lazarus and Steinthal stated explicitly that the *Volksgeist* 'lives' within the individual and has no separate existence. Yet they also referred to the *Volksgeist* as though it were a distinct superordinate entity that exerts power over the individual, much as Kroeber ([1917] 1952) did when he called culture 'the superorganic'. Some of Lazarus and Steinthal's phrasing could be interpreted as mere metaphorical usage – for instance, when they say that the elements of the *Volksgeist*, such as language or myth, 'constitute the various forms or stages of the self-consciousness of a *Volk*' (1860, p. 38). But there is no escape from the implication of their claim that the *Volksgeist* is governed by laws analogous to those governing individual minds – that the *Volksgeist* can, in some sense, be differentiated from individual minds. Since they also defined the *Volksgeist* as 'the inner activity common to all individuals' (1860, p. 29), it is hard to avoid the conclusion that they fell into the very trap they had been anxious to avoid. However, unlike others who sought to cut the Gordian knot by postulating a 'group mind',[4] Lazarus and Steinthal searched for the answers to a problem that has occupied many scholars and is by no means adequately resolved as yet.

Clearly, individuals are the carriers of culture, but only collectively; for any given individual, culture is not only part of her or his make-up but also, in an important sense, part of the external environment. This applies most obviously to what has been called 'material' (i.e. artefacts of every kind) as distinct from 'symbolic' culture, a distinction also made by Lazarus and Steinthal; but it also applies to symbolic culture – customs, language, beliefs and values, and so on. There is still an active debate as to how culture might best be conceptualized, in general as well as in specific relation to psychology (see Van de Vijver and Hutschemaekers, 1990). Yet in spite of all these reservations, the *Volksgeist*–culture equation still holds fairly well in much of Lazarus and Steinthal's writings, and the kinds of problems they tried to tackle by postulating a *Volksgeist* are often similar to those we still tend to interpret in terms of 'culture'.

What can now be seen as their main weakness, rooted in the modes of thought prevalent in the period, was their excessive ambition. They sought to find ways of portraying both the development of the human mind in general and its particular forms within national communities. It is easy to dismiss their efforts, as Whitman did when he wrote: 'These men shared, not a scientific approach, but a set of metascientific myths . . .' (1984, p. 219). While there is no doubt some truth in such a view, it does less than justice to Lazarus and Steinthal. These men had a grand, if unrealistic, vision of a field of research whose problems are still with us and remain to some extent unresolved.

The previously mentioned *Zeitschrift* launched by Lazarus and Steinthal, whose burden was shouldered mainly by the latter, continued to be published in its original form until 1890. It had many distinguished contributors – including, for instance, Bastian and Dilthey. What Lazarus and Steinthal considered the most powerful methodological tool for *Völkerpsychologie*, philology, figured most prominently among the articles, followed by folklore and religion; the rest was widely scattered among such spheres as psychology, philosophy, art and literature, and ethnology. *Völkerpsychologie* as such was one of the minority topics and consisted mainly of theoretical speculation.[5] Given the grandiose aims, coupled with the limitations of the approaches available at the time, it is not surprising that the *Zeitschrift* did relatively little to further the goals of its founders. In particular, one finds precious little about the 'laws' that supposedly govern the development of the human mind in general, and its varied manifestations within national communities.

The status of these 'laws' was extensively discussed by Lazarus and Steinthal, who were vacillating between the view of humans as the products of historical developments and that of humans as natural organisms and, as such, within the purview of natural science.[6] In the course of the following decades this became a widely and hotly debated topic, especially among German scholars. It still remains at the heart of the currently renewed debate about the status of psychology and its relation to 'culture', and is therefore of more than mere historical interest.

Notes

1. The founders of nineteenth-century psychology's adherence to *Naturphilosophie* and also philology was conducive to the establishment of a link between culture and mind. A case in point is that of Hermann Lotze (1817–81), whose *Mikrokosmus: Ideen zur Naturgeschichte und Geschichte der Menschheit* was one of Lazarus and Steinthal's sources of inspiration.
2. For instance, Beuchelt (1974, p. 12) states that the coining of the word is

attributed to Humboldt, citing two references; following these up, one again encounters mere assertion.

3. There does not appear to be any literature on Lazarus and Steinthal in English; useful sources are Belke (1971), Lambrecht (1913), Schneider (1990) and Sganzini (1913).

4. Among psychologists, McDougall (1920) followed that path, subdividing the field much as Lazarus and Steinthal had done:

Group psychology consists properly of two parts, that which is concerned to discover the most general principles of group life and that which applies these principles to the study of particular kinds and examples of group life. (p. 6)

5. For a content analysis of the *Zeitschrift*, see Krewer and Jahoda, 1990.

6. Towards the end of their original article, Lazarus and Steinthal almost seem to have come off the fence on the side of science:

What matters in psychology is essentially the same as that towards which the natural sciences are striving and in which they succeed so well, namely to reduce things and qualities to relationships. (1860, p. 70)

10

Psychology: A Science or a Culture-historical Discipline?

In their 'invitation to *Völkerpsychologie*' Lazarus and Steinthal had made a somewhat tentative effort to show where *Völkerpsychologie* stood in relation to other scholarly and scientific disciplines. During the latter part of the nineteenth century the dichotomy between *Naturwissenschaften* and *Geisteswissenschaften* became the subject of a great debate in Germany. Its ostensible aim was the purely scholarly one of conceptual clarification, but the fact that it was conducted mainly by exponents of *Geisteswissenschaft* indicates that it was the status of the *Geisteswissenschaften* that was chiefly at stake. Although the debate as such was not about psychology, and hardly any of the titles of the participants' writings contain this term, psychology was nevertheless to be found at the heart of the controversy. The reason, no doubt, is the hybrid character of psychology, which spans the divide separating the sciences from the humanities and social studies.

What I shall discuss here is not the wide-ranging debate as such – which is no great loss, as much of it was, in my opinion, pedantic and tiresome – but only those aspects reflecting varying perceptions of the nature and tasks of psychology. As will be evident from previous chapters, psychology of a kind had long been associated with speculations about history in the sense of the historical development of humankind. Now it came to be discussed in novel perspectives, notably its relevance for the academic discipline of history. More important from the present standpoint was the re-emergence, in more elaborated form, of Vico's ideas about the culture-historical roots of mentalities, implying a rejection of the view that psychology is primarily an experimental science. It was also in the context of this debate that psychology first became explicitly linked with *Kultur*. I use the German term advisedly, since it overlaps but is not identical with our term 'culture', but corresponds to some extent to what in English is called 'civilization'.[1]

Before embarking on the story, I should like to remind the reader of the meaning of the cumbersome terminology that has to be used. First, there are the *Naturwissenschaften*, or natural sciences and the more or less synonymous term *Gesetzeswissenschaften* – literally 'sciences that enunciate laws'. Before the debate it was generally taken for granted that the sciences could be contrasted with the *Geisteswissenschaften*, which I render as 'humanities and social studies'.

Paul on *Kulturwissenschaften*

The term *Geisteswissenschaften* was first criticized by Hermann Paul (1846–1921), a prominent philologist who, in 1880, published a book on the principles of the history of language. In it he argued that strictly speaking there could be only one *Geisteswissenschaft* – namely, psychology as a *Gesetzwissenschaft* – and he explicitly categorized it as one of the exact sciences. For him the opposite of nature was not *Geist* but *Kultur*, so he proposed the expression *Kulturwissenschaften*, which subsequently gained wide currency. The characteristic mark of *Kultur*, Paul maintained, lies in the involvement of psychic factors. Since these are also present in animals, he drew the curious conclusion that one has to recognize the existence of animal *Kultur*, so that animal life would form part of the *Kulturwissenschaften*. By this he meant the beehive as an early stage of social organization, or birdsong as the beginning of art.

Paul's main arguments, however, are focused on humans: it is society that makes proto-humans into historical beings through their joint interactions for common purposes. But when we look at historical development it is clear that not only psychological but physical factors were at work, so that an adequate approach to the *Kulturwissenschaften* requires consideration of physical as well as psychological laws. Paul did not elaborate on how these 'psychological laws' might be applied in the study of historical development, and thereby saved himself from running into the difficulties this would have entailed. Instead, he advocated the creation of something forbiddingly called *Prinzipienlehre der Gesellschaftswissenschaft* (loosely translatable as *The Principles of the Study of Society*), which would be charged with the task. From there he went on to attack Lazarus and Steinthal's *Völkerpsychologie* in a manner which evoked a strong response from Wundt.

Paul began his critique by reproaching Lazarus and Steinthal for ignoring the 'physical forces'; he claimed, for instance, that they should have considered bodily movements, which are the business of physiology. From this rather feeble argument he moved on to more substantive matters. Above all, Paul took issue with Lazarus and Steinthal's basic notion that the relationship of *Völkerpsychologie* to both particular peoples and humanity as a whole is analogous to that between psychology and the individual person. They had maintained that the processes occurring in the *Volksgeist* and its component elements are essentially the same as those characterizing individuals, only more complicated. Paul would have none of that:

> This involves concealing, through the hypostatization of a series of abstractions, the true state of affairs. All psychic processes take place within the individual mind, and nowhere else. ... Therefore, away with these abstractions. (Paul, [1880] 1898, p. 11)[2]

These views also constituted a threat to Wundt's own position, since at that time he was contemplating the elaboration of his new version of *Völkerpsychologie*. Paul exposed a weak flank when seeking to reinforce his arguments by referring to Herbart:

> Hence if we conceive psychology in the Herbartian sense as the science of the interrelations of representations, then there can be only an individual psychology to which one cannot juxtapose any *Völkerpsychologie* or whatever one might care to call it. (Paul, 1898, pp. 12–13)

Wundt was later to pounce on this as a misconception arising from an unjustified reliance on Herbart, yet in other ways Paul's ideas were not unlike those he himself adopted later. In his classification of the spheres of knowledge, Paul introduced the term *Kulturwissenschaften* and attempted to blur the distinction between them and the natural sciences, without suggesting any truly radical changes. By contrast, a totally fresh perspective was proposed by the neo-Kantian school of Windelband and Rickert.

Windelband on Psychology as a Natural Science

The famous rectorial address of 1894 by Wilhelm Windelband (1848–1915) was entitled 'History and natural science'. In it he called into question the whole basis of the system of classification of spheres of learning hitherto taken for granted. This basis had been the object or content of the discipline, but he suggested various reasons why this is unsatisfactory. Windelband's clinching argument related to psychology:

> This incongruity of the formal principle of division is above all evident from the fact that one cannot classify an empirical discipline of such significance as psychology into either *Naturwissenschaft* or *Geisteswissenschaft*; in terms of its

content it can only be a *Geisteswissenschaft*, and in a certain sense the foundation of all others; but all its procedures, its whole methodological approach, is from beginning to end that of the *Naturwissenschaften*. (Windelband, [1894] 1924, p. 143)

As an alternative, Windelband favoured a classification according to method, resulting in a dichotomy between *Gesetzeswissenschaften* and *Ereigniswissenschaften* – that is to say, establishing general laws versus describing particularistic phenomena. For describing the modes of thinking involved in the two approaches he coined the terms 'nomothetic' and 'ideographic', which have been appropriated by psychology. Windelband reflected on the relationship between these two, asking whether specific events could be referred to general laws and, conversely, whether it is not the case that a specific event or historical '*Gestalt*' attains its causal significance only within the framework of general lawfulness. He likened this to a syllogism: the major premiss is a natural law, the minor premiss a set of particular conditions, and the conclusion the real singular event. In this sense the nomothetic and ideographic modes should be viewed as complementary.

Accordingly, he believed that in principle a causal explanation of historical events based on natural laws, especially psychological laws, should be possible, at least in principle. Yet almost in the same breath he was led to voice some misgivings on that score:

> To be sure, it is actually most curious how modest have been the demands of history on psychology. The notoriously very limited extent to which it has hitherto been possible to formulate the laws of psychic life has never unduly troubled the historians; through natural judgement of men and intuition they have known enough to understand their heroes and their heroes' behaviour. This gives one pause and makes it appear rather doubtful whether the recently planned mathematical-natural law formulation of elementary psychic processes is likely to yield a worthwhile contribution to our understanding of real human life. (Windelband, [1894] 1924, p. 157)

It would seem that despite the fact that he made psychology the linchpin of his argument, Windelband had no very clear ideas about its nature and scope. There is no indication that he was familiar with the different positions espoused at the time.

Rickert: Nature Versus *Kultur*

The same cannot be said of his follower, Heinrich Rickert (1848–1936), who was responsible for what is regarded as the classic exposition of the neo-Kantian school. In 1902 he published a book on *The Limits of Scientific Conceptualizations*, in which he sought to reinforce Windelband's thesis and defend it against the objections raised by people like Dilthey and Wundt. Little purpose would be served by rehearsing his arguments, which were essentially logical and epistemological, and based on philosophical assumptions that are no longer accepted. Suffice it to say that Rickert was prepared to concede some differences between psychology and what he still insisted were the other natural sciences, but contended that such differences were relatively minor and thus did not affect Windelband's main thesis.

In a later work, entitled *Kulturwissenschaft und Naturwissenschaft* (1910), a rather different perspective is presented. As is evident from the title, Rickert had adopted Paul's terminology and decided that the opposite of *Natur* is not *Geist* but *Kultur*. The justification for this change is rather subtle and involved, depending on the polysemy of the word *Geist*, which can mean both 'spirit' and 'mind'. It boils down essentially to the claim that everything that is 'spiritual' has to do with *Kultur*, while 'mind' is narrowly restricted to psychology. It follows, according to Rickert, that the expression *Geisteswissenschaften* is ambiguous and therefore useless for distinguishing scientific from non-scientific fields of knowledge.

Rickert defined the concept of *Kultur* as 'the totality of objects to which generally recognized values are attached' (1910, p. 27). Thus the basic difference between nature and *Kultur* is that the former, unlike the latter, is value-free. Accordingly, the *Kulturwissenschaften* such as philosophy, economics, jurisprudence, and so on – and, above all, history, which is concerned with all of them – are intimately bound up with values that change over time. They are therefore individualizing or ideographic disciplines, as opposed to the generalizing or nomothetic natural sciences.

Psychology, dealing with mind in general, falls squarely within the natural sciences. Consequently (and here Rickert resolves Windelband's dilemma) it is largely useless as an aid to history, with the possible exception of the 'social psychology' adumbrated by Lamprecht (to be considered shortly). The only psychology that is really useful for history and the arts is not the science but rather the kind of imaginative insight popularly known as 'psychology':

> We call not merely historians, but also poets and artists 'psychologists', for we rightly believe that they must have an intuitive grasp of human nature [*Menschenkenner*] if they are to fulfil their tasks. But the 'psychology' practised by artists surely has nothing but its name in common with the formal science of psychic life; no one would recommend to a poet that he should embark on studies of scientific psychology with a view to improving his poetry. (1910, p. 62)

Rickert correctly characterized the psychology of his time when he said that its aim was to understand mental life by treating it as a combination of simple elements, an approach that has nothing to offer to the historian or literary scholar. Thus when he introduced the notion of *Kultur*, it was to mark off a sphere to which scientific psychology had nothing to contribute. The only slight concession Rickert made was in allowing for a possible contribution, at some time in the future, by a scientific *social* psychology of the kind envisaged by Lamprecht. The ideas of Lamprecht, a controversial figure who outraged his fellow-historians and became involved in the famous *Methodenstreit* (quarrel over methods), merit some attention.

Karl Lamprecht: History, Culture and Social Psychology

Karl Lamprecht (1856–1915) was an unorthodox historian whose vanity and arrogance did not endear him to his colleagues. In contrast to Windelband and Rickert, he believed that the scientific method can be applied to the *Geisteswissenschaften* as well as the natural sciences, and is the only path leading to 'truth'. Accordingly, his aim was to make history into one of the generalizing sciences rather than remaining merely descriptive and interpretative. This went radically against the then dominant trend of viewing history in terms of the actions of particular 'heroic' figures, a view quite incompatible with the objective of establishing universal laws of culture-historical development. Lamprecht proposed that the means for arriving at such laws could be found in a scientific *Sozialpsychologie* that concerned itself with cultural conditions influencing the psyche at different historical epochs, rather than with individual processes.

For Lamprecht, historical phases and events are essentially of a psychic nature, so that any cultural stage is characterized by a *collective* psychic state [*seelischer Gesamtzustand*]. This he regarded as a kind of diapason, pervading all mental states, and thereby also activities, in any given period. Lamprecht also sought to demonstrate that cultural stages succeed each other in a definite order, displaying increasing differentiation in a manner somewhat reminiscent of Herbert Spencer's social evolutionary scheme.

Lamprecht's main work was concentrated on historical civilizations in general, and German history in particular. However, he did not consider that his method was confined to these, as shown by the following example – close, as he put it, to the main task of *Völkerpsychologie*:

> It is possible to determine the development of certain low levels of culture ... through half a millennium, by collecting the oral transmission of epics. We possess, for instance, for certain Kaffir tribes, an epic tradition of such a

time depth. We can analyze it, in terms of its inner psychological motives, into a sequence of increasingly intensive forms of epic representation. (Lamprecht, 1912, p. 134)

He did not elaborate on how such an analysis could be carried out, though he mentioned that the conclusions could be verified by checking the sequence of real events by referring to the records of the Cape Colony – hardly a convincing procedure. Lamprecht himself must have been aware of the limitations of such an approach, because he cast around for some method of validating it independently. He thought that he had found it in child psychology, considered in the light of the 'biogenetic principle'. This was based on the work of Haeckel, who had put forward the so-called 'biogenetic law', which stated that ontogeny, in the sense of the individual's embryological development, is a concise and compressed recapitulation of phylogeny. Lamprecht assumed that this holds not merely for embryology but also for postnatal development; and he writes with complete confidence:

[that] one will be able to establish a sequence of stages of psychogenetic development valid for children all over the world; as regards the higher of these stages, it will be possible to order the character of the known phylogenetic, *and that means cultural* [emphasis added], stages of development; this will be done to the extent that one can allocate ethnographic material and folklore to a sequence of relative stages of development. (Lamprecht, 1912, p. 137)

He was convinced that by this means one would be able to trace cultural evolution right back to the earliest emergence of humanity on earth. While Lamprecht did make an attempt at empirical studies in applying his method (see Jahoda, 1991), he mostly engaged in daring speculation. Again basing himself on the biogenetic principle, he tried to show that there were common elements between the cognitive functioning of the child and that of prehistoric as well as medieval man. But he was never clear about which psychological elements were supposed to remain constant and which he regarded as undergoing progressive differentiation under the impact of historical change; nor did he seem aware of the circularity involved in treating psychological features simultaneously as both causes and consequence.

Lamprecht's notion of 'social psychology' was far broader than our understanding of its scope, as is apparent from the general scheme set out in Table 10.1, overleaf.

Some aspects of this scheme – notably the ecological and subsistence factors – correspond to more recent ones put forward by some cross-cultural psychologists; and if the subcategories of the 'cultural' now appear

Table 10.1 *Social-psychological factors in the course of history*

Cultural			Natural
Material		Ideal	
will	representation	feeling	soil
experience	opinion	insight	climate
			flora
economy	language	art	fauna
(production,			human
nutrition,			biology
population)			
custom	myth/religion	ornamental-	
		symbolic art	
law	science	fine arts	

rather odd, it must be remembered that they are based on conceptualizations of human life, mind and activity that are rather different from our own.

Lamprecht's critics who accused him of positivism, psychologism and other 'isms' were perhaps not too far off the mark. His theories were often vague, if not confused. Like Lazarus and Steinthal he regarded *Sozialpsychologie* more or less as individual psychology writ large, and as an admirer of Darwin he wanted to make biology the model for a scientific history. Yet Lamprecht has been vindicated in his rejection of the exclusive focus on historical personalities in favour of a concern with prevailing conditions. In this he was strongly supported by Wundt, who praised him in his *Logik der Geisteswissenschaften* (1908) and repeatedly stressed that the task of history was to give an account of 'social conditions'. Lamprecht himself often referred to Wundt's *Völkerpsychologie*, believing that his own theories complemented those of Wundt. This was quite unjustified as regards Lamprecht's favourite 'biogenetic principle', which Wundt considered simplistic and quite incapable of accounting for culture-historical development. In other respects, however, they did share a good deal of common ground. For instance, most of the factors listed by Lamprecht also found a place in Wundt's *Völkerpsychologie*, though he dealt with them in a far more coherent and less deterministic manner. Lamprecht and Wundt also agreed on the need to complement the experimental psychology of their time with an approach that could help to understand culture-historical developments. The same was true of another great figure of the period, Dilthey. In contrast to Lamprecht, who yearned to transform history into a science with the aid of a scientific *Sozialpsychologie*, Dilthey considered the causal, hypothesis-testing approach unsuitable for humans as culture-historical beings.

Dilthey's Descriptive Psychology

Lamprecht and Wilhelm Dilthey (1833–1911) shared a keen interest in *Völkerpsychologie*. Dilthey had first come across it in the course of his studies in Berlin, where he met Lazarus and worked with him at the time when the first seminal issue of the *Zeitschrift* appeared. His initial enthusiasm was later tempered by reservations related to the speculative nature and diffuseness of the enterprise. Attracted by the more concrete empiricism emanating from France and Britain, Dilthey turned towards anthropology and the natural sciences. He became a pupil of Helmholtz, studied Fechner's *Psychophysics*, and attended lectures on physiology in Basel. It is important to know that when he later came to reject the natural sciences as the main model for psychology, he did not do so as an ignorant and prejudiced 'arts' man.

When Dilthey obtained a chair in philosophy – first in Basel and eventually in Berlin – he became increasingly preoccupied with problems of psychology, philosophy and history. His life and thought stand in sharp contrast to the then prevailing type of hidebound German academic 'mandarin'. The fastidious William James (1842–1910) met him in Berlin and was taken aback by Dilthey's somewhat unusual attire and behaviour at table; but he was also extraordinarily impressed by the range and depth of Dilthey's learning.

Here I shall concentrate on Dilthey's interest in the nature and aims of psychology, a theme which began with Lazarus and continued – with interruptions – throughout his career. With hindsight one might well label it 'psychology and culture', though this would be anachronistic. Rickert and Lamprecht had to some extent discussed such issues, but taken it for granted that psychology is a natural-science discipline and nothing else. There were also philosophical idealists who denied the possibility of any psychology, since they believed the 'soul' to be beyond the reach of systematic study.

Dilthey avoided both these extreme positions in his extensive writings on the epistemological foundations of psychology and its position with regard to natural science on the one hand the the humane disciplines [*Geistes-wissenschaften*] on the other. In his *Ideas Concerning a Descriptive and Analytical Psychology* ([1894]; in Dilthey 1977) he proposes that there are two distinct aspects to the subject. One is the empiricist approach, essentially concerned with hypothesis-testing by means of experiments. Dilthey accepted this as entirely valid, calling it 'explanatory psychology', which considers mental processes as consisting of causal chains [*Kausalzusammenhang*]. However, he points out some important limitations of such a conception. First, it is too formal and atomistic, dividing consciousness into elementary sensations and feelings (taken to be manifestations of underlying physiological processes) in order to make it amenable to rigorous study. Such compartmentalization ignores the fact that the acting self has a functional unity which eludes any approach that concentrates merely on the constituent parts. Moreover, it cannot tell us anything about the higher mental processes such as thinking and creative imagination.

While this kind of objection has since lost a good deal (though by no means all) its force, the same cannot be said of the other: psychology's emphasis on the self-contained individual. Dilthey characterized the notion that man has a permanent nature which already existed prior to history and society – prevalent in much of Enlightenment thought – as a fiction. He gained this conviction early on, when he was still involved with *Völkerpsychologie* and the then-emerging anthropology; at that time he cited with approval Bastian's optimistic forecast that psychology would be the science of the future, focusing on mankind as a whole and dealing with individuals only within that broad context. In spite of later disappointments, Dilthey continued to hold on to his grand vision of new kind of psychology as the key discipline [*Grundwissenschaft*] for all human studies. For this purpose he proposed a 'descriptive and analytical psychology', based on a recognition of the culture-historically contingent nature of humans. He singled out Waitz as one of his predecessors in making a distinction between explanatory and descriptive psychology. After publishing his *Lehrbuch der Psychologie als Naturwissenschaft* in 1849, Waitz conceived a plan for a complementary descriptive psychology that would, as it were, provide the raw material for explanatory psychology. According to Dilthey, Waitz's monumental *Anthropologie der Naturvölker* was a partial realization of this plan. This view is questionable, since Waitz had emphasized universal 'psychic unity' rather than cultural variations of the psyche. Moreover, in his *Anthropologie* Waitz had effectively confined himself to straightforward descriptions, based on ethnographic accounts. Dilthey's conception of the new psychology was far richer and subtler, and can be sketched here only rather superficially.

The cornerstone of Dilthey's psychology is based on the concept of *Erlebnis*, or lived experience, constituting a person's response to a situation. Psychology is in essence the systematic elaboration of common experience, irreducible to such entities as sensations. This is not to say that one cannot distinguish between various cognitive or affective functions, provided that they are analyzed within the context of a unitary structural system. In a manner comparable to that of Vico, Dilthey drew a fundamental distinction between explanations of physical phenomena and understanding ourselves and our fellows. In the former case we can establish causal relationships, but can never get at the underlying reality; but personal experience *is* its own reality, and we cannot get beyond it. Thus 'We explain nature, we understand psychic life' (Dilthey, [1894] 1977, p. 27). The concept of

Verstehen, central to Dilthey's theory, has given rise to much critical debate (see Ermarth, 1978). This cannot be reviewed here in detail, but since *Verstehen* is sometimes translated without qualification as 'understanding', it is important to point out that this is misleading.

The term *Verstehen* refers not to 'comprehension' in general, but to a particular kind of understanding relating primarily to human behaviour; hence the German term will be retained. Moreover, contrary to what is sometimes suggested (see Abel, 1953), it does not refer to a method, but to a specifically human capacity. It was not, for Dilthey, merely intuitive, but a cognitive process dependent upon representations of mental content. Such representations may be at any level of abstraction, but they are ultimately anchored in the structure of experience.

Closely related to *Verstehen*, in the sense that it is the object of *Verstehen*, is 'meaning' [*Bedeutung*]. This refers not only – or even primarily – to the apprehension of an expression, or of verbal or non-verbal symbols, but to a grasp of the significance of the relationships between life-events. Thus any particular experience becomes intelligible within that wider context of organizational unity. Dilthey regarded *Verstehen* as a kind of induction, albeit different from the usual sense of the term whereby a set of particular instances are generalized into a law. Instead, the instances lead to the recognition of a structure, a system of order in which the parts make up a unified whole.

In his later years, and in response to some criticism, Dilthey came to acknowledge that his original starting point, the description of inner experience, is problematic. There can be no pure, value-free, objective description based on introspection. This led him to put increasing stress on *hermeneutics* as a method for approaching the cultural products of the human mind.

Hermeneutics began as an ancient method of interpreting text, which was widened by Friedrich Schleiermacher (1768–1834) into a more general theory of *Verstehen*, which in turn inspired Dilthey. Hermeneutics is inevitably a circular process, as may be illustrated by the example of understanding a sentence. In order to grasp the meaning of a sentence, one must understand the words composing it; but these words in isolation can have different meanings, depending upon the context. This is particularly clear when it comes to translation. Thus the German word *Geist* can mean spirit, mind or intellect, depending on the context. One could therefore say that the whole makes no sense without the parts, nor the parts without the whole. The same applies, for instance, to the interpretation of a work of literature, or to what influenced the thinking of its author. Logically it would seem that we must remain imprisoned for ever within the hermeneutic circle. In practice we break through it by moving alternatively from the parts to the whole and back again.

While hermeneutics is to some extent formalized into rules, Dilthey held that it also involves a certain intuitive element that contributes to *Verstehen*; it allows us to gain insight not merely into individual minds, but into the nature of the human mind in general and its historical transformations. I might add here a brief comment about later 'critical theorists' who carried Dilthey's ideas much further in an anti-positivist direction. Some, such as Habermas (1972), argue that Dilthey's account of hermeneutics is itself tainted by the empiricist influences to which he had been exposed. Thus the notion that hermeneutic interpretation can obtain direct access to the state of mind of the text's originator is fallacious: 'Hermeneutic knowledge is always mediated through [this] preunderstanding, which is derived from the interpreter's initial situation' (Habermas, 1972, p. 310). This initial situation is a function of culture-historical background; therefore hermeneutics cannot achieve 'objective' knowledge, as Dilthey had erroneously supposed.

While such a critique seems pertinent, it certainly does not mean that Dilthey remained unaware of the importance of culture. On the contrary, under a different label it was central to much of his argument. Like Lazarus and Steinthal, he had taken over from Hegel the notion of 'objective spirit', modifying it to correspond closely to what we refer to as 'culture':

> I understand objective spirit to be the various forms in which the common context [*Gemeinsamkeit*] that exists is objectified in the world of the senses. In this objective spirit, the past is a continuing presence for us. Its domain extends from the style of life and the forms of economic interaction to the system [*Zusammenhang*] of ends which society has formed: to morality, law, the state, religion, art, science, and philosophy. (Dilthey, [1894] 1977, p. 126)

One could also gloss this as a reference to intersubjectively shared meaning-systems, which brings out the sociocommunicative basis of Dilthey's psychology as expounded by Habermas. At any rate, the broad congruence between 'objective spirit' and what we know as culture is supported by the manner in which Dilthey characterizes what we would call the acquisition of culture:

> From earliest childhood our self receives its nourishment from this world of objective spirit. It is also the medium in which the *Verstehen* of other persons and their expressions of life comes about. For everything in which the human spirit has been objectified contains in itself something which is common to the I and the thou. Each square planted with trees, each room in which the chairs are arranged is intelligible to us from our childhood, because human goal-setting, ordering and value-determining, as something common to us

all, has assigned to each square and to each object in a room its place. The child grows up within the order and mores of the family, which he shares with the other members, and his mother's instruction is absorbed by him in this context. Before he learns to speak, the child is already completely immersed in the medium of common contexts. And he learns to understand gestures and facial expressions, motions and exclamations, words and sentences only because they confront him as being always the same, and as always bearing the same relation to that which they signify and express. In this way, the individual becomes oriented in the world of objective spirit. (Dilthey, [1894] 1977, pp. 126–7)

In another part of the same work Dilthey states that descriptive psychology requires a theory of development. Just as the botanist traces the stages from the acorn to the oak, so it is the task of the psychologist to study the developmental laws and the uniformities of succession in a psychic structure. It is important to remember that – in accordance with the ideas prevailing at the time – the primary meaning of 'development' for Dilthey was 'historical development', not that of the child:

One could not understand the development of man without insight into the cross-sectional nexus of his existence; even more, the point of departure of every study bearing on his development is this apprehension and analysis of the nexus in the already developed man. Here alone is the reality given in the inner experience of the psychologists with the bright light of day, whereas we can only obtain uncertain glances into the dawning of the first stages of development by means of observing and experimenting with children. On the other hand, the nexus of historical development explicates that of structure. (Dilthey, [1894] 1977, p. 94)

It appears, therefore, that Dilthey took the transmission of culture through the generations to be obvious and non-problematic. What interested him was the way in which the cultural features of a given period interacted with the dynamic and teleological properties of the mind to create a certain type of what he called 'psychic nexus', perhaps crudely rendered as 'mentality'. These processes, he suggested, could be inferred at the individual level from such material as biographies, memoirs or letters; and at the collective level from phonetic and semantic changes in language, or from modifications in the ideas related to concepts like that of God. Dilthey referred indiscriminately to this area of study as either 'content psychology' or 'anthropology'; he tended to use 'anthropology' either in the sense of what we would call 'cultural psychology' or, later, to characterize the hermeneutic approach to the study of humans.

It should, perhaps, be added that in Dilthey's developmental theory the 'objective spirit' seems to be confined to the cultural features of 'civilized' societies. This is apparent from a discussion in which Dilthey traces the emergence of 'historical consciousness' from Roman times to Herder:

> Finally, the study of primitive peoples provided the link between the theory of natural evolution and the insights of developmental history based on national politics, religion, law, customs, language, poetry and literature. So the point of view of developmental history could be applied to the study of the whole natural and historical development of man . . . (Dilthey, [1911] in Rickman [ed.], 1976, p. 135)

This conformed to the – then prevalent – view that such peoples were, from an evolutionary perspective, closer to nature in the raw than the 'civilized'; and it had semantic support in the German term for 'primitive' peoples: *Naturvölker*. While we now know that this notion is flawed, Dilthey had the great merit of stressing the relationship between culture, history and mind, to which most experimental psychologists of the period remained blind. While Vico had already said that man can understand history because he makes it, Dilthey pointed out that man is also a creature of history, individually as well as collectively:

> it would be wrong to confine history to the co-operation of human beings for common purposes. The individual person in his independent existence is a historical being. He is determined by his position in time and space and in the interaction of cultural systems and communities. The historian has, therefore, to understand the whole life of an individual as it reveals itself at a certain time and place. It is the whole web of relationships which stretches from individuals furthering their own existence to the cultural systems and communities and, finally, to the whole of mankind, which makes up the character of society and history. Individuals, as much as communities and contexts, are the logical subjects of history. (Dilthey, [1910] in Rickman [ed.], 1976, p. 181)

Moreover, he felt that humans could learn more about themselves by looking to history than by conducting psychological experiments. Such views were not always well received by psychologists anxious to distance themselves from phiolosophy and aspire to scientific status. The attack on Dilthey was spearheaded by Ebbinghaus, concentrating mainly on his comments regarding the limitations of an 'explanatory' and hypothesis-testing psychology, and the complementary descriptive approach he advocated; the ideas on culture, which appear so important to us now, remained peripheral to the debate. The Ebbinghaus episode was traumatic for Dilthey, who thereafter ceased to lecture on psychology, began to draw a line between the 'psychic' and the 'psychological' and concentrated his work on the former, as well as on hermeneutics in the wider context of the *Geisteswissenschaften*.

Yet while there was a great deal of opposition among experimental psychologists, Dilthey regarded the greatest of them, Wilhelm Wundt, as an ally. In his *Descriptive and Analytical Psychology* he wrote that Wundt 'found himself constrained by the vast experience he acquired in this domain to adopt a conception of psychic life which abandoned the point of view which had until then prevailed in psychology' ([1894]; in Dilthey, 1977, p. 49). Although their ideas did not always coincide, the similarities between them are more striking than the differences: both held that there are two distinctive traditions in psychology, equally valid but sharply contrasting in terms of both content and method.

Notes

1. See Note 2 on p. 9 concerning the discussion by Elias.
2. The quotation is from the third edition, substantially unchanged from the first except for footnote answers to critics.

11

Wundt's *Völkerpsychologie* and *Kultur*

Wilhelm Wundt (1832–1920) had no fixed position in relation to the debate described in the last chapter, since his views about the status of psychology underwent progressive transformations. In his early *Lectures on the Human and Animal Mind* (1863) he scathingly dismissed mere philosophical speculations about the mind. While he was careful to dissociate himself from materialism of the kind advocated by Haeckel and adumbrating the parallelism he was later to defend, Wundt then regarded psychology as essentially a *Naturwissenschaft*. About a decade later he began to locate psychology as intermediate between *Natur-* and *Geisteswissenschaften*, and it was from then onwards that Dilthey was able to claim him as an ally. After the 1880s he frequently referred to psychology as a *Geisteswissenschaft*, but continued to hedge. For instance, close to the end of the century he published an article 'On the definition of psychology' (1896). After dismissing the definition of psychology as mere 'applied physiology', he characterized its status as follows:

> The mode of acquiring knowledge [*Erkenntnisweise*], in contrast to that of *Naturwissenschaft*, is a direct one, without the intermediary of abstract auxiliary concepts ... it follows that psychology is an empirical science co-ordinated with natural science [*eine der Naturwissenschaft coordinierte Erfahrungswissenschaft*], and that the modes of approach of both are complementary ... (1896, p. 12)

Thus he still seemed loath to abandon the close link with natural science, but gradually moved ever more firmly towards regarding psychology as a *Geisteswissenschaft* – and, indeed, the indispensable basis of all other *Geisteswissenschaften*. It is not possible here to discuss in detail the broader and very complex contexts within which these changes in Wundt's thinking must be understood.[1] However, there is little doubt that one important strand was his growing preoccupation with the problems of *Völkerpsychologie*. This is not to say that his concern with such issues came late – on the contrary, the theme of *Völkerpsychologie* runs as a constant thread throughout his life.

In his autobiography (Wundt, 1920a), which is not very informative about his personal life, Wundt traces his interest back to his childhood in a vicarage. There, it is reported, he laboriously penned his first plans in an exercise book:

> The earliest theme I had in mind was a general history of religions. Bringing out what the various religions had in common appeared to me a question well worth an effort of research. Later the other one that also came to mind was the general course of world history ... the idea underlying these fantastic projects was that of a comparative study of the mental products of man, in which the highest and most mysterious ones played a dominant role. (1920a, p. 199)

Wundt was clearly referring here to his early school years, and without the evidence of what he described as 'unreadable manuscripts' it is impossible to know the extent to which the passage might be a backward projection of more mature thoughts, and possibly even a retrospective attempt to show that these ideas had always been his own. What is certain is that his interest began early, and by his late twenties he was familiar with the first volume of Waitz's *Anthropologie der Naturvölker* (1859, translated into English as *Introduction to Anthropology*) and with Lazarus and Steinthal's *Zeitschrift*, first published in 1860. There can be no doubt that the famous first article in the *Zeitschrift*, with its invitation to *Völkerpsychologie*, made a profound impression on Wundt, though he later sought to play this down; in the *Elemente* ([1912] 1916), for example, he made only passing and not very complimentary reference to Lazarus and Steinthal.

It is hardly likely to have been merely coincidental that when, early in his career, Wundt was planning a book on experimental psychology, he decided to supplement this with a discussion of the mental products of the social life of peoples. This became a substantial part of the second volume of his *Lectures on the Human and Animal Mind* (1863), whose theoretical conception is fairly close to that of Lazarus and Steinthal. One basic difference is that Wundt, unlike them, had already come to see *Völkerpsychologie* not as a field separate from psychology, but as an essential part of it. Another way in which he went beyond Lazarus and Steinthal was by going into details about 'primitive peoples' in a somewhat unfortunate manner; and it was that, presumably, which he later came to regret. Some of the salient aspects of that work will now be summarized.

The First Formulation – a 'Youthful Sin'

The main concern is with *Sitte*, a term that covers both 'morality' and 'custom' and will be used henceforth for the sake of brevity, with occasional reminders of its meaning. Wundt points out that the process of development of *Sitten* (plural) cannot be studied in the consciousness of single individuals – one must look for it in the historical life of peoples. This can most readily be done by examining the historical changes of civilized peoples [*Kulturvölker*]. It has the advantage of providing a coherent sequence, yet also the drawback that it tells us nothing about origins. By contrast, natural history takes as its object humanity as it is in the present, so that one can observe synchronically several different developmental stages that can be compared in order to infer what the 'state of nature' must have been like. While ahistorical peoples have no doubt also undergone some development, one can safely assume that they remain relatively close to their point of origin.

Among civilized peoples, 'great men', founders of religions and reformers have a powerful influence; but among ahistorical peoples the individual has little significance, being submerged in the tribe. *Sitten* always relate to collectivities, be they peoples, tribes or families. In advanced societies customs and morals become embodied in laws. But *Sitten* are not invented, neither by individuals nor simultaneously by the collectivity. Rather, they arise from instinctive tact, prompting everybody to adjust their behaviour to certain norms.

Sitten are not innate, for they change in the course of the development of nations. Their beginnings coincide with the beginnings of society. But what arises from the common life cannot be original, since the individual exists prior to society. Therefore we cannot discover anything about first origins. Thus when Wundt first dealt with the theme of historical development, his primary focus was on the individual. Already in that work he explicitly dissociated himself from the approach to *Völkerpsychologie* adopted by Lazarus and Steinthal. While they, in the Romantic tradition, were pursuing the *Volksgeist* (spirit of a people), Wundt was concerned with understanding individual consciousness and its laws. None the less, for the remainder of his life he was to wrestle with an adequate formulation of the psychological aspects of the relationship between individual and society.

When it came to the discussion of ahistorical peoples, Wundt was ready to grant that they 'cannot be described as being absolutely without culture' (1863, vol. 2, p. 125). (He used the term *Kultur* in the restricted sense common at that time.) With regard to the causes of backwardness, Wundt believed, like David Hume and many others before him, that extremes of temperature seem to be unfavourable to moral culture, though there are exceptions. The influence of climate is readily explained: in the far north, conditions are so harsh that the natural state of the peoples is one where the vices of crude gluttony and drunkenness prevail, coupled with sloth; and they live in dirty conditions. Much the same faults are attributed to people of the tropics, though for the opposite reason: nature provides everything in abundance, so they are shy of any effort. If these people have any moral culture, it is due to immigrants from more temperate climes. None the less, there are no *Naturvölker* in the strict sense; all peoples have at least small traces of culture.

This general discussion is followed by pen pictures drawn from the contemporary travel literature, presenting highly unflattering portraits. South Sea islanders appear mild and gentle at first, but closer acquaintance reveals traits of wild cruelty and beastly crudity – so much for the image of the tropical paradise! There is a lot about cannibalism, said probably to have been universal in the state of nature, and its horrors are graphically described:

> In the South Seas human flesh is a privilege of the well-to-do just as with us the daily roast in the kitchen; and the poor there content themselves with bananas and breadfruit, as they do here with potatoes and dark bread. (1863, vol. 2, p. 131)

The main stages of development are then listed, with hunters at the bottom (cruel, bloodthirsty Indians); then nomads (the moral culture of the Mongols has always remained in the most rudimentary state); then comes agriculture, and the Negro is regarded as transitional between *Natur-* and *Kulturmensch*. However, this applies only to the collectivity, for the individual Negro remains a raw child of nature [*Naturmensch*].

In the initial argument the germs of Wundt's later approach may be discerned, but much of it merely reiterates stereotyped notions widely prevalent in the mid nineteenth century. When he had completed the book Wundt felt, as he reports in his autobiography, that the section on *Völkerpsychologie* constituted its crowning achievement. Subsequently he gained a better insight into its weaknesses – so much so that he regretted having written it; and when a second edition was published in 1892, he suppressed that 'sin of youth'. In the meantime, however, Wundt continued his interest in the area, which also found expression in a series of lectures on *Völkerpsychologie*. These began in the summer of 1875 in Zürich, followed by others at Leipzig, where he had been newly appointed.

During this period when Wundt was revising his ideas and beginning to prepare for the *magnum opus*, he published (Wundt, 1887–8) a critical article directed simultaneously at two different targets. One was Hermann

Paul who, as mentioned above, had denied the possibility of any *Völkerpsychologie* and thus had to be answered. The other target was Lazarus and Steinthal's whole theoretical edifice, which Wundt dismissed as being too vague and all-embracing as well as vitiated by a reliance on outdated Herbartian doctrines. Although Wundt's critique was not unjustified, its harshness was perhaps somewhat ungracious, given his initial indebtedness to Lazarus and Steinthal. He seemed clearly anxious to demonstrate the distinctiveness of his own approach.

So much for what might be called the 'prehistory' of Wundt's *Völkerpsychologie*, which already contained the germs of his later ideas. At this stage a preliminary sketch of successive later developments will perhaps be useful, to provide an overall perspective. The new model of *Völkerpsychologie* made its initial appearance in print in the first two editions of the *Principles of Physiological Psychology* (1873, 1880), where it features as a descriptive psychology – a relatively minor appendage to the experimental psychology central to the main body of the work. Then, in the second volume of Wundt's *Logik* (1883), known as *Methodenlehre* (theory or philosophy of scientific method), two sections deal with the 'comparative' and 'historical-psychological' methods respectively. Curiously enough, this contains no direct mention of *Völkerpsychologie*, though the discussion of historical methods refers to the trinity central to *Völkerpsychologie*: language, myth, and *Sitten* (customs and morals).

Thereafter a decisive shift took place in the third edition of the *Principles* (1887), where experimental and *Völkerpsychologie* were said to belong together, having different but complementary tasks. The following year saw the publication of the polemic against Herman Paul and Lazarus and Steinthal. In the fourth edition of the *Principles* (1893) *Völkerpsychologie* was further promoted, now being described as forming, together with experimental psychology, 'the two main branches of scientific psychology' (1893, p. 5).

From 1900 onwards the vast ten-volume *Völkerpsychologie* began to appear, confined very largely to Wundt's psychological interpretations of a mass of ethnographic material. Its general aim was to throw light on the products of collective mental development, before the rise of civilization, within several specific domains. While engaged on this immense labour – and, it should be remembered, aged eighty – Wundt also wrote the *Elemente der Völkerpsychologie* (1912). Contrary to a common belief, this is by no means a summary of the larger work, though it draws on much of its material. It constitutes an attempt to outline the historical stages of human psychological evolution from prehistory to modern times.[2] Apart from these major works, Wundt also wrote various pieces during that period answering his critics, some of which will be mentioned later.

The Theoretical Foundations of
Völkerpsychologie

Wundt's ten-volume *Völkerpsychologie* is not infrequently mentioned in the literature as though it were the essential source for his theory. This notion is seriously misleading. If someone embarked upon the heroic task of reading all ten volumes of the *Völkerpsychologie* for that purpose, he or she would probably be disappointed.[3] Although one does find theoretical statements scattered throughout, often modified in successive editions, it would be very difficult to form a coherent impression on that basis.

Fortunately, Wundt himself has provided a comprehensive summary in the third edition of his *Logik*, whose third volume is entitled *Logik der Geisteswissenschaften* (1908). In the earlier part of this work, before dealing with *Völkerpsychologie* itself, Wundt had been concerned to establish the position of psychology in general in relation to other *Geisteswissenschaften*:

> there can be no doubt that it is in truth the most general of the *Geisteswissenschaften* and at the same time the indispensable foundation for all the others. (1908, p. 19)

In seeking to justify this strong claim, Wundt stresses that psychology is not concerned solely with individual phenomena. Individual development depends largely on the 'mental environment' resulting from the concatenation of multiple inter-individual effects. This environment mainly takes the form of language, custom and belief, without which a person could not exist 'in his own mental individuality'. While one cannot assess such influences in a quantitative fashion, they are none the less crucial. What Wundt calls 'mental environment' is in fact more or less equivalent to what we understand by 'culture'. It is important to point out here a source of confusion arising not only from the different connotations of the term *Kultur* in Wundt's time, but also from his frequently inconsistent usage, which will be examined more closely in the Appendix to this chapter. When Wundt refers to *Kultur* he often means the level of development achieved, rather than 'culture' in the modern, wider sense. This is not to deny that a postulate of cultural influences on mental processes is central to his whole approach, but it rests partly on his concept of the 'mental environment' and partly on his rather nebulous notion of the 'folk-soul' [*Volksseele*]; both of these sometimes, though by no means invariably, overlapped with his usage of *Kultur*.

From the principle of dependence upon the mental surroundings, it follows that one can investigate the nature of this medium in a particular period and *Kultur*, determining its salient characteristics in a scientific manner. Thus one can study a particular period or population and examine its major mental products like language, literature and art. While Wundt recommended that this should be done, it is important to note that he did *not* regard such studies as falling within the scope of *Völkerpsychologie*: it excludes anything *singular* – that is, unrelated to *general psychological laws*.

This brings us to the section specifically concerned with *Völkerpsychologie*, which is formally defined as follows:

> We shall call *Völkerpsychologie* the field of psychological investigations relating to those processes which, owing to their conditions of origin and development, are tied to mental collectivities. Since the individual and the community mutually imply each other, this name does not indicate a field whose content is totally separate from individual psychology; rather, it indicates an abstraction complementary to that of individual psychology. (1908, vol. 3, p. 226)

In subsequent passages Wundt explains how he conceives the relationship between individual psychology and *Völkerpsychologie*. He starts with the assumption that the ultimate sources of mental products are bound to be the individuals composing the collectivity; and from this he draws some far-reaching conclusions. Before citing these, it is necessary to explain that Wundt drew a distinction between 'principles' and 'laws'. Psychological 'principles' he held to be just as generally valid as those of the natural sciences, while psychological 'laws' apply only within certain sets of conditions. Now Wundt's own 'principle of creative synthesis' postulates that in the course of mental development new elements always emerge, so that these conditions are bound to change, leading to different psychological 'laws'. A principle (such as 'creative synthesis') always underlies 'laws' and, unlike the latter, cannot be empirically verified or form the basis for inferences. Thus in the passage below the terms 'principles' and 'laws' have distinct technical meanings:

> from the outset it is out of the question that one could come across any general psychological laws in *Völkerpsychologie* that are not already completely contained in the laws of individual consciousness.
>
> In so far as *Völkerpsychologie* can find any psychological laws of independent content, these will always be *applications* of principles valid for individual psychology. But one can also assume that the conditions of mutual mental interaction will bring out new and special manifestations of the general psychic forces that could not be predicted from the mere knowledge of the properties of individual consciousness; these again will augment our insight into the functioning of individual mental life. Thus only individual psychology and *Völkerpsychologie* together constitute the whole of psychology [*das Ganze der Psychologie*] . . . just there, where the experimental method reaches its limit, the methods of *Völkerpsychologie* provide objective results. . . . As in

the interpretation of its findings *Völkerpsychologie* must necessarily fall back on individual psychology, the latter is certainly the more general discipline, while the former has more of an applied character. But this relationship is here, as in many other cases, substantially modified by the following fact: in order to achieve a complete solution of its tasks, notably in the sphere of the higher mental functions, individual psychology already uses certain results of *Völkerpsychologie* in order to make inferences concerning the laws of individual consciousness. (1908, vol. 3, pp. 227–8)

Wundt's dilemma, evident from these highly convoluted arguments, is that he wanted to assert at least two things that do not seem readily compatible: (a) individual psychology and *Völkerpsychologie* are equally important and complementary parts of a unified whole; (b) yet ultimately it is individual psychology that is more fundamental, and *Völkerpsychologie* somewhat derivative. Perhaps not surprisingly, Wundt was afraid of being misunderstood and devoted a lengthy footnote to explaining that he did not share the views of Lazarus and Steinthal, who had conceived the relationship between individual psychology and *Völkerpsychologie* as a merely analogical one. Wundt contends that the objects of *Völkerpsychologie*, such as language and myth, are privileged sources of psychological insight for which there is no substitute within individual psychology; and these can be approached only through historically based psychological research. He goes on to delimit the scope of *Völkerpsychologie* to *general* psychological aspects, describing the study of the characteristics of particular peoples as a mere applied subfield. Such a study must be related to that of the physiological characteristics of peoples which, together with the psychological ones, is the business of ethnology.[4]

The justification for the claim that *Völkerpsychologie* is fundamental for the historical and social disciplines – a tricky issue – is dealt with at some length. In essence, Wundt argues that it is not so much a question of the subject matter, but of the standpoint from which it is being treated. This may be illustrated in connection with his discussion of linguistics and philology [*Sprachwissenschaft*]:

Thus both *Sprachwissenschaft* and *Völkerpsychologie* are concerned with language. But while the former examines the connections among the various linguistic phenomena, these linguistic events are [for *Völkerpsychologie*] only a means whereby one first finds the psychological laws of linguistic phenomena and then draws conclusions therefrom about the general links between psychic processes. (1908, p. 230)

This leads us to ask on what basis such conclusions may be drawn. Wundt's answer assumes a close parallel between individual and collective mental phenomena. The relationship is not one of analogy, but is at least quasi-causal in the sense that collective phenomena are *manifestations* of individual ones. This emerges very clearly from Wundt's discussion of the major subdivisions of *Völkerpsychologie* – language, myth, art and *Sitte*:

> They [i.e. language, myth, etc.] are of similar general significance for the collective consciousness [*Völkerbewusstsein*] as, say, cognition [*Vorstellung*], feeling and will are for individual consciousness. At the same time they correspond to the general components of psychic processes, in the sense that in language the laws of the internal linkages between cognitions and their gradual modifications find expression, while art and myth reflect the influence of feelings and drives on the general content of cognitions ... finally *Sitte* encompasses the directions of the will, stemming from these cognitions and drives, in their effects upon the organization of society. These four areas of communal mental life are very closely connected, much as in the individual mind [*Seele*] cognition, feeling and will are in reality not different processes but merely different facets of a single, unitary set of events. (1908, p. 232)

Wundt goes on to postulate that *Völkerpsychologie* is confined to the 'generally valid products' of human communal life, and that these products encompass all the essential directions of mental development. While the major categories selected are those of language, art, myth and *Sitte*, these are not meant to be exhaustive, and the concern is in a wider sense with the general foundations of mental life:

> Thus the psychological value of language consists essentially in its giving expression to the lawfulness of thinking; consequently the various linguistic forms constitute at the same time particular stages in the development of this fundamental psychological function. In the same way myth is very closely connected with the activity of fantasy and art. (1908, p. 232)

Wundt then proceeds to sketch the intricate interrelationships between these various elements and their modifications over time – processes so complex that *Völkerpsychologie* cannot hope to unravel them all. What it can do, for instance, is to trace the motives that lie at the origin of myths and thereby, ultimately, the development of religion and art. Yet he draws a distinction between, on the one hand, language and myth and, on the other, art and religion:

> But while language and myth are in their entirety subject to *völkerpsychologische* study, art and religion in their more advanced forms reach beyond *Völkerpsychologie* into the realm of history. (1908, p. 233)

It is necessary to understand how Wundt conceptualized the transition from *Völkerpsychologie* to history, since it is a key notion implicit in many of the discussions in his ten-volume work. He believed that during the early stages of humanity the psychological processes, both individual and collective, were relatively uniform. Under the influence of changing cultural conditions, and of particular forceful personalities that had begun to emerge, a progressive differentiation set in. As a consequence, collective phenomena – for instance, art and religion – began to take on a variety of distinctive forms. Once that had happened, it was no longer the surface content but the underlying, most general mental content [*geistiger Inhalt*] that revealed the universally valid *völkerpsychologische* motives at the root of these phenomena. *Völkerpsychologie* seeks to tease out these underlying common principles from existing historical records and ethnographic data. History, by contrast, is concerned with understanding singular events, and for this purpose it has recourse to psychology as an aid to the interpretation of historical phenomena. *Völkerpsychologie*, however, cannot fulfil that purpose – only individual psychology, which deals with the actions of particular persons, can do so. Wundt stresses the close link between cultural history and *Völkerpsychologie*, which has 'as its last and noblest task to provide evidence about the origin of *Kultur* and its main forms of development' (1908, p. 234). It is clear that *Kultur* refers, in this context, to human culture in general.

The last section on the methods of *Völkerpsychologie* is rather disappointing; much of it consists of little more than vague generalities. Possible bias in ethnographic and historical sources is discussed, and it is stated that such material should always be looked at in the light of psychological considerations. Problems of diffusion and the question of progress versus retrogression are touched upon, as are a number of other rather marginal issues. The basic method of *Völkerpsychologie* is said to be comparison, which, if accurately applied, is equivalent to the experimental method in individual psychology. Coupled with it is the historical-psychological method, said to yield developmental laws. However, the term 'law' in this context has a special meaning, as has already been indicated. Wundt distinguished between 'physical' and 'psychological' causality, referring to the latter also as 'teleological causality'. In the physical world there is a symmetry between cause and effect, while in the psychic domain there is a transmutation and a growth in accordance with the complementary principles of 'creative synthesis' and the 'heterogeny of ends'; hence there is asymmetry between cause and effect – the latter being, as it were, greater than the cause.[5] It follows that the 'laws' of psychology (other than those, like Fechner's, which concern simple responses dependent largely on physical conditions) are entirely different in character from those of natural science. This is not merely a matter of the greater complexity of psychic events, but a qualitative difference. In the case of *Völkerpsychologie* Wundt assumed a principle of 'historical causality':

according to which it [i.e. historical causality] can acquire the attribute of necessity only in relation to the past; as regards the future, it can at best approach the region of the probable. For however great might be the significance of material physical conditions, culture and history are merely different forms of psychic events [*geistigen Geschehens*]. (Wundt, 1920, p. 217)

Thus in this sphere causes can be discerned only by an insightful analysis of the records of the past. Wundt believed that such insight can be trained by critical self-observation, leading to an objective assessment of psychic products and the elicitation of underlying processes. He did not comment on the risk of subjective bias in such a procedure, which does not readily lend itself to any verification other than that of the consensus of independent interpreters of the records.

Völkerpsychologie and Some of Its Critics

The ten volumes of *Völkerpsychologie* consist of separate treatments of what Wundt regarded as its major domains. The modern reader finds some material that will clearly be seen as psychological; but much – if not most – of it has nothing to do with psychology as we know it, and this is why Wundt's vast labour has often been dismissed as irrelevant.

The volumes on language, one section of which is the only part of the ten volumes available in English translation (Wundt, 1973), clearly fall into the former category. It is no accident that the first volumes were devoted to 'language', since Wundt, like Steinthal before him, regarded language as most intimately connected with human psychological functioning, and especially all higher cognitive processes.[6] The first volume deals, among other things, with expressive movements and the language of gestures, considered by Wundt to be universal modes of communication which form the basis of all human social life. Generally in this sphere, the contribution of Wundt – whom Blumenthal (1970) called 'The Master Psycholinguist' – was outstanding. Other examples may be found in the volume on art, where Wundt discusses the development of drawing skills in children and makes many interesting observations on the psychology of child art.

By contrast, in one of the volumes on myth and religion (Wundt, 1909), totalling almost 800 pages, there is nothing but detailed accounts of myths, rituals and religious forms. Even where the section subheading includes the term 'psychology' – as in 'The psychological development of the forms of prayer' (1909, p. 661) – there is nothing in the text that one would recognize as such nowadays.

How might one account for this fact, so strange to the modern reader? I believe that there are two probable answers: one personal, and the other theoretical. Wundt seems to have become captivated by the ethnographic material he pursued so tirelessly, imagining that he had acquired special insight into 'primitive' mental processes which he wanted to communicate. It almost seems to have been some sort of 'mystical participation'; this comes out very clearly in the graphic description by one of his students of his lectures on *Völkerpsychologie*, Wundt's favourite theme in his mature years. Volkelt-Leipzig (1921–2) explains that Wundt had a special feeling for problems of development, particularly cultural development:

> One could sense this most directly in his lectures on *Völkerpsychologie*, and here most intensely when Wundt immersed himself in the mental life of the most primitive peoples. . . . As soon as the names of the most ancient tribes, the Vedda, the Semang, the Senoi, the Bushmen, fell from his lips, his voice took on instinctively a deep, velvety timbre. Yes, as soon as he selected the phrase he often used to refer generally to the distant past, 'already in the early period' [*frühe schon*], a startling breath of primordial life was apt to pervade the lecture theatre. (pp. 92–3)

Another – more important – clue to this apparent puzzle of why Wundt presented such a stream of what, for us, is pure ethnography is to be found in the general theory discussed above. Myths are mental products, and as such were themselves treated by Wundt as psychological data, and therefore as entirely pertinent. In the preceding volume he had in fact initially spelled out his ideas about the psychological processes that lie at the origin of myths. He saw them in a universal tendency for sense perception to be fused with subjective affective responses of an imaginative type, which animate or even personify nature. While this kind of perception holds sway among primitive peoples, it is kept in check among the civilized by critical reflection, though it continues to exist. His theory thus runs counter to the rationalist one of the so-called 'English School' of Tylor and Frazer, who interpreted magic and myths as attempted explanations of natural phenomena.

Although the idea is presented here in a highly condensed manner that makes it sound somewhat simplistic, it is a powerful one; it was taken up by Lévy-Bruhl ([1910] 1951) when he wrote: 'les primitifs ne perçoivent rien comme nous' (p. 37), and later by Werner (1957), who referred to it as 'physiognomic perception'. But whatever its merits, the inordinately long and detailed recitation of purely ethnographic material on myths adds nothing. For even if one shared Wundt's view that such material is in itself psychological, it cannot be considered as supporting, nor even illustrating, the kinds of 'apperceptive' processes postulated; and such 'mental products' remain open to alternative interpretations of their origin.

A related problem was noted by Marcel Mauss, a contemporary critic and follower of Durkheim. Having initially expressed his discomfort [*nous sommes très mal à l'aise*] at having to review the volume on myth and religion by the greatest encyclopaedic mind of Germany, he voiced a shrewd judgement:

> The actual theory of Monsieur Wundt reduces itself in the last analysis to a very small number of assertions, mostly of a psychological order, where, in short, it is the general, philosophical theory of his preceding works that plays the explanatory role, rather than the scientific detail of that psychology. (Mauss, 1907, p. 214)

Elsewhere Mauss complained – in my view with ample justification – about the difficulty of following Wundt's thought, which often loses itself in a labyrinth of divisions, subdivisions and subtle distinctions. Mauss's major criticism is Wundt's reliance on individual psychology, completely ignoring the work of Durkheim and his followers on 'collective representations'. In fact, Wundt's concept of the *Volksseele* (folk-soul) has a good deal in common with Durkheim's notion of a set of 'collective representations', as the following passage shows:

> *Völkerpsychologie* and history both presuppose the community to be a psychic [*geistige*] entity superordinate to the individual. *Völkerpsychologie* is founded on the fact that the community creates independent psychic values [*geistige Werte*], rooted in the mental [*seelischen*] properties of the individual, but themselves of a specific kind that in turn contributes to the individual mental life [*Seelenleben*] its most important contents. (Wundt, 1911a, vol. 1, p. 19)

It was precisely to this kind of formulation by Wundt that Herman Haeberlin (1916) took exception. His critique – too lengthy to be summarized here – is considerably more subtle and sophisticated than the older one of Hermann Paul. In particular, Haeberlin in no way questioned what he called 'the social factor in cultural development'. What he objected to was Wundt's 'would-be science of over-individual synthesis' (1916, p. 294), which implies a belief in the reality of the 'folk-soul'; and on this ground Haeberlin characterized 'folk-psychology' as an *Unding* (an absurdity). Wundt had laid himself open to such attack by some of his formulations, which could be construed as asserting the existence of a supra-individual 'group mind'. However, in another publication answering his critics he explicitly disclaimed such an interpretation: 'nobody any longer entertains the notion of a disembodied entity independent of the individual; even Hegel's attempt to rationalize the notion is no longer acceptable' (Wundt, 1911b, p. 60). Nowadays most writers give Wundt the benefit of the doubt, agreeing that he was concerned with the cumulative effects of social interactions over time, considered as a developmental process (see Danziger, 1983).

There is no doubt that Wundt viewed his *Völkerpsychologie* as a developmental discipline, although he rejected Felix Krueger's (1915) suggestion that it should be renamed 'developmental psychology'. He did so mainly on the grounds that nine-tenths of German psychologists would understand that term to refer to child psychology, whose importance he believed to be generally overestimated (*'übertriebene Bewertung der Kinderpsychologie'*: Wundt, 1917a, p. 195) and whose methods have nothing in common with those of *Völkerpsychologie*. This echoes the views of Lazarus and Steinthal (1860, p. 24), who had commented that child psychology is significant and fruitful for individual psychology but of limited value for *Völkerpsychologie*. Wundt seems to have had no more inkling than his predecessors that child development could provide the key to understanding the link between the 'mental environment' or culture and individual psychological processes. This, of course, does not imply that he was ignorant of the link, already clearly set out during the Enlightenment (see Part I above). It means that the link was regarded as something self-evident and non-problematic, and therefore not in need of special study.[7] Wundt's standpoint emerges clearly from his list of the various fields of psychology employing a 'genetic' approach – which, apart from *Völkerpsychologie*, includes child and animal development, and that of the human individual! In any case, Wundt was no doubt justified in rejecting the term 'developmental psychology' as liable to give rise to confusion.

Interestingly, Wundt also considered the possible substitution of the term 'cultural psychology' [*Kulturpsychologie*], but decided against it for the following reason:

> as it, combined with the concept of development as 'developmental psychology of *Kultur*', not merely altogether excludes those parts of humanity that have not made any demonstrable contribution to such a development, but also emphasizes, in the case of the so-called *Kulturvölker*, only that aspect of culture which, important though it might be, does not encompass the whole of the mental life of peoples. (Wundt, 1917a, p. 198)

In this sentence the meaning of *Kultur* is roughly equivalent to 'civilization', illustrating once again the vagaries of Wundt's usage.

The Subsequent Fate of Wundt's Contribution

It will have become evident by now that in order to gain an adequate understanding of Wundt's lifelong preoccupation with *Völkerpsychologie*, one has to labour one's way through a terminological thicket in order to arrive at the core ideas. In crude summary, the main aim of his theory was to provide an account of the *universally* operating psychological processes which he regarded as accounting for cultural development in general.[8] He viewed these processes as the outcome of the cumulative effects of social interaction over many generations. The ways in which these interactions function in generating collective products which in turn affect individuals remained unspecified, but he left as an important heritage the idea of an intimate link between culture and mind, mediated by developmental processes over time.

The impact of this aspect of Wundt's ideas was mainly confined to Germany. Its extent is not easy to assess, since by the early years of the twentieth century the term *Völkerpsychologie* had, in a much broader sense, become part of the vocabulary of the educated German public. Thus an international psychoanalytical journal had a section for '*Völkerpsychologisches*' – to which, for instance, Reik (1915) contributed a piece on 'The cave as a *völkerpsychologisches* symbol of the female body'. The term was often used in a similarly broad manner by ethnographers (see Danzel, 1928).

The strictly Wundtian version was discussed extensively and rather negatively by Vierkandt (1914) and then more neutrally by Thurnwald (1924), both under the identical title 'The current status of *Völkerpsychologie*'. In a subsequent, more extensive discussion, Thurnwald (1929) was highly critical of Wundt's handling of ethnographic reports and departed widely from the Master. An earlier effort by Hurwicz (1920) to extend and systematize the whole approach has been largely forgotten. The last detailed exposition of Wundt's *Völkerpsychologie* – as a viable theory rather than history – was by Hellpach (1938), one of his former students.

The interpretation of *Völkerpsychologie* in the English-speaking world is illuminated by a study of the several ways in which the term came to be translated (Gundlach, 1983). These included 'ethnic psychology'[9] and even 'racial psychology', indicating total misunderstanding. Next to the most common term, 'folk-psychology' – which is close, although 'folk' has the wrong connotations – came 'social psychology'. Not only had this expression been used by Lamprecht, but Wundt himself had considered it at one stage. Unfortunately, that happened to be the period when McDougall and Ross, whose ideas had little in common with those of Wundt, published their books on 'social psychology'. It was their interpretation of the term that prevailed, and the theme of *Völkerpsychologie* soon disappeared from the texts.

There is therefore no direct line of descent from Wundt's *Völkerpsychologie* to present-day 'cultural psychology'. Vygotsky, the founder of the Soviet sociohistorical school, was certainly familiar with Wundt's writing, but he drew his inspiration from a whole range of different sources (see Valsiner, 1988). Only after cultural psychology had gained a solid foothold was Wundt rediscovered as an ancestor.

Appendix: The Concept of *Kultur* in Wundt's Writings

In his earliest relevant publication, Wundt (1863) employed the term *Kultur* in the sense – then prevalent – of the expression of the higher forms of human intellect and creativity; it meant art, science, knowledge and high-level skills, sophistication and *savoir-faire*. Wundt's statement that there are no longer any peoples totally lacking in *Kultur* is to be understood in this context. Stocking's (1982) apt observation on Tylor's famous definition applies equally well to Wundt: 'his notion of culture in its actual usage lacked certain elements crucial to the modern concept: historicity, plurality, integration, behavioral determinism, and relativity' (p. 200).

In the *Methodenlehre* (1883) Wundt referred to *Kulturvölker* as meaning 'civilized peoples'. In the later edition of the *Logik* he mentions *Kulturkreise* (culture areas), a term that had gained wide currency as a result of the teachings of Friedrich Ratzel; it implies the universality of 'culture'. Moreover, in the same work Wundt made a passing comment anticipating the now widespread view that a particular culture is not merely a random assembly of features but possesses unity and coherence:

> Cuvier maintained that one can reconstruct from a single bone the typical form of the whole vertebrate to whom it belongs; similarly, each single part of a culture provides an approximate mirror image of all the remaining parts. (1908, vol. 3, p. 434)

A more detailed treatment is to be found in Volume 7 of the *Völkerpsychologie*, dealing with 'Society' (1917b). This contains a critical discussion of the dichotomy of *Natur-* versus *Kulturvölker*. The distinction had usually been drawn on the basis of the absence of history and an organized state, but Wundt pointed out that these criteria are too vague for any clear division to be possible. There is no *Naturvolk* without elements of *Kultur*, generated by the immanent developmental drive in the spheres of language, myth and custom, and there are different levels of culture among these peoples. Hence the dichotomy is becoming redundant:

> [It is for this reason] that the concept of *Kultur* in its actual extension to the peoples of the earth has become ever broader, while the concept of *Naturvolk* is gradually disappearing. (Wundt, 1917b, p. 121)

From this passage one might imagine that Wundt had begun to think of 'culture' in much the same way as we do today. But one is rapidly disabused of this by an immediately subsequent – and rather confused – discussion of the concept of 'culture-minimum'. In this discussion he reverted to a usage of *Kultur* as more or less synonymous with 'civilization'.

This same theme is taken up in the tenth and final volume on 'Culture and History' (Wundt, 1920b). The absolute lower limit of *Kultur* is set by the possession of language, which presupposes at least a modicum of mental life [*geistiges Leben*]. The question of origins is a futile one, and it is more profitable to ask what cultural products and events have been critical for development. Wundt reviews various turning points that have been proposed, like the invention of the plough or the printing press, but raises various objections to such simple schemes – in particular, that they leave out qualitative aspects of cultural values. These are implicit in the concept of 'civilization', which is felt to be something that has been actively achieved, while culture is merely the outcome of historical processes – a rather curious distinction. At any rate, this means that civilization leads to a sense of superiority and of a mission both to civilize and to dominate more backward peoples. Wundt regarded this as a valuable aspect of civilization, since it contains a purposive element that is absent from 'culture'.

Shortly afterwards there is a radical shift in the meaning attributed to *Kultur*:

> *Kultur* is national. It is confined to the particular national community [*Volksgemeinschaft*] which constitutes a coherent unity in terms of language, custom and intellectual cultivation [*geistige Bildung*]; but it lacks the tendency to go beyond these limits by spreading the acquired cultural achievements more broadly . . . (Wundt, 1920b, pp. 20–1)

Here Wundt suddenly identifies 'culture' with something very much like Herder's *Volksgeist*, seemingly unaware of the change. He concludes that the notions of *Kultur* and 'civilization' are complementary: *Kultur* is bound to nationality, while 'civilization' embodies an ideal of humanity as a unity under the leadership of the advanced nations [*Kulturvölker*].

The next section, entitled 'Animal antecedents of cultural man', reverts again to a wider concept of *Kultur*, applying to humans in general. However far back one goes, what one finds universally, among all those who have the physical characteristics of humans, are language, myth and *Sitte*:

> As these three labels designate only the major directions in which human mental life is distinguished from that of other organic beings, and although each of these directions comprises very different forms, so all these factors and their influences on men can be subsumed under the collective name of *Kultur*, so that in view of this *Völkerpsychologie* and cultural psychology are equivalent concepts. (Wundt, 1920b, p. 57)

In the end, therefore, Wundt overcame his misgivings and accepted that what he had been doing could be described as 'cultural psychology', because he seems to have arrived at a conception of 'culture-in-general' that is close to our own. The path that led him to this position was not a straight one. For a long time Wundt swivelled between several different and mutually exclusive notions of 'culture', varying according to context, as well as between an objective stance and one that uncritically accepted the prevailing ethos. One must remember that he wrote that last volume at an advanced age, and under the impact of the trauma of Germany's defeat in World War I, which had affected him deeply. This is probably the reason for the patriotic aberration about 'national culture'. Wundt rarely drew a sufficiently explicit distinction between 'human culture in general' and the varied cultures of different peoples; nor did he seek to relate these, respectively, to general *Völkerpsychologie* and what he regarded as its applied aspect, which he called 'ethnic characterology' – that is, dealing with the psychological characteristics of particular peoples. There is no indication that any echoes of the radical rethinking of the notion of 'culture' by Franz Boas and his students ever reached Wundt.

Notes

1. A lucid account of the development of Wundt's ideas in this sphere, also relating them to those of Dilthey and Windelband, may be found in Van Hoorn and Verhave (1980); Farr (1983) provides a useful general survey; a recent German work is Schneider (1990).
2. The two are not infrequently confused. For instance, Miller (1964), in a chapter devoted to Wundt, referred to 'the ten volumes of his *Elements of Folk Psychology*'.
3. I must confess that I cannot claim to have read them properly myself, nor have I ever encountered anyone who has; much of the work is well-nigh unreadable today. What I have done is to scan all the volumes, concentrating on some specific parts.
4. In this connection the then prevailing preoccupation with skull shapes should be remembered.
5. For an excellent discussion of the theoretical ideas underlying the distinction, see Danziger (1980a).
6. Hellpach (1938) relates that in his classical lectures on *Völkerpsychologie* Wundt devoted more than half the semester to language, barely a third to myth, and all the remainder was compressed into two or three hours.
7. It is an intriguing question meriting further exploration when and by whom the link first came to be defined as a topic for research. It was certainly so considered by such students of Franz Boas as Margaret Mead, who also came under the influence of Freudian theories about the critical effects of early childhood. Vygotsky ([1930] 1978) explicitly stated that 'The developmental roots of two cultural forms of behavior arise during infancy' (p. 46).
8. It should perhaps be noted that Wundt was not always clear about this, and at times it would appear that he had two rather different objectives, often not distinguished in his discussions: (a) to trace the development of the psyche as

manifested in socio-culturally mediated constructions; (b) to undertake a psychological analysis of human cultural development. The first of these would be relativistic and related most closely to the function of psychology as a *Geisteswissenschaft*, the second universalistic and conceived in the context of psychology as a natural science. This uncertainty probably also accounts for his inconsistencies when dealing with the relationships between the individual and society, and between general and *Völkerpsychologie*. The summary expresses what, in my judgement, seems to have constituted his dominant aim.

9. Such misinterpretations are by no means confined to the past; Bourguignon (1979), for instance, suggested that *Völkerpsychologie* should be translated as 'ethnic psychology', since Wundt was concerned with cultural differences!

Epilogue:
Old Wine in New Bottles

[T]he historical process is a process in
which man creates for himself this or that
kind of human nature by re-creating in
his own thought the past to which he is
heir.

This inheritance is not transmitted by
any natural process. To be possessed, it
must be grasped by the mind that
possesses it, and historical knowledge is
the way in which we enter upon the
possession of it. (Collingwood, 1946,
p. 226)

In this book, an attempt has been made to 're-create' some past
thought about the nature of human nature. The purpose was
twofold. One of my aims has been to show that something corresponding at
least roughly to the *concept* of culture (whatever the actual terminology) runs
as a more or less constant thread through the web of reflection and
speculation about human nature and the human mind. Thus in historical
perspective the narrow natural-science ethos in psychology – an ethos that
resolutely ignores culture, and remained dominant for a considerable part
of the present century – can be seen as probably constituting a temporary
aberration. This is a point to which I shall return.

The other aim was to tell the story of a heritage that has contributed to
the shaping of our current ideas. In many spheres of knowledge concerning
nature, truly revolutionary changes have occurred, and we now view the
physical world in a manner radically different from that of our predecessors. Great advances have also been made in our understanding of what
might be called the 'mechanical' aspects of psychology, such as the
functioning of the central processing system. While the great value and
importance of such knowledge should be fully accepted, it must be said

that this is not all there is to the human mind – it is merely the machinery. As Matthew Arnold, the Victorian poet who described culture as 'the pursuit of sweetness and light', put it:

> Know man hath all which Nature hath, but more,
> And in that *more* lie all his hopes of good.

It is the 'more' that has been largely neglected by mainstream psychology, which has mistakenly regarded it as 'soft', 'unscientific' and 'out of date'. An increasing number of writers now advocate a broadening of the scope of psychology, if not a fundamental change in its orientation. Even among their ranks there are some who – either through ignorance or through anxiety to appear original and up to date – make only casual, if not patronizing, references to ideas of the past. Thereby it is implied, if not actually stated, that most of the old questions have either been answered or shown to be irrelevant. In reality, however, matters are seldom so clear-cut.

In conclusion, therefore, I propose to review in outline the major themes, in a manner that does not pretend to be either systematic or comprehensive. It is merely designed to show how few issues have been completely settled, and that it is the continuities of problem areas that are most striking. Although no sharp distinctions can be drawn, it will be noted that in what follows the earlier points are more closely connected with the topics of Parts I and II, and the later ones with those of Part III.

Within the problem areas considered in this book, one of the few instances of a question decisively resolved by the advancement of science is that of the boundary between human and non-human – or, in other words, between organisms capable or incapable of creating culture. The period when this boundary was being drawn saw the rise of an optimistic faith in the inevitable and potentially infinite progress of the human mind and consequent improvement of culture, enunciated most clearly by Condorcet. What Bury (1920) called 'the illusion of finality' persisted in its essentials until it was shaken by the slaughter of the First World War and shattered by the spectre of nuclear holocaust. 'Progress', of course, constituted a value-laden dogma – as such it is even less susceptible to proof or disproof than the rival view of an eternal cycle of advance and decay dating back to Antiquity.

The belief that every section of humanity moved forward through a fixed succession of stages, associated with the eighteenth-century doctrine of progress, still held sway for most of the nineteenth century. Although it was disproved by archaeological and other evidence, certain ideas connected with it are still relevant. The most important one concerns a postulated relationship between the psychological characteristics of a people and their level of material culture and mode of subsistence. What, for the philosophers of the Scottish Enlightenment, had been the four 'stages of society' – hunting, pastoral, farming and commerce – are closely similar to the categories atemporally treated by modern cross-cultural psychologists as 'independent variables' (see Berry, 1976).

The more general notion of connections between ecology, social institutions and character already existed in Ancient Greece,[1] as did the belief in innate mental differences between peoples. This belief lost its significance and virtually disappeared during the Middle Ages, when the dividing line was between Christians and the rest; this meant that one could cross the line by becoming converted. The notion of 'race' emerged during the eighteenth century and – later becoming associated with evolutionary biology – led to the view that 'race' determines both psychology and culture. It was salient during the nineteenth century and persisted well into the twentieth before becoming discredited. Now the question of 'race' is regarded as resolved, at least by the scientific community.[2]

In the mid nineteenth century, when racial theories were in the ascendant, their opponents raised the banner of 'psychic unity'. This concept had been implicit in much of the more tolerant eighteenth-century thought, but it was more fully expounded and given a label a century later. This label has not only survived; it has become an article of axiomatic faith that is seldom questioned. It seems to me, however, that it requires reconsideration in the light of modern circumstances, and I shall briefly seek to justify this opinion.

The early advocates of 'psychic unity' were progressive opponents of racial doctrines, though not usually egalitarians in our sense. They sought to show that underlying what we would now call wide 'cultural differences' is a constant human nature. From being a mainly theoretical concept, 'psychic unity' has acquired powerful emotional overtones and survived the demise of the theories with which it was once associated; therefore it may seem somewhat heretical even to raise the question of whether it still serves a useful purpose in psychological discourse.

If one tries to define what 'psychic unity' means today, it soon becomes apparent that it is an exceedingly vague notion. Attempts to identify the existence of psychological universals, such as Lonner's (1980), have not been very fruitful. Furthermore, the implication of uniformity runs counter to our newly acquired insights that cultural influences can have important psychological effects. Indeed, the banner of 'psychic unity' is sometimes being used in an effort to justify the neglect of cultural factors.[3] Hence there appear to be good grounds for arguing that at the present time, when 'race' has ceased to be theoretically relevant, the notion of 'psychic unity' has also outlived its usefulness.

These comments refer, of course, to the old-fashioned nineteenth-century concept of 'race as biologically given destiny'. But with the further development of evolutionary thought, the old problems have begun to appear in a new light. The question of the relationship between evolutionary biology, genetics, culture and mind has become very much a live issue. Here I am referring not so much to the specific 'sociobiology debate', which has subsided somewhat, but to the broader discussion of the role of culture in human evolution.[4] A somewhat paradoxical consequence has been that a number of eminent biologists and geneticists have become more concerned with problems of culture than the general run of mainstream psychologists, who are anxious to preserve what they imagine to be the 'scientific' image of psychology. The distinguished biologist Robert Hinde (1987, p. 5), for example, after considering animal 'proto-cultures', stated: 'the human language-based capacity for culture has consequences much more fundamental than those of these animal traditions, affecting virtually all aspects of our behaviour and experience'.

This brings me to the theme of the relationship between culture, language and thought, a very ancient one that has fascinated thinkers of varied persuasions. Empiricists were no less concerned than their opponents with the nature of this relationship, and it even became entangled in the 'race' debate during the latter part of the nineteenth century, when a temporary confusion reigned between 'races' and certain linguistic groups. Leaving this aberration aside, there is a long tradition, going back to Francis Bacon and Vico, which regards particular languages as bearing the traces of the thoughts and feelings of the community of its speakers. For instance, the Scottish moral philosopher Thomas Reid (1710–96) noted that one can trace the 'sentiments of nations' prior to any records by the structure of their language. Others, like Vico and Humboldt, believed – much like Sapir and Whorf – that a people's language constrains their modes of thought. This whole set of problems remains an active field of research and debate.[5]

A somewhat related aspect concerns the role of language as a key element in the transmission of the cultures of particular human groups. This has long been recognized – notably by Herder in his discussion of the *Volksgeist*. Moreover, he saw language as a crucial component of the cement that binds an individual to his or her *Volk*. It was his answer to the question of the relationship between an individual and the community, a question that goes back to Rousseau's '*moi commun*' or 'general will'. It preoccupied Lazarus and Steinthal, as well as subsequently Wundt, and gave rise to speculations about a 'group mind'. While this term as such has ceased to be respectable, the notion persists under other labels, and the kind of problem it was intended to solve still remains.[6]

One of the ways in which it has returned takes the form of questions about the locus of culture: should it be regarded as something in people's heads, or as external to individuals? These questions have been widely discussed in anthropology,[7] but have aroused little interest in mainstream psychology which, by and large, focuses on the individual, paying little more than occasional lip-service to culture. On the other hand, the need for a 'cultural psychology' has become the rallying cry for an important section of those opposed to the positivist orientation of the mainstream, still dominant but increasingly under attack.

Such conflicting viewpoints reflect divisions within psychology at large – that constitute, in essence, a continuation of the debate at the end of the nineteenth century. The current debate – in a different key, since it takes account of the advances of knowledge, and in a greater variety of forms – is still about the status of the discipline: is it to be a *Naturwissenschaft* or a *Geistes-* or *Kulturwissenschaft*? Over a large part of the twentieth century the former view prevailed, for historical reasons that have been analyzed by several scholars (Danziger, 1979; Fischer, 1977; Graham, 1986). From the 1960s onwards a series of counter-movements arose, including 'humanistic psychology' (Rychlak, 1977), ethogenics (Harré and Secord, 1972), social constructionism (Gergen, 1985) and existential or phenomenological psychology (Valle and Halling, 1989). While culture as such does not appear in their banner heading, their discussions have much in common with – and sometimes explicitly refer to – Dilthey's culture-historical arguments, Wundt's *Völkerpsychologie*, or Franz Brentano's (1838–1917) 'Descriptive Psychology'. Moreover, the main method advocated by some of them is the 'hermeneutic' one in the tradition of Schleiermacher and Dilthey, involving the interpretation of 'texts' (Messer *et al.*, 1988). As already mentioned (p. 138), the modern prophet of this approach was Gadamer (1965), who inspired Habermas to use hermeneutics in his anti-positivist writings.

While Habermas's polemics are directed at the empirical social sciences as a whole, there is also a more specifically psychological version. Erich Stern ([1920] 1990) had written an article on problems of cultural psychology, and a few years later had come Karl Bühler's (1927) famous proclamation of the 'crisis of psychology', in which he had discussed 'the idea of a cultural psychology'. Subsequent events stifled further progress, and after the Second World War German psychology became thoroughly Americanized for a time. More recently the old threads have been taken up again, and there is now a flourishing movement calling itself *Kulturpsychologie* (Allesch and Billmann-Mahecha [eds], 1990). Somewhat amorphous in its aims and scope, it provides a broad umbrella for all those disillusioned with what they call 'nomothetic-experimental psychology'. Although it claims to be deeply concerned with 'the psychology of everyday life', one gets the impression that the main emphasis is not so much on 'culture' in the Anglo-Saxon sense as on *Hochkultur* (high culture) as manifest, for instance, in literary and artistic creation. Accordingly, the *Kultur* in question is essentially European with barely a mention of other cultures.

The work of some other German scholars, notably Boesch (1991) and Eckensberger (1990) involves a broader conception of culture, closely in line with that of the American advocates of a 'cultural psychology'. Among these, two outstanding figures are Michael Cole and Richard Shweder, who share a clear awareness of their intellectual ancestry but have rather different conceptions of 'cultural psychology'. Cole was primarily responsible for the dissemination and further elaboration of the ideas of the Soviet sociohistorical school of Vygotsky and Luria.[8] Their approach is a subtle blend of Marxism (which, via Hegel, is of course an 'inverted' German idealism) with the teachings of such psychologists as Pierre Janet and James Baldwin. Cole, somewhat like Boesch, takes the view that culture provides the basic context of meaning and action, so that all psychology ought to be cultural psychology using comparative and developmental approaches. He has recently set out the far-reaching implications of this view, displayed on a broad historical canvas (Cole, 1990).

Unlike Cole, whose style is in the universalist tradition of the Enlightenment, Shweder (in Shweder and LeVine, 1984) is more inclined towards the 'romantic rebellion against the Enlightenment'. Hence his blueprint for a 'cultural psychology' (Shweder, 1990) is rather different, and he appears to see it as a specialized field concerned with – as it were – entering the spirit of particular cultures through a hermeneutic approach. As such, cultural psychology would be complementary to allied fields like cross-cultural psychology and psychological anthropology.

In spite of their divergences of views, Shweder and Cole are in full agreement on one crucial point, expressed by Cole and his associates in the statement that 'mind and culture are different aspects of the same phenomenon' (Laboratory of Comparative Human Cognition, 1983, p. 349), and by Shweder when he says that 'culture and psyche make each other up' (Shweder, 1990, p. 24).

At present, such a view is as yet far from general acceptance. But as the old debate is renewed, there is a growing consensus on the need to recognize culture as the medium through which the drama of human action is performed. Perhaps the time will come when a psychology that treats humans as isolated, timeless organisms, and fails to take account of culture and history, will seem like a *Hamlet* with the Prince of Denmark as the only character.

Notes

1. A modern neo-Freudian version of this theme, known as the 'culture-and-personality school', flourished during the 1940s and 1950s. Although it has since become unfashionable, the problems with which it was concerned continue to be studied (Barnouw, 1973; Bock, 1980; Jahoda, 1982; Spindler [ed.], 1978).

2. There are still occasional attempts to give it scientific respectability, such as Rushton's (1988).

3. Such an attitude is least defensible in social psychology, yet it has been put forward even in that connection: 'Given the abiding faith in basic universals of humankind, the social psychologist might just as well work with a subject population he knows something about and that is close at hand – the students in his classes' (Gerard and Conolley, 1972).

4. See Boyd and Richerson (1985); Cavalli-Sforza and Feldman (1981).

5. See Goodenough (1981); Holland and Quinn (1987); Scribner (1979); Tyler (1978).

6. A concise exposition of 'group mind' theories may be found in Ginsberg (1944). As can readily be illustrated, the idea persists, even though it is clothed in up-to-date terminology: 'When people act correctly and talk appropriately, control is exercised, not by the conditions of individual brains, but by the collective cognitions of the group fractionated and distributed among the members' (Harré, Clarke and De Carlo, 1985, p. 91); or again, some, like Fuhrer (1991–2), refer to 'external minds'.

7. See the chapter in Service (1985) entitled 'The locus of cultural reality: Is it in the mind or is it an entity *sui generis?*'

8. Wertsch (1991) offers a concise and lucid account of the essentials of their theory.

Bibliography

Where two dates are given, the original date of publication is shown in square brackets.

Abel, T. (1953) 'The operation called *"Verstehen"*, in H. Feigl and M. Brodbeck (eds), *Readings in the Philosophy of Science*, New York: Appleton-Century-Crofts.

Adkins, A. W. H. (1970) *From the Many to the One*, London: Constable.

Albano, M. E. (1986) *Vico and Providence*, New York: Peter Lang.

Allen, G. (1879) *The Colour-Sense*, London: Trübner.

Allesch, C. G. and Billmann-Mahecha (eds) (1990) *Perspektiven der Kulturpsychologie*, Heidelberg: Asanger.

Anonymous (1825) 'On the coincidence between the natural talents and dispositions of nations, and the development of their brains', *Phrenological Journal* II: 1–19.

Anonymous (1826) 'Sandwich Islanders and South American Indians', *Phrenological Journal* III: 421–36.

Anonymous (1834) 'Skull of a Hottentot and character inferred from it', *Phrenological Journal* VIII: 68–9.

Anonymous (1904) 'Kleinere Mitteilungen', *Archiv für Kriminalanthropologie und Kriminalstatistik* XV: 287–8.

Ariès, P. (1973) *Centuries of Childhood*, Harmondsworth: Penguin.

Askevis-Leherpeux, F. (1988) *La Superstition*, Paris: Presses Universitaires de France.

Bache, R. M. (1895) 'Reaction time with reference to race', *Psychological Review* 2: 457–586.

Baldry, H. C. (1965) *The Unity of Mankind in Greek Thought*, Cambridge: Cambridge University Press.

Banton, M. (1987) *Racial Theories*, Cambridge: Cambridge University Press.

Barnard, F. M. (1969) *J. G. Herder on Social and Political Culture*, Cambridge: Cambridge University Press.

Barnouw, V. (1973) *Culture and Personality*, Homewood, IL: Dorsey Press.
Bartlett, F. C. (1932) *Remembering*, Cambridge: Cambridge University Press.
Barzun, J. (1938) *Race: A study in modern superstition*, London: Methuen.
Bastian, A. (1860) *Der Mensch in der Geschichte* (3 vols), Leipzig: Wigand.
Bastian, A. (1868a) *Beiträge zur vergleichenden Psychologie*, Berlin: Dümmler.
Bastian, A. (1868b) *Das Beständige in den Menschenrassen*, Berlin: Reimer.
Bastian, A. (1888) *Allerlei aus Volks- und Menschenkunde* (2 vols), Berlin: Mittler.
Bedani, G. (1988) *Vico Revisited*, Oxford: Berg.
Beddoe, J. (1874) 'Psychology', in *Notes and Queries on Anthropology*, London: Stanford.
Belke, I. (1971) *Moritz Lazarus und Heymann Steinthal*, Tübingen: Mohr.
Benedict, R. ([1935] 1945) *Patterns of Culture*, London: Routledge.
Berlin, I. (1976) *Vico and Herder*, London: Hogarth.
Bernheimer, R. (1952) *Wild Men in the Middle Ages*, Cambridge, MA: Harvard University Press.
Berry, J. W. (1976) *Human Ecology and Cognitive Style*, New York: Wiley.
Berry, J. W., Poortinga, Y. H., Segall, M. H. and Dasen, P. R. (eds) (1992) *Cross-Cultural Psychology: Research and applications*, Cambridge: Cambridge University Press.
Beuchelt, E. (1974) *Ideengeschichte der Völkerpsychologie*, Meisenheim-am-Glan: Anton Hain.
Bevan, W. (1991) 'A tour inside the onion', *American Psychologist* 46: 475–83.
Billig, M. (1984) *Ideology and Social Psychology*, Oxford: Blackwell.
Blumenbach, J. F. ([1775] 1865) *The Anthropological Treatises of Johann Friedrich Blumenbach*, transl. and ed. Thomas Bendyshe, London: Longmans Green.
Blumenthal, A. L. (1970) *Language and Psychology*, New York: Wiley.
Boas, F. (1911) *The Mind of Primitive Man*, New York: Macmillan.
Bock, P. K. (1980) *Continuities in Psychological Anthropology*, San Francisco: Freeman.
Boesch, E. E. (1980) *Kultur und Handlung*, Bern: Huber.
Boesch, E. E. (1991) *Symbolic Action Theory and Cultural Psychology*, Berlin: Springer.
Bond, M. (ed.) (1988) *The Cross-Cultural Challenge to Social Psychology*, Newbury Park, CA: Sage.
Bornstein, M. H. (1973) 'Color vision and color naming', *Psychological Bulletin* 80: 257–85.
Bourguignon, E. (1979) *Psychological Anthropology*, New York: Holt, Rinehart & Winston.
Bowerman, M. (1985) 'What shapes children's grammars?', in D. I. Slobin (ed.), *The Cross-Linguistic Study of Language Acquisition*, vol. 2: *Theoretical Issues*. Hillsdale, NJ: Erlbaum.
Bowler, P. J. (1989) *The Invention of Progress*, Oxford: Blackwell.
Boyd, R. and Richerson, P. J. (1985) *Culture and the Evolutionary Process*, Chicago: University of Chicago Press.
Bradley, R. (1721) *A Philosophical Account of the Works of Nature*.
Braudel, F. (1980) *On History*, London: Weidenfeld & Nicolson.

Brislin, R. W. (ed.) (1990) *Applied Cross-Cultural Psychology*, Newbury Park, CA: Sage.

British Association for the Advancement of Science (1853) *Report of the Twenty-Second Meeting*, London: Murray.

Broca, P. (1879) *Instructions Générales pour les recherches anthropologiques*, Paris: Masson.

Brosses, Président C. de (1760) *Du culte des dieux fétiches*.

Bryson, G. (1945) *Man and Society: The Scottish inquiry of the eighteenth century*, Princeton, NJ: Princeton University Press.

Bühler, K. (1927) *Die Krise der Psychologie*, Jena: Fischer.

Burke, J. G. (1972) 'The wild man's pedigree: Scientific method and racial anthropology', in E. Dudley and M. E. Novak (eds), *The Wild Man Within*, Pittsburgh, PA: University of Pittsburgh Press.

Burke, P. (1985) *Vico*, Oxford: Oxford University Press.

Burnet, J. (Lord Monboddo) (1773) *On the Origins and Progress of Language*, Edinburgh.

Burrow, J. W. (1966) *Evolution and Society*, Cambridge: Cambridge University Press.

Burton, R. F. (1864) *A Mission to Gelele, King of Dahomey* (2 vols), London: Tinsley.

Bury, J. B. (1920) *The Idea of Progress*, London: Macmillan.

Cabanis, P. J. G. ([1802] 1824) *Rapports du physique et du moral de l'homme* (new edn; 3 vols), Paris.

Camper, P. (1794) *The works of the late professor Camper on the connexions between the science of anatomy and the arts of drawing, painting, statuary etc. containing a treatise on the natural differences of features in persons of different countries and periods of life*, transl. from the Dutch by T. Cogan, London.

Carraher, T. N., Carraher, D. W. and Schliemann, A. D. (1985) 'Mathematics in the streets and in schools', *British Journal of Developmental Psychology* 3: 21–9.

Cassirer, E. ([1942] 1961) *Zur Logik der Kulturwissenschaften*, Darmstadt: Wissenschaftliche Buchgesellschaft.

Cassirer, E. (1989) *The Question of Jean-Jacques Rousseau* (2nd edn), New Haven, CT: Yale University Press.

Cavalli-Sforza, L. L. and Feldman, M. W. (1981) *Cultural Transmission and Evolution*, Princeton, NJ: Princeton University Press.

Cole, M. (1988) 'Cross-cultural research in the sociohistorical tradition', *Human Development* 31: 137–57.

Cole, M. (1990) 'Cultural psychology: A once and future discipline?', in J. J. Berman (ed.), *Cross-Cultural Perspectives, Nebraska Symposium on Motivation 1989*. Lincoln, NB: University of Nebraska Press.

Collingwood, R. G. (1946) *The Idea of History*, Oxford: Clarendon Press.

Combe, G. (1842) 'Observations on the heads and mental qualities of the Negroes and North American Indians', *Phrenological Journal* XV: 147–54.

Combe, G. (1850) *Elements of Phrenology* (7th edn), Edinburgh: Maclachan & Stewart.

Condillac, E. B. de ([1746] 1971) *An Essay on the Origin of Human Knowledge*, Gainesville, FL: Scholars' Facsimiles and Reprints.

Condillac, E. B. de (1754) *Traité des sensations* (2 vols), Paris.
Condorcet, M. J. ([1794] 1966) *Esquisse d'un tableau historique des progrès de l'esprit humain*, Paris: Editions Sociales.
Cook, T. D. and Campbell, D. T. (1979) *Quasi-Experimental Design and Analysis Issues for Field Settings*, Chicago: Rand McNally.
Cooter, R. J. (1976) 'Phrenology: The provocation of progress', *History of Science* 14: 211–34.
Copans, J. and Jamin, J. (1978) *Aux origines de l'anthropologie française*, Paris: Le Sycomore.
Cuvier, G. (n.d.) 'Note instructive sur les recherches à faire relativement aux différences anatomiques des diverses races d'hommes', reprinted in Copans and Jamin (1978).
Cuvier, G. (1817) 'Extraits d'observations faites sur le cadavre d'une femme connue à Paris et à Londres sous le nom de Vénus Hottentotte', *Mémoires du Musée d'Histoire Naturelle* 3: 259.
D'Amico, R. (1989) *Historicism and Knowledge*, New York: Routledge.
Danzel, T. H. (1928) 'Probleme der afrikanischen Ethnographie im Lichte völkerpsychologischer Fragestellung', *Mitteilungen des Museums für Völkerkunde Hamburg*, XIII.
Danziger, K. (1979) 'The social origins of modern psychology', in A. R. Buss (ed.), *Psychology in Social Context*, New York: Wiley.
Danziger, K. (1980a) 'Wundt's theory of behavior and volition', in R. W. Rieber (ed.), *Wilhelm Wundt and the Making of Scientific Psychology*, New York: Plenum.
Danziger, K. (1980b) 'Wundt and the two traditions of psychology', in R. W. Rieber (ed.).
Danziger, K. (1983) 'Origins and basic principles of Wundt's *Völkerpsychologie*', *British Journal of Social Psychology* 22: 303–13.
Darwin, C. ([1874] 1901) *The Descent of Man* (2nd edn), London: John Murray.
Davey, J. G. (1847) 'The character of the Cingalese phrenologically considered', *Phrenological Journal* XX: 147–56.
Degérando, J.-M. ([1800] 1969) *The Observation of Savage Peoples*, transl. F. T. C. Moore, London: Routledge & Kegan Paul.
De Mause, L. (1976) *The History of Childhood*, London: Souvenir Press.
Deregowski, J. B. (1980) 'Perception', in H. C. Triandis and W. Lonner (eds): *Handbook of Cross-Cultural Psychology*, vol. 3: *Basic Processes*, Boston, MA: Allyn & Bacon.
Descartes, R. ([1637] 1937) *A Discourse on Method*, London: Dent.
Diderot, D. ([1772] 1875) *Œuvres complètes*, vol. 2, Paris: Garnier Frères.
Dilthey, W. ([1894] 1977) *Descriptive Psychology and Historical Understanding*, The Hague: Nijhoff.
Duchet, M. (1971) *Anthropologie et histoire au siècle des Lumières*, Paris: François Maspéro.
Duijker, H. C. J. and Rijswijk, M. J. (eds) (1975) *Trilingual Psychological Dictionary*, 3 vols, Bern: Huber.
Eckensberger, L. H. (1990) 'On the necessity of the culture concept in psychology',

in F. J. R. van de Vijver and G. J. M. Hutschemaekers (eds), *The Investigation of Culture: Current issues in cultural psychology*, Tilburg: Tilburg University Press.

Eisenstädter, J. (1912) *Elementargedanke und Übertragungstheorie in der Völkerkunde*, Stuttgart: Strecker and Schröder.

Elias, N. (1977) *The Civilizing Process*, Oxford: Blackwell.

Elliot Smith, G. (1926) 'Introduction', in W. H. R. Rivers, *Psychology and Ethnology*, London: Kegan Paul, Trench, Trübner.

Ermarth, M. (1978) *Wilhelm Dilthey: The critique of historical reason*, Chicago: University of Chicago Press.

Fabian, J. (1983) *Time and the Other*, New York: Columbia University Press.

Farr, R. M. (1980) 'Sunk with hardly a trace: On reading Darwin and discovering social psychology', in R. Gilmour and S. Duck (eds): *The Development of Social Psychology*, London: Academic Press.

Farr, R. M. (1983) 'Wilhelm Wundt (1832–1920) and the origins of psychology as an experimental and social science', *British Journal of Social Psychology* 22: 289–301.

Ferguson, A. ([1767] 1966) *An Essay on the History of Civil Society*, Edinburgh: The University Press.

Figlio, K. M. (1976) 'The metaphor of organization: An historiographical perspective on the bio-medical sciences of the early nineteenth century', *History of Science* XIV: 17–53.

Fischer, C. T. (1977) 'Historical relations of psychology as an object-science and a subject-science', *Journal of the History of the Behavioral Sciences* 13: 369–78.

Forichon, Abbé and Maupied, Abbé (1844) *De l'origine de l'homme et de l'unité de l'espèce humaine*, Louvain: Fonteyn.

Forster, G. ([1786] 1969) *Werke* (4 vols), Frankfurt: Insel.

Freud, S. ([1912/13] 1950) *Totem and Taboo*, New York: Norton.

Friedman, J. B. (1981) *The Monstrous Races in Medieval Art and Thought*, Cambridge, MA: Harvard University Press.

Fuhrer, U. (1991–2) 'Living in our own footprints - and those of others: Cultivation as intensive coping', *Reports from the Group for Environmental and Cultural Psychology*, University of Bern.

Gadamer, H. G. (1965) *Wahrheit und Methode*, Tübingen: Mohr.

Gall, F. J. (1819) *Anatomie et physiologie du système nerveux en général et du cerveau en particulier*, vol. 4: *Physiologie du cerveau*, Paris.

Galton, F. ([1892] 1914) *Hereditary Genius* (2nd edn), London: Macmillan.

Gay, P. (1989) 'Introduction' to E. Cassirer: *The Question of Jean-Jacques Rousseau*.

Gebhard, W. (1984) *Der Zusammenhang der Dinge*, Tübingen: Max Niemeyer.

Geertz, C. (1973) *The Interpretation of Cultures*, London: Hutchinson.

Gerard, H. B. and Conolley, E. S. (1972) 'Conformity', in C. G. McClintock (ed.), *Experimental Social Psychology*, New York: Holt, Rinehart & Winston.

Gergen, K. J. (1982) *Toward Transformation in Social Knowledge*, New York: Springer.

Gergen, K. J. (1985) 'The social constructionist movement in modern psychology', *American Psychologist* 40: 266–75.

Ginsberg, M. (1944) *The Psychology of Society*, London: Methuen.

Gladstone, W. E. (1858) *Studies on Homer and the Homeric Age*, Oxford: Oxford University Press.

Goodenough, W. H. (1981) *Culture, Language and Society* (2nd edn), Menlo Park, CA: Cummings.

Goody, J. (1976) *Production and Reproduction*, Cambridge: Cambridge University Press.

Gould, S. J. (1981) *The Mismeasure of Man*, New York: Norton.

Graham, H. (1986) *The Human Face of Psychology*, Milton Keynes: Open University Press.

Greverus, I.-M. (1987) *Kultur und Alltagswelt*, Frankfurt: Institut für Kulturanthropologie.

Gundlach, H. (1983) *Folk psychology oder social psychology oder?* Bericht aus dem Archiv für die Geschichte der Psychologie; Psychologisches Institut der Universität Heidelberg. Historische Reihe No. 5.

Gusdorf, G. (1972) *Dieu, la nature, l'homme au siècle des Lumières*, Paris: Payot.

Habermas, J. (1972) *Knowledge and Human Interests*, London: Heinemann.

Haddon, A. C. (ed.) (1901) *Reports of the Cambridge Anthropological Expedition to Torres Straits*, vol. 2: *Physiology and Psychology*, Cambridge: Cambridge University Press.

Haddon, A. C. (1934) *History of Anthropology*, London: Watts.

Haeberlin, H. K. (1916) 'The theoretical foundations of Wundt's folk-psychology', *Psychological Review* 23: 279–302.

Haller, J. S. (1970) 'The species problem: Nineteenth century concepts of racial inferiority in the origin of man controversy', *American Anthropologist* 72: 1319–29.

Hampson, N. (1982) *The Enlightenment*, Harmondsworth: Penguin.

Happel, J. (1887) 'Über die Bedeutung der völkerpsychologischen Arbeiten Adolf Bastians', *Zeitschrift für Völkerpsychologie und Sprachwissenschaft* 17: 1–20.

Harré, R. (ed.) (1976) *Life Sentences*, Chichester: Wiley.

Harré, R., Clarke, D. and De Carlo, N. (1985) *Motives and Mechanisms*, London: Methuen.

Harré, R. and Secord, P. F. (1972) *The Explanation of Social Behaviour*, Oxford: Blackwell.

Harris, M. (1968) *The Rise of Anthropological Theory*, London: Routledge & Kegan Paul.

Harris, P. and Heelas, P. (1979) 'Cognitive processes and collective representations', *Archives of European Sociology* 20: 211–41.

Heelas, P. and Lock, A. (1981) *Indigenous Psychologies*, London: Academic Press.

Hellpach, W. (1938) *Einführung in die Völkerpsychologie*, Stuttgart: Enke.

Helvétius, C. A. ([1758] 1973) *De l'esprit*, Verviers: Gérard.

Herbart, J. F. ([1816] 1901) *A Textbook in Psychology*, transl. M. K. Smith, New York: Appleton.

Herbart, J. F. ([1821] 1890) 'Über einige Beziehungen zwischen Psychologie und Staatswissenschaft', in K. Kehrbach (ed.), *Herbart's Sämmtliche Werke*, vol. 5, Langensalza: Beyer.

Herbart, J. F. ([1824] 1890) 'Psychologie als Wissenschaft neu gegründet auf

Erfahrung, Metaphysik und Mathematik', in K. Kehrbach (ed.), *Joh. Fr. Herbart's Sämmtliche Werke*, Langensalza: Beyer.

Herder, J. G. (1969) *Herder's Werke* (5 vols), Berlin: Aufbau.

Hertz, F. (1925) 'Die Theorien über den Völkercharakter bei den Hellenen', *Kölner Vierteljahrshefte für Soziologie* 4: 174–87.

Hinde, R. A. (1987) *Individuals, Relationships and Culture*, Cambridge: Cambridge University Press.

Hodgen, H. T. (1964) *Early Anthropology in the Sixteenth and Seventeenth Centuries*, Philadelphia, PA: University of Pennsylvania Press.

Holland, D. and Quinn, N. (1987) *Cultural Models in Language and Thought*, Cambridge: Cambridge University Press.

Home, H. (Lord Kames) ([1774] 1819) *Sketches of the History of Man* (new edn in 3 vols), Glasgow.

Hoorn, van W. and Verhave, T. (1980) 'Wundt's changing conceptions of a general and theoretical psychology', in W. G. Bringmann and R. D. Tweney (eds), *Wundt Studies: A centennial collection*, Toronto: Hogrefe.

Horton, R. (1970) 'African traditional thought and Western science', in B. R. Wilson (ed.), *Rationality*, Oxford: Blackwell.

Hoyme, L. E. (1953) 'Physical anthropology and its instruments: An historical study', *Southwestern Journal of Anthropology* 9: 408–30.

Hsu, F. L. K. (1961) *Psychological Anthropology*, Cambridge, MA: Schenkman.

Humbolt, W. von ([1820] 1969) *Schriften zur Sprachphilosophie* (5 vols), vol. 3, Stuttgart: Cotta.

Humboldt, W. von (1836) *Über die Verschiedenheit des menschlichen Sprachbaues und ihren Einfluss auf die geistige Entwicklung des Menschengeschlechtes*, Berlin.

Humboldt, W. von ([1836] 1988) *On Language*, transl. P. Heath, Cambridge: Cambridge University Press.

Hume, D. (1779) *Dialogues Concerning Natural Religion*, London.

Hume, D. (1894) *Essays Literary, Moral and Political*, London: Routledge.

Hunt, E. and Banaji, M. R. (1988) 'The Whorfian hypothesis revisited: A cognitive science view of linguistic and cultural effects on thought', in J. W. Berry, S. H. Irvine and E. B. Hunt (eds), *Indigenous Cognition: Functioning in cultural context*, Dordrecht: Martinus Nijhoff.

Hunt, J. (1863a) *The Negro's Place in Nature*, London: Trübner.

Hunt, J. (1863b) 'On the Negro's place in nature', *Anthropological Review* I: 386–91.

Hunt, J. (1867) 'Retiring address', *Anthropological Review* V: xvii.

Hurwicz, E. (1920) *Die Seelen der Völker: Ideen zu einer Völkerpsychologie*, Gotha: Perthes.

Itard, J.-M. ([1801] 1932) *The Wild Boy of Aveyron*, New York: Century.

Itard, J.-M. (1807) *Rapport sur les nouveaux développements du sauvage de l'Aveyron*.

Jahoda, G. (1961) *White Man*, London: Oxford University Press.

Jahoda, G. (1969) *The Psychology of Superstition*, London: Allen Lane.

Jahoda, G. (1971) 'Retinal pigmentation, illusion susceptibility and space perception', *International Journal of Psychology* 6: 199–208.

Jahoda, G. (1980) 'Cross-cultural comparisons', in M. H. Bornstein (ed.), *Comparative Methods in Psychology*, Hillsdale, NJ: Erlbaum.

Jahoda, G. (1982) *Psychology and Anthropology*, London: Academic Press.

Jahoda, G. (1991) 'Dessins primitifs, dessins d'enfant, et la question de l'évolution, *Gradhiva* 10: 60–70.

Jamin, J. (1983) 'Faibles sauvages . . . corps indigènes corps indigents: le désenchantement de François Péron', in J. Hainard and R. Kaehr (eds), *Le Corps en jeu*, Neuchâtel: Musée d'ethnographie de Neuchâtel.

Janet, P. (1926) *Psychologie expérimentale et comparée*, Compte-rendu du Cours au Collège de France, Paris: Chaline.

Jensen, A. R. (1973) *Educability and Group Differences*, London: Methuen.

Jüthener, J. (1923) *Hellenen und Barbaren*, Leipzig: Dietrich.

Kames, H. H. (Lord) See Home.

King, P. (ed.) (1983) *The History of Ideas*, London: Croom Helm.

Knox, R. (1862) *The Races of Man: A philosophical enquiry into the influence of race on the destiny of nations* (2nd edn), London: Renshaw.

Koch, J. (1931) 'Sind die Pygmäen Menschen?', *Archiv für Geschichte der Philosophie* 40: 194–213.

Koepping, K.-P. (1983) *Adolf Bastian and the Psychic Unity of Mankind*, St Lucia: University of Queensland Press.

Koffka, K. (1935) *Principles of Gestalt Psychology*, London: Routledge & Kegan Paul.

Kohlberg, L. (1976) 'Moral stages and moralization: The cognitive-developmental approach', in T. E. Lickona (ed.), *Moral Development and Behavior*, New York: Holt, Rinehart & Winston.

Kollmann, J. (1911) 'Das Problem der Gleichheit der Rassen', *Archiv für Rassen und Gesellschaftliche Biologie* 8: 339–48.

Kragh, H. (1987) *An Introduction to the Historiography of Science*, Cambridge: Cambridge University Press.

Kramer, F. (1977) *Verkehrte Welten*, Frankfurt am Main: Syndicat.

Kramer, F. (1985) 'Empathy – reflections on the history of ethnology in pre-fascist Germany: Herder, Creuszer, Bastian, Bachofen and Frobenius', *Dialectical Anthropology* 9: 337–47.

Krewer, B. (1990) 'Psyche and culture', *Quarterly Newsletter of the Laboratory of Comparative Human Cognition* 12: 24–36.

Krewer, B. and Jahoda, G. (1990) 'On the scope of Lazarus and Steinthal's "Völkerpsychologie" as reflected in the *Zeitschrift für Völkerpsychologie und Sprachwissenschaft* (1860–1890)', *Quarterly Newsletter of the Laboratory of Comparative Human Cognition* 12: 4–12.

Kroeber, A. L. ([1917] 1952) 'The superorganic', in A. L. Kroeber (ed.), *The Nature of Culture*, Chicago: University of Chicago Press.

Kroeber, A. L. and Kluckhohn, C. (1952) *Culture: A critical review of concepts and definitions*, Cambridge, MA: Peabody Museum.

Krueger, F. (1915) *Über die Entwicklungspsychologie*, Leipzig: Engelman.

Laboratory of Comparative Human Cognition (1983) 'Culture and cognitive development', in P. H. Mussen (ed.), *Handbook of Child Psychology* (4th edn), vol. 1, New York: Wiley.

Lafitau, J. F. (1724) *Mœurs des sauvages Amériquains comparés aux mœurs des premiers temps* (2 vols), Paris.

Lambrecht, G. (1913) *La Notion de 'Völkerpsychologie'*, Paris: Annales de l'Institut Supérieur de Philosophie.

La Mettrie, J. O. de (1748) *L'Homme machine*, Leiden.

Lamprecht, K. (1912) *Einführung in das historische Denken*, Leipzig: Voigtländer.

Lawrence, W. (1819) *Lectures on Physiology, Zoology and the Natural History of Man*, London: Callow.

Lazarus, M. (1851) 'Über den Begriff und die Möglichkeit einer Völkerpsychologie', *Zeitschrift für Literatur, Kunst und Öffentlichkeitsleben* 1: 112–26.

Lazarus, M. (1865) 'Einige synthetische Gedanken über die Völkerpsychologie', *Zeitschrift für Völkerpsychologie und Sprachwissenschaft* III: 1–94.

Lazarus, M. and Steinthal, H. (1860) 'Einleitende Gedanken über Völkerpsychologie, als Einladung zu einer Zeitschrift für Völkerpsychologie und Sprachwissenschaft', *Zeitschrift für Völkerpsychologie und Sprachwissenschaft* 1: 1–73.

Leicht, A. (1904) *Begründer der Völkerpsychologie*, Leipzig: Dürr.

Leopold, J. (1980) *Culture in Comparative and Evolutionary Perspective: E. B. Tylor and the making of primitive culture*, Berlin: Reimer.

Lepointe, F. H. (1970) 'The origin and evolution of the term "psychology"', *American Psychologist* 25: 640–6.

LeVine, R. A. and Campbell, D. T. (1972) *Ethnocentrism*, New York: Wiley.

Lévi-Strauss, C. (1962a) *Le Totémisme aujourd'hui*, Paris: Presses Universitaires de France.

Lévi-Strauss, C. (1962b) *La pensée sauvage*, Paris: Plon.

Lévy-Bruhl, L. ([1910] 1951) *Les Fonctions mentales dans les sociétés inférieures*, Paris: Presses Universitaires de France.

Locke, J. ([1690] 1975) *An Essay Concerning Human Understanding*, ed. P. H. Nidditch, Oxford: Clarendon Press.

Lonner, W. J. (1980) 'The search for psychological universals', in H. C. Triandis and W. W. Lambert (eds), *Handbook of Cross-Cultural Psychology*, Boston, MA: Allyn and Bacon.

Lotze, H. ([1852] 1966) *Medizinische Psychologie*, Amsterdam: Bonset.

Lovejoy, A. O. (1957) *The Great Chain of Being: A study of the history of an idea*, Cambridge, MA: Harvard University Press.

Luria, A. R. (1976) *Cognitive Development: Its cultural and social foundations*, Cambridge, MA: Harvard University Press.

MacCormack, C. (1980) 'Nature, culture and gender: A critique', in C. MacCormack and M. Strathern (eds), *Nature, Culture and Gender*, Cambridge: Cambridge University Press.

McDougall, W. (1920) *The Group Mind*, Cambridge: Cambridge University Press.

Magnus, H. (1880) *Untersuchungen über den Farbensinn der Naturvölker*, Jena: Fraher.

Malefijt, A. de Waal (1974) *Images of Man*, New York: Knopf.

Marsella, A. J., de Vos, G. and Hsu, F. L. K. (eds) (1985) *Culture and Self*, New York: Tavistock.

Mauss, M. (1907) 'Review of Wundt's Völkerpsychologie, vol. II, *Mythus und Religion*, part I', *L'Année Sociologique* X: 210–16.

Mead, G. H. ([1934] 1956) in A. Strauss (ed.), *The Social Psychology of George Herbert Mead*, Chicago: University of Chicago Press.

Meiners, C. (1785) *Grundriss der Geschichte der Menschheit*, Lemgo: Meyer.
Meiners, C. (1815) *Untersuchungen über die Verschiedenheiten der Menschennatur* (3 vols), Tübingen: Cotta.
Messer, S., Sass, L. and Woolfolk, R. (eds) (1988) *Hermeneutics and Psychological Theory*, New Brunswick, NJ: Rutgers University Press.
Messick, D. (1988) 'On the limitations of cross-cultural research in social psychology', in M. H. Bond (ed.), *The Cross-Cultural Challenge to Social Psychology*, Newbury Park, CA: Sage.
Millar, J. ([1771] 1806) *The Origin of the Distinction of Ranks*, Edinburgh: William Blackwood.
Miller, G. A. (1964) *Psychology: The science of mental life*, London: Hutchinson.
Miller, G. A. (1990) 'The place of language in a scientific psychology', *Psychological Science* 1: 7–14.
Montagu, A. M. F. (1943) *Tyson, MD, FRS, 1650–1708*, Philadelphia, PA: American Philosophical Society.
Montaigne, M. ([1580] 1954) *Montaigne: Selected essays*, ed. A. Tilley and A. M. Boase, Manchester: Manchester University Press.
Montesquieu, C. de Secondat (1964) *Œuvres complètes*, Paris: Editions du Seuil.
Moore, F. C. T. (1969) see Degérando ([1800] 1969).
Moravia, S. (1977) *Beobachtende Vernunft*, Frankfurt: Ullstein.
Moreau, J. (1973) *Jean-Jacques Rousseau*, Paris: Presses Universitaires de France.
Morgan, L. H. ([1877] 1964) *Ancient Society*, Cambridge: MA: Harvard University Press.
Morgan, M. J. (1977) *Molineux's Question*, Cambridge: Cambridge University Press.
Morton, S. G. (1839) *Crania Americana*, Philadelphia, PA: Dobson.
Mühlmann, W. E. (1986) *Geschichte der Anthropologie* (4th edn), Wiesbaden: Aula.
Murphy, G., Murphy, L. B. and Newcomb, T. M. (1937) *Experimental Social Psychology* (rev. edn), New York: Harper.
Myers, C. S. (1925) *A Textbook of Experimental Psychology* (2 vols, 3rd edn), Cambridge: Cambridge University Press.
Naroll, R., Michik, G. L. and Naroll, F. (1980) 'Holocultural research methods', in H. C. Triandis and J. W. Berry (eds), *Handbook of Cross-Cultural Psychology*, vol. 2: *Methodology*, Boston, MA: Allyn & Bacon.
Notes and Queries on Anthropology (1874), published by a Committee of the British Association for the Advancement of Science, London: Stanford.
Oelze, B. (1991) *Wilhelm Wundt: die Konzeption der Völkerpsychologie*, Münster: Waxmann.
Opler, M. K. (ed.) (1959) *Culture and Mental Health*, New York: Macmillan.
Osgood, C. E., May, W. H. and Miron, S. (1975) *Cross-Cultural Universals of Affective Meaning*, Urbana, IL: University of Illinois Press.
Park, K. and Daston, L. J. (1981) 'Unnatural conceptions: The study of monsters in 16th and 17th century France and England', *Past and Present* 92: 21–54.
Parry, J. H. (1963) *The Age of Reconnaissance*, London: Weidenfeld & Nicolson.
Pattison, R. (1982) *On Literacy*, New York: Oxford University Press.
Paul, H. ([1880] 1898) *Prinzipien der Sprachgeschichte* (3rd edn), Halle: Niemeyer.

Peel, J. D. Y. (1971) *Herbert Spencer: The evolution of a sociologist*, London: Heinemann.

Penrose, B. (1967) *Travel and Discovery in the Renaissance, 1420–1620*, Cambridge, MA: Harvard University Press.

Piéron, H. (1909) 'L'Anthropologie psychologique', *Revue de l'Ecole d'Anthropologie de Paris* **XIX**: 113–27.

Pike, L. O. (1870) 'On the methods of anthropological research', *Anthropological Review*, **VIII**: iii–xiii.

Pollack, R. H. and Silvar, S. D. (1967) 'Magnitude of the Müller–Lyer illusion in children as a function of the pigmentation of the Fundus Oculi', *Psychonomic Science* **8**: 83–4.

Porter, R. and Teich, M. (eds) (1981) *The Enlightenment in National Context*, Cambridge: Cambridge University Press.

Price-Williams, D. R. (1980) 'Toward the idea of a cultural psychology', *Journal of Cross-Cultural Psychology* **11**: 75–88.

Prichard, J. C. ([1843] 1848) *The Natural History of Man* (3rd edn), London: Baillière.

Quatrefages, A. de (1879) *The Human Species*, New York: Appleton.

Quatrefages, A. de Bréau (1884) *Hommes fossiles et hommes sauvages*, Paris: Baillière.

Quatrefages, A. de Bréau (1887) *Histoire générale des races humaines*, Paris: Hennuyer.

Quetelet, A. (1869) *Physique sociale ou essai sur le développement des facultés de l'homme* (2 vols), Brussels: Muquard.

Reik, T. (1915) 'Die Höhle als völkerpsychologisches Symbol des Frauenkörpers', *Internationale Zeitschrift für Ärtzliche Psychoanalyse* **3**: 180–3.

Richards, A. L. (1932) *Hunger and Work in a Savage Tribe*, London: Routledge.

Rickert, H. (1902) *Die Grenzen der naturwissenschaftlichen Begriffsbildung*, Tübingen: Mohr.

Rickert, H. (1910) *Kulturwissenschaft und Naturwissenschaft*, Tübingen: Mohr.

Rickman, H. P. (ed.) (1976) *W. Dilthey: Selected writings*, Cambridge: Cambridge University Press.

Rickman, H. P. (1979) *Wilhelm Dilthey*, London: Paul Elek.

Rivers, W. H. R. (1901) 'Part I. Introduction, and vision', in A. C. Haddon (ed.), *Reports of the Cambridge Anthropological Expedition to Torres Straits*, vol. 2, Cambridge: Cambridge University Press.

Rivers, W. H. R. (1926) 'Intellectual concentration in primitive man', in W. H. R. Rivers, *Psychology and Ethnology*, London: Kegan Paul, Trench, Trübner.

Robertson, W. ([1777] 1808) *The History of America*, 4 vols, London.

Rogoff, B. and Lave, J. (1984) *Everyday Cognition*, Cambridge, MA: Harvard University Press.

Rohner, R. P. (1984) 'Toward a conception of culture for cross-cultural psychology', *Journal of Cross-Cultural Psychology* **15**: 111–38.

Romanes, G. J. (1888) *Mental Evolution in Man*, London: Kegan Paul & Trench.

Rothacker, E. (1927) *Logik und Systemik der Geisteswissenschaften*, Munich: Oldenburg.

Rousseau, J.-J. (1964) Œuvres complètes, vol. 3, Paris: Gallimard.

Rowe, J. H. (1965) 'The Renaissance foundations of anthropology', American Anthropologist 67: 1–20.

Rumney, J. (1934) Herbert Spencer's Sociology, London: Williams & Norgate.

Rushton, J. P. (1988) 'Race differences in behaviour: A review and evolutionary analysis', Personality and Individual Differences 9: 1009–24.

Rychlak, J. F. (1977) The Psychology of Rigorous Humanism, New York: Wiley.

Schaefer, J. M. (1977) 'The growth of hologeistic studies 1889–1975', Behavior Science Research 12: 71–108.

Schneider, C. (1990) Wilhelm Wundt's Völkerpsychologie, Bonn: Bouvier.

Schultze, F. (1900) Psychologie der Naturvölker, Leipzig: von Veit.

Scribner, S. (1979) 'Modes of thinking and ways of speaking: Culture and logics reconsidered', in R. O. Freedle (ed.), New Directions in Discourse Processing, Norwood, NJ: Ablex.

Scripture, E. W. (1897) The New Psychology, London: Walter Scott.

Segall, M. H. (1983) 'On the search for the independent variable in cross-cultural psychology', in S. H. Irvine and J. W. Berry (eds), Human Assessment and Cultural Factors, New York: Plenum.

Segall, M. H., Campbell, D. T. and Herskovits, M. J. (1966) Influence of Culture on Visual Perception, Indianapolis, IN: Bobbs-Merrill.

Segall, M. H., Dasen, P. R., Berry, J. W. and Poortinga, Y. H. (eds) (1990) Human Behavior in Global Perspective, New York: Pergamon.

Service, E. R. (1985) A Century of Controversy, Orlando, FL: Academic Press.

Sganzini, C. (1913) Die Fortschritte der Völkerpsychologie von Lazarus bis Wundt, Bern: Franke.

Shotter, J. (1975) Images of Man in Psychological Research, London: Methuen.

Shweder, R. A. (1990) 'Cultural psychology – what is it?', in J. W. Stigler, R. A. Shweder and G. Herdt (eds), Cultural Psychology, Cambridge: Cambridge University Press.

Shweder, R. A. and LeVine, R. A. (1984) Culture Theory, Cambridge: Cambridge University Press.

Smith, C. H. (1848) The Natural History of the Human Species, Edinburgh.

Smith, R. (1988) 'Does the history of psychology have a subject?', History of the Human Sciences 1: 147–77.

Soemmering, S. T. (1785) Über die körperliche Verschiedenheit des Negers vom Europäer, Frankfurt.

Spearman, C. (1923) The Nature of Intelligence and the Principles of Cognition, London: Macmillan.

Spencer, H. (1876a) 'The comparative psychology of man', Mind 1: 7–20.

Spencer, H. (1876b) The Principles of Sociology (3 vols), London: Williams & Norgate.

Sperber, D. (1985) 'Anthropology and psychology: Towards an epidemiology of representations', Man 20: 73–89.

Spiess, E. (1946) 'Die Gesetze der Kulturentwicklung nach Karl Lamprecht', Studia Philosophica (Jahrbuch der Schweizerischen Philosophischen Gesellschaft) VI: 120–75.

Spindler, G. D. (ed.) (1978) *The Making of Psychological Anthropology*, Berkeley, CA: University of California Press.

Spurzheim, J. C. (1815) *The physiognomic systems of Drs. Gall and Spurzheim. Founded on an anatomical and physiological examination of the nervous system in general and of the brain in particular; and indicating the dispositions and manifestations of the mind*, London: Baldwin, Cranbock & Joy.

Stanton, W. (1960) *The Leopard's Spots: Scientific attitudes toward race in America 1815–59*, Chicago: University of Chicago Press.

Starobinski, J. (1971) *Jean-Jacques Rousseau: la transparence et l'obstacle*, Paris: Gallimard.

Steinthal, H. (1858) *Der Ursprung der Sprache*, Berlin: Dümmler.

Steinthal, H. (1887) 'Begriff der Völkerpsychologie', *Zeitschrift für Völkerpsychologie und Sprachwissenschaft* **XVII**: 233–64.

Stepan, N. (1982) *The Idea of Race in Science: Great Britain 1800–1960*, London: Macmillan.

Stern, E. ([1920] 1990) 'Problems of cultural psychology', *Quarterly Newsletter of the Laboratory of Comparative Human Cognition* **12**: 12–24.

Stern, W. and Lipmann, O. (1912) *Vorschläge zur psychologischen Untersuchung primitiver Menschen*, Beihefte zur Zeitschrift für angewandte Psychologie und psychologische Sammelforschung, No. 5, Leipzig: Barth.

Stocking, G. W., Jr (1982) *Race, Culture and Evolution*, Chicago: University of Chicago Press.

Stocking, G. W., Jr (1987) *Victorian Anthropology*, New York: The Free Press.

Thurnwald, R. (1912) 'Einleitung', in Stern and Lipmann (1912).

Thurnwald, R. (1913) *Ethno-psychologische Studien an Südseevölkern*, Beihefte zur Zeitschrift für angewandte Psychologie und psychologische Sammelforschung, No. 6, Leipzig: Barth.

Thurnwald, R. (1924) 'Zum gegenwärtigen Stande der Völkerpsychologie', *Kölner Vierteljahresheft für Soziologie* **IV**: 32–43.

Thurnwald, R. (1929) 'Grundprobleme der vergleichenden Völkerpsychologie', *Zeitschrift für die gesamte Staatswissenschaft*, **87**: 240–96.

Tiedemann, D. (1787) 'Beobachtungen über die Entwicklung der Sellenfähigkeiten bei Kindern', *Hessische Beiträge zur Gelehrsamkeit und Kunst* 2: 313–33.

Tiedemann, F. (1837) *Das Hirn des Negers mit dem des Europäers und Orang-Outans verglichen*, Heidelberg: Winter.

Titchener, E. B. (1916) 'On ethnological tests of sensation and perception', *Proceedings of the American Philosophical Society* 55: 204–36.

Trevarthen, C. (1983) 'Interpersonal abilities of infants as generators for transmission of language and culture', in A. Oliverio and M. Zapella (eds), *The Behavior of Human Infants*, New York: Plenum.

Triandis, H. C. (ed.) (1980) *Handbook of Cross-Cultural Psychology* (6 vols), Boston, MA: Allyn & Bacon.

Turgot, A. R. ([1750] 1973) 'A philosophical review of the successive advances of the human mind', in R. L. Meek (ed.), *Turgot*, Cambridge: Cambridge University Press.

Tyler, St A. (1978) *The Said and the Unsaid: Mind, meaning and culture*, New York: Academic Press.

Tylor, E. B. (1865) *Researches into the Early History of Mankind and the Development of Civilization*, London: John Murray.

Tylor, E. B. ([1871] 1958) *Primitive Culture*, New York: Harper.

Tylor, E. B. ([1881] 1930) *Anthropology* (2 vols), London: Watts.

Tylor, E. B. (1889) 'On a method of investigating the development of institutions', *Journal of the Royal Anthropological Institute of Great Britain and Ireland* 18: 245–72.

Valle, R. S. & Halling, S. (eds) (1989) *Existential-Phenomenological Perspectives in Psychology*, New York: Plenum.

Valsiner, J. (1988) *Developmental Psychology in the Soviet Union*, Brighton: Harvester.

Vaughan, F. (1972) *The Political Philosophy of Giambattista Vico*, The Hague: Martinus Nijhoff.

Vico, G. ([1725] 1948) *The New Science*, transl. T. G. Bergin & M. H. Fish, Ithaca, NY: Cornell University Press.

Vierkandt, A. (1914) 'Der gegenwärtige Stand der Völkerpsychologie', *Neue Jahrbücher für das klassische Altertum, Geschichte, und deutsche Literatur, und Pädagogik* 33: 625–41.

Vijver, van de, F. J. R. & Hutschemaekers, G. J. M. (eds) (1990), *The Investigation of Culture*, Tilburg: Tilburg University Press.

Voget, F. W. (1967) 'Progress, science, history and evolution in eighteenth- and nineteenth-century anthropology', *Journal of the History of the Behavioral Sciences* 3: 132–55.

Voget, F. W. (1973) 'The history of cultural anthropology', in J. J. Honigmann (ed.), *Handbook of Social and Cultural Anthropology*, Chicago: Rand McNally.

Vogt, C. (1864) *Lectures on Man*, London: Longman.

Volkelt-Leipzig, H. (1921–2) 'Die Völkerpsychologie in Wundt's Entwicklungs- gang', *Beiträge zur Philosophie des deutschen Idealismus* 2: 74–105.

Voltaire, F. M. A. ([1756] 1963) *Essai sur les mœurs* (2 vols), Paris: Garnier Frères.

Vygotsky, L. S. (1978). *Mind in Society*, Cambridge, MA: Harvard University Press.

Wagner, D. A. (1981) 'Culture and memory development', in H. C. Triandis and A. Heron (eds), *Handbook of Cross-Cultural Psychology*, vol. 4, Boston, MA: Allyn & Bacon.

Waitz, T. (1849) *Lehrbuch der Psychologie als Naturwissenschaft*, Braunschweig: Vieweg.

Waitz, T. ([1859] 1863) *Introduction to Anthropology*, London: Anthropological Society.

Werner, H. (1957) *Comparative Psychology of Mental Development*, New York: International Universities Press.

Wertsch, J. V. (ed.) (1985) *Culture, Communication and Cognition*, Cambridge: Cambridge University Press.

Wertsch, J. V. (1991) *Voices of the Mind*, Hemel Hempstead: Harvester Wheatsheaf.

White, C. (1799) *An Account of the Regular Gradation in Man*, London: Dilley.

Whitman, J. (1984) 'From philology to anthropology in mid-nineteenth-century Germany', in G. W. Stocking (ed.), *Functionalism Historicized*, Madison, WI: University of Wisconsin Press.

Windelband, W. ([1894] 1924) 'Geschichte und Naturwissenschaft', in *Präludien, Aufsätze und Reden zur Philosophie und ihrer Geschichte* (2 vols), Tübingen: Mohr.

Winterbottom, T. (1803) *Account of the Native Africans in the Neighbourhood of Sierra Leone* (2 vols), London: Hatchard.

Wundt, W. (1863) *Vorlesungen uber die Menschen- und Thierseele* (2 vols), Leipzig: Voss.

Wundt, W. (1873) *Grundzüge der physiologischen Psychologie*, Leipzig: Engelmann.

Wundt, W. (1880) *Grundzüge der physiologischen Psychologie* (2nd edn, 2 vols).

Wundt, W. (1883) *Logik*, vol. 2: *Methodenlehre*, Stuttgart: Enke.

Wundt, W. (1887) *Grundzüge der physiologischen Psychologie* (3rd edn, 2 vols).

Wundt, W. (1887–8) 'Über Ziele und Wege der Völkerpsychologie', *Philosophische Studien* 4: 1–27.

Wundt , W. (1893) *Grundzüge der physiologischen Psychologie* (4th edn, 2 vols).

Wundt, W. (1896) 'Über die Definition der Psychologie', *Philosophische Studien*, 12: 1–66.

Wundt, W. ([1900] 1973) *The Language of Gestures*, The Hague: Mouton.

Wundt, W. (1908) *Logik*, vol. 3: *Logik der Geisteswissenschaften* (3rd edn), Stuttgart: Enke.

Wundt, W. (1909) *Völkerpsychologie*, vol. 2: *Mythus und Religion* (2nd edn), part 3, Leipzig: Engelmann.

Wundt, W. (1911a) *Völkerpsychologie*, vol. 1: *Die Sprache* (2nd edn), Leipzig: Engelmann.

Wundt, W. (1911b) *Probleme der Völkerpsychologie*, Leipzig: Wiegandt.

Wundt, W. ([1912] 1916) *Elements of Folk Psychology*, London: Allen & Unwin.

Wundt, W. (1917a) 'Völkerpsychologie und Entwicklungspsychologie', *Psychologische Studien* X: 189–238.

Wundt, W. (1917b) *Völkerpsychologie*, vol. 7: *Die Gesellschaft*, Leipzig: Kröner.

Wundt, W. (1920a) *Erlebtes und Erkanntes*, Stuttgart: Kröner.

Wundt, W. (1920b) *Völkerpsychologie*, vol. 10: *Kultur und Geschichte*, Leipzig: Kröner.

Young, R. M. (1970) *Mind, Brain and Adaptation in the Nineteenth Century*, Oxford: Clarendon Press.

Name Index

Subject Index